Contents

Energy Policies and the Greenhouse Effect
Volume One: Policy Appraisal

To Anne-Christine Davis

ENERGY POLICIES AND THE GREENHOUSE EFFECT
Volume One: Policy Appraisal

Michael Grubb

The Royal Institute of International Affairs
Dartmouth

The Royal Institute of International Affairs is an independent body which promotes the rigorous study of international questions and does not express opinions of its own. The opinions expressed in this publication are the responsibility of the author.

Published by Dartmouth Publishing Company, Gower House, Croft Road, Aldershot, Hants, GU11 3HR, England

Dartmouth Publishing Company, Old Post Road, Brookfield, Vermont 05036, USA

Reprinted 1991

ISBN 1 85521 175 0

Cover by Twenty Twenty Design

Printed in Great Britain by
Billing & Sons Ltd, Worcester

Text Boxes

Foreword

This study represents the culmination of two years of research on the Greenhouse Effect by the Energy and Environmental Programme. It is the fourth study which we have published on the policy aspects of this subject, following *Issues for Policymakers*, *Negotiating Targets*, and our report of October 1990 *Formulating a Convention*.

The first volume of the study concentrates on the policy issues arising from attempts to reduce greenhouse gas emissions from the energy sector. The second volume on 'country studies and technical options' provides the detailed analysis on which the conclusions of this book have been based, and will be published in early 1991. Although it was not our intention to produce such a large work at the outset, the upsurge of interest in the subject has expanded the framework of measures being considered to address environmental issues in general and the greenhouse effect in particular. These developments have had a major impact on the size and content.

In this book, as in our previous publications, the Programme's work is aimed at moving the policy debate forward as quickly as possible into areas which seem to offer the best prospects for effective policy action. Michael Grubb is the principal co-ordinator and author of the Programme's work in this area. He has become an internationally known authority in this field and his work has helped enormously in placing our Programme and the name of Chatham House in the forefront of such research. The workload involved in preparing this study has been colossal given the breadth of the subject and speed of events. It is a tribute to him that the work has been brought to a successful conclusion at such an important point in the policymaking process and a tribute to the rest of the Programme that we have survived the experience.

Jonathan Stern, September 1990

About the Author

Dr Michael Grubb is a Research Fellow at the Energy and Environmental Programme of the Royal Institute of International Affairs, where he is leading studies on the implications of the greenhouse effect, and on emerging energy technologies. Following publication of his report *The Greenhouse Effect: Negotiating Targets* (RIIA, 1989) he was appointed as an adviser to the United Nations Environment Programme, and has been involved in working groups of the Intergovernmental Panel on Climate Change and the World Energy Council. His studies prior to joining the Institute resulted in a range of publications on renewable energy sources and on electricity system operation and planning.

The Energy and Environmental Programme would like to thank the organisations below for their contribution to funding our research

Arthur D. Little • British Coal • British Gas
British Nuclear Fuels • British Petroleum • Caltex
Chubu Electric Power Co • Department of Energy
Department of Environment • Elf UK • Enterprise Oil
Eastern Electricity • East Midlands Electricity • Esso UK
Japan National Oil Corp • Kuwait Oil • LASMO
National Energy Administration, Sweden • National Power
Petroleos de Venezuela • Petroleum Economics • PowerGen
Sedgwick Energy • Shell • Statoil (UK)
Tokyo Electric Power Company
United Kingdom Atomic Energy Authority

Acknowledgments

Any serious international study draws upon the inputs and criticisms of many people. It is possible to thank only a fraction of those who have helped in the development of this study.

Many people took time out from pressured jobs to read material and to attend the study groups which met to consider earlier versions; they considered sometimes hurried and incomplete drafts, which often argued unpalatable conclusions, with great tolerance. Their comments remained thoughtful and helpful throughout. To all of them I am very grateful.

The efforts of the country case study authors has been crucial; the full fruits of their labours will appear in Volume II. My thanks go to various people who provided detailed comments on particular chapters of this volume: Geoff Jenkins on Chapter 1; Jonathan Fisher and David Pearce on Chapters 3 and 4; Donald Donaldson, Peter Jones and Walter Patterson on Chapter 5; David Hall on Chapters 1 and 5; and Lee Schipper on Chapters 4, 6, and 7. Gerald Leach offered various helpful comments and advice. Richard Eden, Bob Rowthorn and Matthew Paterson read the full text and returned comments with admirable promptness. The editor, Margaret Cornell, did likewise. All helped to note areas of doubt and provided new insights; the product owes much to their input. Needless to say, this should not be taken to imply that they agree with the views expressed here, which remain the sole responsibility of the author.

The statistical analyses in the study drew primarily on the labours and co-operation of BP and the IEA statistical services; the work involved in gathering good data and making it accessible should not be underestimated. For keeping up to date with the torrent of literature and international events in the field, the Global Environmental Change Report and the mailings of the Climate Action Network have been invaluable; special thanks are due to Stewart Boyle and Annie Ronceral.

Nicola Steen, the Programme Assistant in the Energy and Environmental Programme, has managed the production in all aspects, from early gestation through to final camera-ready copy. Along the way she sought out and mastered the graphics package, and coaxed it into meeting the unreasonable demands made by the author. She was never short of good ideas either on the content or presentation of diagrams and the text. She also ensured that material (including the author) arrived at the right place at the right time, and bore the brunt of phone calls, publicity and other administration surrounding the work.

Rosina Pullman, the Programme Administrator, has juggled brilliantly the conflicting pressures of doing many projects at once. Jonathan Stern, the Head of Programme, has as ever proved his extraordinary ability to manage a rapidly expanding programme of research - including his own book - and still read all the draft material thrown at him by various authors, responding promptly with invaluable comments on content, structure, presentation and the overall development of this and other projects. Silvan Robinson, the Chairman, has likewise given valuable guidance and support - including the ever important raising of funds to support our work.

My deepest thanks and appreciation go to my wife, Anne-Christine. Her love and support have been central, and she has borne unreasonable pressures for someone with her own career to follow. For my young daughter Tara, I can only say that life would have been easier, but much less fun, if her zest and energy had been less boundless. I can only hope that both of them consider the final product to be worth the irritations of waking to a father whose body remained half asleep while his mind was in the next century.

Acronyms, units, and conversion factors used in text

Acronyms:
  GDP   Gross Domestic Product
  IPCC Intergovernmental Panel on Climate Change
  NGOs Non-Government Organisations
  OECD Organisation for Economic Cooperation and Development
  CPE   Centrally Planned Economies

Primary units in this study:
  tC   tonne of carbon
  GtC   Gigatonnes (billion tonnes) of carbon
  Mtoe Million tonnes of oil equivalent (industrial unit of energy)

Prefixes:
  Kilo (Thousand)   k 10^3
  Mega (Million)   M 10^6
  Giga (Billion, milliard) G,B 10^9
  Tera (Trillion)   T 10^{12}
  Peta (Quadrillion)   P 10^{15}

Energy units and conversion factors:
  1 kilocalorie (kcal)   = 4.2kJ (kilojoule)
  1 British Thermal Unit (Btu) = 1.05kJ
  1 quad   = 10^{15}Btu = 1.05EJ = 10^{10} therms
  1 terawatt-hour (TWh)   = 3.6PJ
  1 tonne oil equivalent (toe)[*]   = 10400 Mcal = 44.6 GJ GHV[*]
  1 barrel oil   = 0.136tonnes
  1 million m^3 nat gas equiv[*] = 9555 Mcal = 40PJ = 0.90Mtoe GHV
  1 tonne coal equivalent[*]   = 7220 Mcal = 30.4PJ = 0.68Mtoe GHV

Other units:
  1km   = 3330 feet = 0.62 miles
  $1km^2$ = 100 hectares = 247 acres
  $1m^3$ = 1000 litres = 220 Imperial gallons = 264 US gallons

* Energy units use international/World Energy Conference standard
definitions based on Gross Heating Values (GHV), ie including the
energy content of condensed steam from combustion (see Volume II).

For greenhouse gases and their acronyms, see Table 1.4.

Addressing concerns about the greenhouse effect will entail efforts to limit carbon dioxide emissions from fossil fuels. Many technical options for this exist. Improving energy efficiency is the cornerstone technical response; this and other measures have additional environmental and sometimes economic benefits. At present the key questions concern not technologies but the policy tools available, their impact, and the constraints upon them.

Pervasive imperfections in energy markets create many opportunities for cost-effective savings. Some market obstacles can be removed, but tapping most of the potential may require more interventionist policies. Available measures include: product standards, including various flexible and target standards; fiscal incentives, including revenue-neutral measures for transferring operating savings to capital cost savings; and major changes in utility regulation. Many of these measures could have economic benefits; the drawbacks concern the managerial and political difficulties of effective intervention.

Energy pricing is important. A carbon tax would be an effective tool for promoting both efficiency in supply and demand, and moves towards lower carbon fuels, especially if market imperfections are also reduced. To some level, which cannot yet be determined, carbon taxes may aid economic growth; even high taxes are unlikely to reduce it significantly in most countries. The key issues concern not gross economic impact but transitional costs, political feasibility, and the long-term effectiveness including international reactions to widely varying tax levels. Tradeable permits do not offer a preferable alternative for domestic carbon control.

Coal would be hardest hit by attempts to limit carbon emissions, though various measures could slow the impact and help coal industries to diversify. Greenhouse concerns alone are unlikely to displace oil from its strongholds in transport and petrochemicals, but could lead eventually to one of several non-fossil transport options when combined with other pressures, notably urban congestion and pollution. Accelerating moves towards natural gas including its use for electricity generation, using carbon taxes and/or more traditional supply-side policies, would help to reduce emissions.

Further expansion of nuclear power faces grave political and other obstacles. Using new nuclear technologies and abandoning reprocessing might ease these difficulties but would require daunting technological and institutional restructuring. The prospects for expansion of a variety of modernised renewable energy technologies, eventually to being major components of supply, appear better. The progress of non-fossil energy sources will depend upon the removal of various market barriers, and the degree of government support for research, development, and initial deployment. More general support for a range of low-carbon technologies, both for supply and demand, is justified if taxes are not used to reflect the environmental costs of fossil fuels.

The structure of energy demand in developed economies is changing, and greenhouse concerns will hasten these changes. Energy utilities will tend increasingly towards energy service and co-ordination companies; the emphasis on cars will reduce as part of a more balanced approach to transport; and industrial activities will reflect growing pressures to reduce wastes, and shifts away from materials-intensive manufacturing. These factors will curtail energy growth but are unlikely in themselves to reduce consumption without additional measures.

Industrialised countries account for over two-thirds of current emissions and action by them will be crucial, but the greatest long-term opportunities for low cost abatement lie in altering the development path of poorer countries. Deep-rooted economic and political obstacles impede this. Improving efficiency depends heavily upon domestic policy reforms, but these are improbable without reduced external pressures notably from debt and the dumping of inferior goods. Additional improvements in efficiency, and expansion of non-fossil sources, will depend upon large-scale international resource transfers. There are important unresolved questions concerning the management, as well as the political feasibility, of such transfers.

Without abatement policies, global fossil carbon emissions are likely to double over the next thirty to forty years and will continue rising just as fast for decades thereafter. The most that can be expected for several decades from abatement policies is to hold net emissions (excluding deforestation) roughly constant at present levels. This falls far short of the changes needed to stabilise the atmosphere, but would greatly reduce risks and predicted rates of change. Even this would require major policy changes in all the important groups, which currently seems unlikely with respect to the big energy producers in particular.

The greenhouse effect poses unique challenges. Scientific challenges are better to understand and to communicate the risks that are being run. Analytic challenges are to improve techniques and assumptions for estimating the costs and impact of abatement policies. Economic challenges are to develop more consistent approaches for dealing with the uncertain, global and intergenerational implications of the greenhouse effect. Industrial challenges are those of starting innovative changes years ahead of legislation - but not so far ahead as to lose existing markets and waste new investments. Political challenges include the development of efficient long-term policies in the face of considerable uncertainty and deep-rooted market imperfections.

The international challenges may be the most daunting of all. The only effective international approach may be one based on the principle that countries should pay in proportion to the pollution they generate, but this raises very large hurdles of political acceptability. In particular, it may be impossible to accommodate both the United States and the major developing countries together without compromises so great as to render the resulting agreement ineffective.

There is no convincing evidence that even extensive measures to limit carbon emissions need damage economic growth, and modest abatement policies could aid it and would bring other benefits. Yet the transitional impacts, the drawbacks of extensive intervention, international inequities and the inertia of existing energy systems and institutions pose immense obstacles. The depth of policy changes, and the consequent impact on emissions, will depend upon the extent to which the key challenges are addressed, and the ways in which they are resolved.

Energy and the Greenhouse Effect: An Overview

Civilisation depends on energy. Fossil fuels provide it in a cheap and concentrated form, and as a result they dominate commercial supplies. At the same time they emit billions of tonnes of carbon dioxide (CO_2) and a range of other gases which increase the degree to which heat is trapped near the earth's surface. The concentration of all these 'greenhouse gases' in the atmosphere is rising. This is likely to warm the earth's surface on average, resulting in various changes of climate and a slow rise in sea level. The conclusions of the Intergovernmental Panel on Climate Change, set up to consider the issue, confirm the existence of the greenhouse problem.

Much remains uncertain, and further research is clearly required. Societies and ecosystems may adapt to some slow climate change without difficulty; measures taken in advance can enhance their ability to do so, and may have other benefits. These factors and other possibilities do not constitute grounds for avoiding efforts to limit the rise of greenhouse gas concentrations, because of the various risks posed by unprecedented and accelerating changes to the earth's atmosphere. The political pressures for such action are likely to grow.

The first focus of abatement measures should be to reduce emissions of chlorofluorocarbons. Measures will also be required to ensure that the shorter-lived gases, primarily methane, do not grow excessively. However, following CFCs, CO_2 forms by far the most important focus for abatement policies.

Many measures can help to slow its accumulation. Slowing deforestation, and large-scale reforestation, could make a significant impact. Moves to stimulate its increased absorption in the oceans or on land might be feasible. However, none of these are of sufficient scale and promise to offset substantially the impact of growing fossil fuel emissions.

It is technically possible to extract most of the CO_2 arising from coal combustion in power stations. The costs are uncertain, though not necessarily exorbitant. However, effective routes for disposal of the extracted CO_2 are limited, and even if feasible this process could not play a major role in limiting emissions. Any serious attempts to slow the accumulation of CO_2 in the atmosphere thus imply reduced use of fossil carbon.

Many technical options for achieving this exist, at varying degrees of readiness and costs. Some are economically attractive now, and many carry benefits in addition to those of limiting carbon emissions. Further technical development will be important, but at present the key questions concern policy options and the issues raised by trying to alter energy trends.

1.1 Energy and society

How does a civilisation survive? It survives by procuring enough energy and enough food without imperilling the provision of irreplaceable environmental services on which it depends. Everything else is secondary.[1]

The development of civilisation has depended upon energy. It provides the main services which underpin human societies: heat, light, materials, transport, communication. The Bronze Age was powered by the fire of wood fuel. The Renaissance drew on the energy of watermills and windmills, and harnessed the winds to drive ships of exploration. The Industrial Revolution fed upon coal for process heating, steam, and later electricity. The pattern of human development has been one of almost uninterrupted rise in energy consumption. With an expanding global population, the majority of whom are still far from the levels of comfort enjoyed in the developed economies, further growth in energy consumption seems inevitable.

Modern societies have developed on the back of fossil fuel reserves, which provide energy in an accessible, concentrated form: first coal, then increasingly oil, now with widely growing use of natural gas as well. Technologies for extracting, converting, and using such fuels is well developed and familiar. For clear economic reasons, fossil fuels dominate energy supplies, and their use globally is still growing rapidly.

Twenty years ago there was concern that the demands of modern societies would outstrip the fossil energy resources available. Known reserves of oil and gas were projected to last little beyond the end of the present century, and even the much larger known reserves of coal seemed inadequate to meet the projected exponential increase through the next century. Today, these fears have largely abated. The steep increases in the price of oil during the 1970s checked the exponential increase in global energy demand; in some countries, demand stabilised or declined. Higher prices made other resources more economic and stimulated more exploration for oil and other fuels; major new discoveries of all fossil fuels, and development of previously ignored deposits and processes, followed.

In 1970, the proven oil reserves amounted to less than thirty years of production at existing rates. In 1990, with twenty of those thirty years

[1] V.Smil, *Energy, Food, Environment: Realities, Myths, Options*, Clarendon Press, Oxford, 1987, p.2.

now passed, oil production is higher than it was in 1970, and the proven reserves remaining amount to over forty years of supply. For gas the figure is nearer sixty years, and for coal, several hundred. There is widespread confidence that even these figures do not represent absolute limits, and that economics can lay to rest the spectre of the world running out of energy: approaching constraints will lead to rising prices which will stimulate responses which will make the constraints recede again, though perhaps not without some severe shocks and dislocations. The process would eventually force a move away from fossil fuels - but not to a significant extent for many decades.

Yet, as concerns over resources have receded, others have emerged to take their place. Environmental concerns about energy are, of course, not a new phenomenon. Complaints about coal dust and smoke date back well into the eighteenth century. The London smogs of the 1950s resulted in thousands of deaths, and in widespread 'smokeless zones' where raw coal burning was banned. The choking fumes from cars and other energy-related emissions were already a serious concern in the 1960s and led to widespread legislation in the United States and Japan to clean up exhausts - as well as more amusing legacies from the first widespread wave of general environmental concerns in wealthy countries.[2]

More regional concerns about energy emerged with Scandinavian claims that their river and lake ecosystems were dying as a result of acid deposition from power stations in other countries, followed by the phenomenon of forest dieback. In Europe and North America this emerged as a major issue in regional diplomacy. Intensive study demonstrated complex links with acid deposition and a range of other pollutants from power stations, cars, and various other energy-related sources, though the full mechanisms are still far from fully understood. In Eastern Europe the ravages left by energy-related pollution provided a focus for political opposition, and have made world news as Western film crews have explored them. Many other countries have experienced acid damage.

---

[2] As in the memorable lines of Tom Lehrer: 'If you visit an American city/You will find it very pretty/Just two things of which you must beware/Don't drink the water and don't breathe the air/Pollution, pollution, wear a gas mask and a veil/Then you can breathe as long as you don't inhale ...', (T.Lehrer, 'Pollution', on *That Was the Year that Was*, Pye records R6179, 1965).

However, all of these problems can ultimately be dealt with, or at least greatly ameliorated, by technical measures to remove the pollutants concerned. Catalytic converters on cars, which remove most exhaust contaminants, have been mandatory in the United States and Japan for many years, and soon will be in Europe. Scrubbers can be installed at power stations, and low-sulphur coal can be used, to remove most of the sulphur emissions, and other steps can be taken to reduce emissions of nitrogen oxides. These measures add to the costs of using fossil fuels and usually reduce the operating efficiency by a few per cent, but in no way have they yet threatened the pre-eminence of the fossil fuel economy.

The greenhouse effect, however, is in a league of its own. The single most important gas involved, CO_2, is not a mere by-product; it is a primary output from combustion. Hydrocarbons are the fuel, and burning them is the process which turns the hydrogen into water and the carbon into CO_2. The amount of CO_2 released is typically around a hundred times greater than the amount of sulphur dioxide emitted, and trying to remove and dispose of it is a task which most have concluded is not a feasible option - with a few caveats discussed below. If there really is a need to curtail CO_2 emissions from fossil fuels, the implications for the hydrocarbon economy are profound.

Why are there such concerns about the greenhouse effect? What are the possible responses to it, and what is the role of CO_2 from fossil fuels? The rest of this chapter sets the background by reviewing these questions.

1.2 The science of the greenhouse effect

If the earth had no atmosphere, the average temperature at the surface would be well below freezing. Various gases in the atmosphere absorb infra-red radiation and act as a blanket which helps to trap the heat absorbed and re-emitted from the surface. Human activity is increasing the concentration of such radiatively active gases, and hence changing the radiative balance in a way that seems certain to increase the surface temperature. The extent of the temperature rise, and its implications, is a matter of considerable uncertainty. A rise in temperature increases the concentration of water vapour in the atmosphere - itself the most important greenhouse gas - and changes the extent and nature of clouds, snow fall and ice cover; these and many other feedbacks, together with the uncertain role of oceans, greatly complicate assessment of the overall temperature change.

It is not yet clear whether human interference with the biosphere has pushed the temperature beyond the considerable range of natural variability. However, the 1980s, which saw the five warmest years on record and some extreme climatic disturbances - the most important of which politically was the US drought of 1988 - have helped to establish the greenhouse effect as a major political issue.

In response to widespread concerns, and the results of a series of international scientific workshops, the Intergovernmental Panel on Climate Change was established in 1988, charged with conducting an 18-month international assessment programme. This effort was divided among three working groups:

- Working Group I: Scientific assessment of the greenhouse effect
- Working Group II: Assessment of potential impacts
- Working Group III: Response strategies.

The conclusions of Working Group I,[3] (summarised in the box, pp.8-9), broadly supported the growing scientific concerns. The basic theory is unchallengeable. Also, the world has been getting warmer. Natural variability means that this cannot conclusively be attributed to the greenhouse effect, but it is consistent with current understanding of it. If trends in carbon emissions continue as projected, global average temperature over the next century is likely to rise by several degrees - comparable to, but considerably faster than, the changes since the last ice age. The changes would not be smooth and there would be considerable regional variations in both temperature and other impacts, most notably rainfall and soil moisture. Storm patterns might change, and sea levels rise.

Naturally not everyone has accepted these conclusions. A few US scientists argue that the likely rate of change is considerably smaller than the IPCC suggest,[4] and that the WGI summary report was unduly pessimistic. Others have expressed the fear that the conclusions were dangerously cautious, and highlighted the possibilities of further feedbacks which would amplify the concentrations of greenhouse

[3] J.T.Houghton, G.J.Jenkins and J.J.Ephraums (eds), *Climate Change:The IPCC Scientific Assessment*, Cambridge University Press, Cambridge, 1990. The publication details of the other two working group reports were not available at the time of going to press, but are available from the World Meterological Organisation.
[4] George C. Marshall Institute, *Scientific Perspectives on the Greenhouse Problem*, George C. Marshall Institute, Washington, DC, 1989. These arguments were considered during the IPCC assessment but gained little support.

gases.[5] The IPCC report itself noted that 'it appears likely that, as climate warms, these feedbacks will lead to an overall increase, rather than decrease, in natural greenhouse gas abundances. For this reason, climate change is likely to be greater than the estimates we have given.'[6]

Working Group II found that, given the uncertainties concerning precipitation and other regional variations, it was not possible to reach clear conclusions about the impacts. Climate change would be combined with other environmental stresses caused by human activities and natural variations. Agricultural impacts could be considerable at the regional level, but 'studies have not yet conclusively determined whether, on average, the global agricultural potential will increase or decrease'. Natural ecosystems, both on land and in the oceans, would be altered. Water resources could be a particular concern because 'relatively small climate changes can cause large water resource problems in many areas ... changes in drought risk represent potentially the most serious impact of climate change on agriculture'. Such factors, combined with changes in disease patterns and the impact of sea level rises combined with storm surges, 'could initiate large migrations of people'. Overall the WGII report emphasised that a key determinant would be the rate of climate change; irrespective of whether a stable warmer world might be better or worse, rapid changes could disrupt both human societies and natural ecosystems.

Set against this, Working Group III, concerned with response strategies, reflected the delicate political nature of its deliberations with broad generalisations hedged with caveats. 'Effective responses would require a global effort which may have a considerable impact on humankind and individual societies ... industrialised countries should adopt domestic measures to limit climate change by adapting their own economies in line with future agreements ... it is imperative that the right balance between economic and environmental objectives be struck.'

The body of the WGIII report noted various technical options which could help with both adaptation to climate change and mitigation of it, but did not review in any depth the actual policy steps which might be

[5] D.Schimel, 'Biogeochemical Feedbacks in the Earth System', and J.Leggett, 'The Nature of the Greenhouse Threat', both in J.Leggett (ed.), *Global Warming - the Greenpeace Report*, Oxford University Press, 1990.
[6] IPCC Working Group 1, *Policymakers Summary*, June 1990, p.19.

Summary of IPCC Working Group I conclusions

We are certain of the following:

There is a natural greenhouse effect which already keeps the earth warmer than it would otherwise be.

Emissions resulting from human activities are substantially increasing the atmospheric concentrations of the greenhouse gases (carbon dioxide, methane, chlorofluorocarbons (CFCs) and nitrous oxide). These increases will enhance the greenhouse effect, resulting on average in an additional warming of the earth's surface.

We calculate with confidence that:

Carbon dioxide has been responsible for over half the enhanced greenhouse effect in the past, and is likely to remain so in the future.

Atmospheric concentrations of the long-lived gases (carbon dioxide, nitrous oxide and the CFCs) adjust only slowly to changes in emissions. Continued emissions of these gases at present rates would commit us to increased concentrations for centuries ahead.

The long-lived gases would require immediate reductions in emissions from human activities of over 60% to stabilise their concentrations at today's levels; methane would require a 15-20% reduction.

Based on current model results, we predict:

The IPCC Business-as-Usual (Scenario A) emissions of greenhouse gases ... will result in a likely increase in global mean temperature of about 1 degree C above the present value by 2025 and 3 degrees C before the end of the next century.

That land surfaces warm more rapidly than the ocean, and high northern latitudes warm more than the global mean in winter.

Regional climate changes differ from the global mean, although our confidence in the prediction of the detail of regional changes is low. For example, temperature increases in Southern Europe and central North America are predicted to be higher than the global mean, accompanied on average by reduced summer precipitation and soil moisture.

An average rate of global mean sea-level rise of about 6cm per decade over the next century.

There are many uncertainties in our predictions particularly with regard to the timing, magnitude and regional patterns of climate change

Our judgement is that:

Global-mean surface air temperature has increased by 0.3 degrees C to 0.6 degrees C over the last 100 years, with the five global-average warmest years being in the 1980s ... These increases have not been smooth with time, nor uniform over the globe.

The size of this warming is broadly consistent with predictions of climate models, but it is also of the same magnitude as natural climate variability.

The unequivocal detection of the enhanced greenhouse effect from observations is not likely for a decade or more.

There is no firm evidence that climate has become more variable over the last few decades.

Ecosystems affect climate, and will be affected by a changing climate and increasing carbon dioxide concentrations.

required to achieve them. The baseline scenarios painted a picture of continuing rapid increases in CO_2 and methane, and WGIII was unable to form a view about whether or how lower scenarios might be achieved. In the light of the WGI conclusions, the case for some kind of serious policy response now seems strong. The political impetus for it is also considerable, and is likely to grow further. Extreme climatic events will occur - some always do. Scientifically it will be impossible to establish for certain whether or not they were caused by the greenhouse effect. But in the public mind, the association has been forged, and each extreme event will add to the pressure for action.

This book examines the possible policy options for trying to limit CO_2 emissions from the energy sector, and their implications for energy worldwide. Before embarking on this, however, it is necessary to review the broader range of policy options, and the role of energy within the greenhouse effect.

1.3 Policy responses: an overview

The main options in the face of this situation may be characterised as:[7]

* wait until scientific research has established greater certainty about the scale and implications of greenhouse impacts;
* focus on policies to adapt to climate change;
* adopt direct countermeasures to offset global warming;
* take measures to limit the increasing concentrations of greenhouse gases.

The first option, backed up by a rapidly expanding programme of research and assessment, is the option which the world has been broadly following to date. The concerns about continuing this state of affairs are well known. In changing the planet without fully understanding the consequences, humanity is clearly running a degree of risk; even if the known impacts were negligible, with only one planet on which to experiment uncertainty argues in favour of caution rather than continued and accelerating changes. Furthermore, the time delays involved in the climate system, and in modifying patterns of greenhouse gas emissions, mean that the world is already committed to significant changes decades

---

[7] For a characterisation and discussion of broad policy options, see D.Everest, *The Greenhouse Effect: Issues for Policy Makers*, Royal Institute of International Affairs, London, 1988.

beyond any decisions to do something about them, thus compounding the risks.

The greatest logical difficulty with a strategy of waiting until sufficient knowledge has been accumulated is the question of what constitutes sufficient knowledge. The IPCC warned that, even if all the modelling studies are accurate, and recent events are related to the greenhouse effect, it will be at least another decade before it is possible to be certain of the fact because of the range of natural variability. In fact, computer models have reached a broad degree of consensus about the likely rate of average warming, and the degree of uncertainty around this; the estimate has scarcely changed in five years, and few believe that further modelling refinements would greatly alter this picture. It therefore seems unlikely that doubters would be convinced by such efforts. More modelling and other studies might well improve regional understanding, but most analysts judge that predicting the long-run regional impacts with much confidence will take at least another decade of effort, and probably more. More extensive observational programmes would certainly help to verify some aspects of the models, but again they cannot give absolute certainty.

For some years to come, therefore, a policy of waiting for firmer evidence is probably equivalent to the second option, namely that of relying on adaptation. In practice, as Boyle and Ardill put it, 'adaptation to climate change is not so much an option as an inescapable necessity'.[8] Some degree of climate change now seems inevitable and societies will have to adapt to it. Everest notes that 'if the warming is relatively limited and slow to emerge, then adaptation to its impacts might well be left to the normal evolution of society, including the action of market forces'.[9] But as he noted this also carries risks, and perhaps high economic and human costs if the changes are rapid.

Adaptive strategies focus on measures which would help to minimise the possible costs and risks arising from climate change. Because so much about regional impacts is uncertain, policies need as far as possible to be both flexible and to give resilience to human and natural systems. Measures could include improvements in coastal defences, water management, and various agricultural practices including greater crop

---

[8] S.Boyle and J.Ardill, *The Greenhouse Effect*, New English Library, UK, 1989, p.137.
[9] Everest, *Greenhouse Effect: Issues for Policy Makers*, p.10.

diversity and tolerant strain selection, and enhanced national and international stocks of food and other resources.[10]

Some economists have attempted to put a value on the likely costs of climate change, and of adapting to it, but as discussed briefly in Chapter 3 below, such efforts are fraught with uncertainty and controversy. At present, all that can usefully be said is that the less the rate of atmospheric change, the less the risks and costs are likely to be. There is an unfathomable trade-off between the costs and risks of adaptation and those of trying to limit climate change. No-one really knows where that trade-off lies, but most people now accept that some limitation is important, and that the long-term prospects of very rapid change implied by current models and emission projections would not be acceptable. Assessing the costs and options for limitation - upon one major component of which this book concentrates - is clearly an essential element in these decisions.

The third broad option is to rely on countermeasures - interventions to counteract directly the warming effects of increasing greenhouse gases. Many suggestions have been made: injecting dust into the stratosphere, to absorb some solar radiation there; using aerosols (small particles) to 'seed' more clouds over the oceans so as to reflect more solar radiation; floating polystyrene on the oceans to achieve a similar result; and launching dust or small plates outside the atmosphere to block some solar radiation before it reaches the earth.

There are several problems with such 'geo-engineering' solutions.[11] First, a denser blanket of greenhouse gases is not the same thing as more solar radiation, and cannot be exactly offset by less. Thus there could still be significant regional climate changes even if the aggregate warming effects were exactly cancelled.[12] Worse, so much remains

---

[10] Various measures are discussed in the IPCC Working Group III report. A concise review of adaptation strategies is given in J.H.W.Karas and P.M.Kelly, *The Heat Trap*, Friends of the Earth, London, 1988 (Chapter 4). The key reference for many aspects of the greenhouse effect and its possible impacts remains the report by the international Scientific Committee on Problems of the Environment: B.Bolin et al. (eds), *The Greenhouse Effect, Climatic Change, and Ecosystems - SCOPE 29*, John Wiley & Sons, Chichester, 1986.

[11] Several of these points are drawn from a slightly longer discussion in S.Schneider, *Global Warming*, Sierra Club Books, San Francisco, 1989.

[12] This may be illustrated by taking the concept to the logical extreme of an almost perfectly insulated world with an average temperature equal to that of the present one

uncertain about the global mechanisms which regulate climate, including the exact magnitude of and delays affecting greenhouse warming, that it would be impossible to know how strong countermeasures should be or how they should be timed. If through ignorance the 'countermeasures' were overdone, the world might cool instead of getting warmer, which might be fine for some countries but not others.

This points to a political problem as serious as any; if there were any attempts deliberately to modify the global climate in this way, then any random and damaging climatic events might be attributed to them. Who would take the decisions, who would accept responsibility for them, and who would arbitrate as to whether climatic impacts were a consequence of the countermeasures? The greenhouse effect itself raises similar questions, but changes caused by deliberate intervention are politically a very different matter from those caused by the by-products of economic activity.

Such reasoning leads inevitably to the fourth option - to limit the build-up of greenhouse gases. This option and the issues that it raises form the main theme of this book, particularly in relation to energy and the use of fossil fuels. First, it is necessary to establish the role of CO_2 and other energy-related emissions within the broader pattern of greenhouse gas changes.

1.4 The greenhouse gases

Many different gases contribute to the greenhouse effect. The main ones which are affected directly by human activities are carbon dioxide (CO_2), various chlorofluorocarbons (CFCs), methane (CH_4), nitrous oxide (N_2O), and tropospheric (low-level) ozone (O_3). Choosing the gases and processes on which abatement measures could best concentrate requires some understanding of relative impacts, trends, sources and control options.

Figure 1.1 shows the relative contribution which the main gases are judged to have made to the changes in the relevant characteristics of the

---

The temperature would be almost the same at the poles as at the equator, and presumably everything would be bathed in a weak dusky light just sufficient to offset the slow heat losses.

Figure 1.1 Relative contribution of greenhouse gases to radiative change in the 1980s

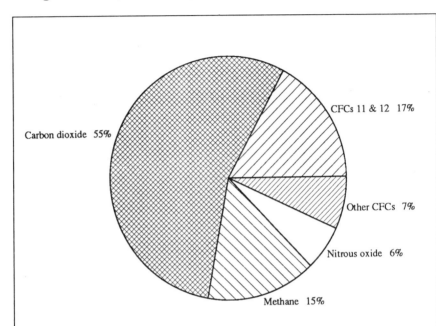

Carbon dioxide 55%

CFCs 11 & 12　17%

Other CFCs　7%

Nitrous oxide　6%

Methane　15%

The contribution from tropospheric ozone may also be significant, but cannot be quantified at present.

Source: J.T.Houghton, G.J.Jenkins and J.J.Ephraums (eds), *Climate Change: The IPCC Scientific Assessment*, Cambridge University Press, Cambridge, 1990.

atmosphere during the 1980s.[13] Of the measurable gases, CO_2 emissions accounted for about 55%, and CFCs nearly a quarter. The rest was divided between methane (15%) and nitrous oxide (6%). Tropospheric ozone made some contribution, but because this is a

---

[13] The greenhouse effect is driven by the 'radiative forcing' of the atmosphere, which depends on the absorption and re-emission of incoming solar radiation compared with that of radiation re-emitted from the earth's surface.

Table1.1 Greenhouse gases: atmospheric characteristics and trends

	Carbon Dioxide	Methane	CFC-11	CFC-12	Nitrous Oxide
Atmospheric concentration	ppmv	ppmv	pptv	pptv	ppbv
Pre-industrial (1750-1800)	280	0.8	0	0	288
Present day (1990)	353	1.72	280	484	310
Current rate of change per year	1.8 (0.5%)	0.015 (0.9%)	9.5 (4%)	17 (4%)	0.8 (0.25%)
Atmospheric lifetime (years)	(50-200)†	10	65	130	150

ppmv = parts per million by volume;
ppbv = parts per billion (thousand million) by volume;
pptv = parts per trillion (million million) by volume;
† The way in which CO_2 is absorbed by the oceans and biosphere is not simple and a single value cannot be given.

Source: IPCC, (see Figure 1.1)

localised and relatively short-lived gas the overall magnitude is extremely uncertain.

Table 1.1 shows some atmospheric characteristics and trends of these gases. The CFCs are increasing most rapidly, followed by methane and then CO_2. CFC-12, CO_2 and N_2O are relatively long-lived; for these, a substantial fraction of emissions made today will still be in the atmosphere at the end of the next century. Other CFCs and replacements have somewhat shorter lifetimes, and methane on average lasts only ten years before it is chemically broken down - although in the process it affects other greenhouse gases, so that it also has an indirect impact which may be of a similar magnitude to the effect of methane itself.

Table 1.2 Relative global warming impact of 1990 emissions over the next 100 years

	Global warming potential (100yr horizon)	1990 emissions (Tg)	Relative contribution over 100yr
Carbon dioxide	1	26000†	61%
Methane*	21	300	15%
Nitrous Oxide	290	6	4%
CFCs	Various	0.9	11%
HCFC-22	1500	0.1	0.5%
Others*	Various		8.5%

* These values include the indirect effect of these emissions on other greenhouse gases via chemical reactions in the atmosphere. Such estimates are highly model dependent and should be considered preliminary and subject to change. The estimated effect of ozone is included under 'others'.
† 26000 Tg (teragrams) of carbon dioxide =7000 Tg (=7Gt) of carbon

Source: IPCC, (see Figure 1.1)

Because of these variations, the relative impact of different gases depends on the timescales considered. Table 1.2 shows the relative global warming impact of estimated emissions in 1990 totalled over the next 100 years, including the more speculative contributions from the less well understood gases: notably, the indirect contributions from unburnt hydrocarbons and nitrogen oxides, which are implicated in the formation of low-level ozone, and carbon monoxide which helps to sustain methane in the atmosphere by competing for the substances which destroy it.

If emissions continue at current rates, the concentration of the different gases will continue rising, with relative impacts not unlike those in

Table 1.3 Emission reductions required to stabilise atmospheric concentrations at current levels

Reductions in the man-made emissions of greenhouse gases required to stabilise concentrations at present day levels:

Carbon dioxide	>60%
Methane	15 - 20%
Nitrous Oxide	70 - 80%
CFC-11	70 - 75%
CFC-12	75 - 85%
HCFC-22	40 - 50%

Note the stabilisation of each of these gases would have different effects on climate.

Source: IPCC, (see Figure 1.1)

Figure 1.1.[14] Actually to stabilise concentrations in the atmosphere at current levels, emissions would have to be reduced as shown in Table 1.3. Emissions of all the long-lived gases would have to be cut by over 60%. The figure for CO_2 is particularly complex because of the interactions with the oceans; a 60% cut might stabilise concentrations for a few years, but if emissions then continued at the reduced rate concentration would start to rise again. More extensive reductions still would be required to prevent a long term increase in CO_2 concentrations.

The anthropogenic sources of these gases, as indicated in Table 1.4, are many and varied. Carbon dioxide emissions are primarily from fossil fuel

[14] Complexities in the CO_2 and methane cycles, and non-linearities in the impact of non-CFC gases, mean that this is a rather broad approximation, but it emphasises the fact that just because the concentration of one gas is growing faster than another, it does not mean that its relative contribution is expanding from previous incremental changes.

Table 1.4 Greenhouse gases and their main anthropogenic sources

Carbon dioxide (CO_2)	Fossil fuel burning Deforestation and land use change Cement manufacture
Methane (CH_4)	Rice paddy cultivation Ruminants (eg. cows, sheep) Biomass (wood,wastes etc) burning and decay Releases from fossil fuel production
Chlorofluorocarbons (CFCs)	Manufactured for solvents, refrigerants, aerosol spray propellants, foam packaging, etc
Nitrous Oxide (N_2O)	Fertilisers Fossil fuel burning Land conversion for agriculture

Precursor gases (involved in ozone and methane chemistry):

Nitrogen oxides (NO_x)	Fossil fuel burning
Non-methane hydrocarbons	Evaporation of liquid fuels and solvents
Carbon monoxide (CO)	Fossil fuel and biomass burning

Source: M.Grubb, *The Greenhouse Effect: Negotiating Targets*, Royal Institute
of International Affairs, London, 1990.

combustion, which accounts for about 6 billion tonnes of carbon annually
at present. Carbon dioxide emissions from deforestation and other land
use are very uncertain. One detailed review suggests 1.0±0.6GtC/yr.[15]
Others argue that such values are based on unduly low estimates of forest
biomass and deforestation rates; another review suggests 0.9-2.5GtC/yr

[15] D.O.Hall, 'Carbon flows in the biosphere: present and future', *Journal of the
Geological Society*, London, Vol.146, 1989, pp.175-81.

in 1980, with mean 1.8GtC/yr - and states that the figure has increased substantially during the 1980s.[16]

The sources of methane are exceptionally complex and varied. In addition to the anthropogenic sources there are many natural ones, including the decay of vegetation and releases from termite mounds, which account for perhaps a third of the total methane emissions. Also it is thought that some methane may be released from tundra and from 'clathrates' (methane locked in ice crystals, mostly below the sea bed) in response to global warming itself. The relative importance of the various sources, and the practical means for controlling them, are poorly understood. As already noted, methane lifetimes are also extended by carbon monoxide.[17]

Chlorofluorocarbons have already received attention because of their role in depleting the stratospheric ozone layer, but they are also powerful greenhouse gases. CFCs are entirely man-made, being manufactured for a wide variety of industrial and domestic uses.

Policy efforts need to focus on the gases which are important and for which the sources are broadly known and controllable. The first priority is clearly to reduce substantially emissions of the long-lived CFCs. Because of their role in depleting the stratospheric ozone layer, measures have already been taken; with a revision of the Montreal Protocol[18] in mid-1990, the developed economies agreed to phase out CFC production by the end of the 1990s, and the future contribution from the developing countries has been effectively capped. Some of the proposed substitutes could also have greenhouse impacts, but these are much more modest than the gases they replace, and attention will be paid to the greenhouse implications in considering them.

Any further steps to slow atmospheric change clearly need to address two different issues. One is to ensure that emissions of the short-lived gases - especially methane but also those contributing to tropospheric ozone - do not grow out of control, so that their total impact is kept modest. The other component is to try and slow as far as possible the

[16] R.A.Houghton and G.M.Woodwell, 'Global climate change', *Scientific American* 260, 1989, pp.36-44.
[17] For a comprehensive review of methane chemistry, sources, and sinks, see R.J.Cicerone and R.S.Orenland, 'Biogeochemical Aspects of Atmospheric Methane', *Global Biogeochemical Cycles*, Vol.2, December 1988, pp.299-327.
[18] First Review Meeting of Parties to the 1987 Montreal Protocol on Substances that Deplete the Ozone Layer, London, June 1990.

build-up of CO_2. Energy is strongly implicated in the first, and central to the second.

Fossil fuel activities contribute to methane emissions in several ways. Methane escapes from coal mines, it is vented from oil wells, and it leaks from gas production and distribution; together, these are estimated to account for perhaps 20% of methane emissions from human-related sources.[19] The impact of methane relative to the carbon dioxide from fuels has been a matter of some debate;[20] for the reasons discussed above it depends strongly upon the timescale over which impacts are considered. Especially in considering long-term impacts, but also given that global coal mine emissions are estimated to be of the same order as those from oil and gas production and distribution,[21] accounting for methane emissions seems most unlikely to change substantially the relative impact of different fuels as judged on the basis of carbon content alone.

In addition, incomplete burning of fossil fuels - for example in poorly maintained car engines - results in carbon monoxide, which, as noted, helps to sustain methane in the atmosphere. Nitrogen oxides are also formed in fossil fuel combustion, which together with the evaporation of volatile hydrocarbons from oil products helps to form tropospheric ozone. Measures to clean up vehicle and power station emissions reduce these impacts considerably.

Combined with the impact of CO_2, these gases make energy consumption the dominant human activity contributing to the greenhouse effect. Estimates vary, but place the contribution from fossil fuel activities in the range 45-70% of the total human impact[22] - a

---

[19] Cicerone and Orenland, 'Biogeochemical Aspects'. The biggest sources are estimated to be natural wetlands and rice paddies, followed by animals and biomass burning, with termites and landfills on the same order as coal mines and gas sources.

[20] J.P.Stern, *European Gas Markets: Challenge and Opportunity in the 1990s*, Dartmouth/Gower, Aldershot, 1990, Appendix III, 'Some observations on methane leakage'.

[21] Cicerone and Orenland, 'Biogeochemical Aspects'.

[22] The IPCC estimated the contribution from fossil fuels to the change in radiative forcing during the 1980s to be 34-54%, but the total impact over time is considerably larger because of the long lifetime of the CO_2. The 1980s were probably also the peak decade for CFC and deforestation contributions. The range given reflects differing timescales and differing assumptions about the contribution of ozone, and of various non-energy activities, notably deforestation.

fraction which is likely to grow further as CFCs are phased out, and more still if fossil fuel use grows and deforestation is curbed.

There is one respect in which fossil fuels may help to offset average warming. Sulphur emissions form aerosols which can reflect sunlight, and when they drift over oceans, they help to create clouds which do likewise. One analysis suggests that the impact of growing sulphur dioxide emissions from power stations might have been sufficient to offset a substantial fraction of greenhouse warming in the northern hemisphere for much of this century, though the calculations are inevitably uncertain.[23] Needless to say, sulphur dioxide emissions leave much to be desired as a countermeasure, even in comparison with the general drawbacks discussed earlier. But it would hardly be a new theme in energy to find that, in addressing a more pressing and visible environmental threat, efforts to clean up sulphur may as a by-product be unwittingly contributing to a longer-term one, by allowing the real impact of greenhouse gas emissions on the earth's radiative balance to show through more clearly.

All these gases could be significant but they are of relatively minor importance in terms of long-term radiative impact, and also for energy, compared with CO_2. Reducing the use of fossil fuels would reduce these emissions but to a large extent the non-CO_2 emissions can be removed by technical measures: efforts to capture methane from mines; greater efforts to flare methane instead of venting it, and to reduce leakages; and various technical measures to reduce CO, NO_x, methane and other volatile hydrocarbon emissions. The real problem lies with CO_2.

1.5 Global carbon flows: oceans, forests and the role of fossil fuels

The earth is a vast system for recycling carbon. Every year, over 100Gt (Gigatonnes, or thousand million tonnes) of carbon as CO_2 is absorbed by plant life, and emitted again as plants decay or respire soil carbon back to the atmosphere. Similar amounts are cycled through the oceans. Set against this, the 6GtC contribution from fossil fuels appears very small. This has led many people to suggest that, rather than trying to

---

[23] T.M.L.Wigley, 'Possible climate change due to SO_2-derived cloud condensation nuclei', *Nature*, Vol.339, 1 June 1989, pp.365-7: 'One can place limits on the possible magnitude of any SO_2-derived forcing. The upper limit is sufficiently large that the effects of SO_2 may have significantly offset the temperature changes that have resulted from the greenhouse effect.'

reduce fossil carbon emissions, it would make more sense to seek small alterations in the natural flows to absorb the extra few per cent input from fossil fuels.

The fact that fossil emissions are small compared with natural flows is not in itself a very helpful observation. Assuming that this makes it easy to absorb the excess is much like assuming that human beings could themselves help to absorb carbon by holding a little air back each time they breathe. Unless there is somewhere for the carbon to go, it doesn't work.

Many hopes have been placed in the oceans as a reservoir for carbon. The oceans act as a vast CO_2 pump. Cold water can hold more CO_2 than warm. Crudely summarised, warm water from the equator picks up CO_2 from the atmosphere as it flows towards the poles, where it tends to sink when its temperature falls towards freezing, carrying dissolved and organic carbon with it. In addition, organisms in the surface layers accumulate carbon which may sink as particles, including shells of some sea creatures when they die. Most of this dissolves on the way down, though some may reach the bottom especially in shallower waters. The relative contribution of these routes is uncertain, but in all over 100GtC is estimated to be taken down through these routes each year.[24]

However, the ocean is essentially saturated with CO_2, so that what goes down comes up. As deep waters well to the surface in the tropics and warm, they give off copious amounts of CO_2.

Overall the oceans do act to take up some CO_2. Rising atmospheric concentrations force more CO_2 into the surface waters, which gives a short-term uptake.[25] As the ocean waters slowly circulate, relatively more carbon is taken down and less is given off, so that in addition carbon is gradually taken up throughout the body of the ocean, over several hundreds to thousands of years. If all the carbon in known fossil fuel resources were put into the ocean-atmosphere system, a stable state

---

[24] H.H.W. de Baar and M.B.C.Stoll, 'Storage of Carbon Dioxide in the Oceans', in P.A.Okken, R.J.Swart, and S.Zwerver(eds) *Climate and Energy: the Feasibility of Controlling CO2 Emissions*, Kluwer Academic Publishers, Dordracht, The Netherlands, 1989.

[25] Recent studies, however, suggest that the oceans are a less important sink for carbon than was previously assumed (P.P.Tans, I.Y.Fing, T.Takahashi, 'Observational constraints on the global atmospheric CO2 budget', *Science* 247, 23 March 1990, pp.1431-8).

would eventually be reached after about 2000 years with an atmospheric concentration about four times pre-industrial levels.[26]

There may be some opportunities for stimulating faster uptake of carbon by the oceans. In particular, if it were possible to stimulate the growth and death of surface water organisms which then sink, this would speed the process; indeed, if it were in a form or location where the organisms reached the bottom the carbon might be taken out of the system for good. Unfortunately, the main factor limiting the growth of organisms is the nutrient supply, and dead organisms take their nutrients along with their carbon. The main source of new nutrients is deep water, but this brings the carbon straight back up again. In all, the options for stimulating oceans to take up carbon much faster seem distinctly limited, though a modest contribution might be possible.[27]

Land routes seem more important on the timescales of interest. Trees are themselves part of the global carbon recycling system, but because they can store carbon for such a long time, on timescales of years to decades they are themselves sources of and sinks for carbon. Currently, as is well known, the destruction of old forests is releasing uncertain but probably large amounts of carbon; the figures cited earlier equate to 5%-50% of the emissions from fossil fuels.

Reducing deforestation would be an important contribution to limiting CO_2 increases, though its effect would be modest compared with projected growth in fossil fuel emissions. It would have many other benefits. However, the causes of deforestation are often deep-rooted; Holdgate[28] describes it as one of six 'unstoppable' trends (the greenhouse effect is another). Because the causes and implications are so different, the contribution is so uncertain, and amelioration would not

---

[26] de Baar and Stoll, 'Storage of Carbon Dioxide'. This is roughly twice the level which would appear from a simple comparison of CO_2 quantities, because the ocean waters absorb roughly one atom of carbon from bottom rocks for each one entering in the form of CO_2, to buffer the acidity created by CO_2.

[27] There is evidence that in Antarctic waters, iron is a factor limiting organism growth, so that some carbon uptake might be stimulated by scattering iron-rich dust on the surface (J.H.Martin, R.M.Gordon, S.E.Fitzwater, 'Iron in Antarctic Waters', *Nature*, Vol.345, pp.156-8, 10 May 1990; A.G.Davies, 'Taking a Cool Look at Iron', ibid., pp.114-5).

[28] M.Holdgate, 'The Environment of Tomorrow's World', Annual Memorial Lecture, David Davies Memorial Institute of International Studies, London, February 1990.

significantly change the situation regarding fossil fuels, deforestation is not considered further in this book.

Reforestation is another matter, and one which to a considerable extent is separate from deforestation. New trees would steadily absorb carbon over the next few decades as they grew, and thus in principle could counteract fossil fuel emissions. However, the scales involved are daunting. Absorbing 1Gt/yr of carbon would require trees sufficient to cover about 1 million square kilometres (again, the figure is a matter of some debate, and certainly over short periods absorption might be greater than this).[29]

A million square kilometres is a lot of land - an area equivalent to the UK, France and West Germany combined. Trees would not all have to be planted in great forests, of course; many could be planted in small stands around villages, along roads, etc. But experience demonstrates that it is not possible simply to plant a seed and walk away; in most environments, trees need nurturing if they are to survive. Though the land exists,[30] absorbing 1GtC/yr from new trees would be a mammoth undertaking. Even then it would only be a temporary fix, lasting some decades; as trees matured they would absorb carbon more slowly, so to keep up the process additional trees would have to be planted, or the old replaced and stored in such a way that they would not decay and release their carbon; burning the wood to displace fossil fuels might make more sense.

There are other possible land-based routes; given limitations on current ocean uptake, land sources must already be absorbing a net several billion tonnes of carbon annually, though no-one is entirely sure what the main routes are. Carbon dioxide stimulates plant growth, other things being equal, and the net standing biomass may be increasing; plants must also be transferring carbon into soils. Less is known about this, but it might be possible artificially to accelerate the transfer in some way. Unfortunately many factors may again limit this process, including the water and nutrient requirements for more rapid fixation of carbon.

[29] N.Myers, 'The Greenhouse Effect: A Tropical Forestry Response', *Biomass* 18, Elsevier Science, 1989. Myers notes that, although 1 million km^2 is a lot of land, it is roughly equal to 'wasted lands' in developing country regions, and that a further 2 million km^2 'needs to be reforested for reasons other than control of the greenhouse effect'.
[30] Ibid.

At present, other human activities are steadily eroding the area of healthy vegetation which may be taking part in the natural uptake, and one of the worst greenhouse scenarios would be if climate changes began to occur so fast that land ecosystems were disrupted to the extent that their current net uptake of carbon was reversed. Perhaps the most important message concerning land routes is to minimise devegetation, land erosion and disruption, so that natural systems have the greatest opportunity to absorb carbon.

In all, options do exist for absorbing some extra CO_2 once it is in the atmosphere, but these seem distinctly limited. If serious efforts are to be made to reduce its build-up in the atmosphere, the trap on fossil fuels by this logic appears to be closing. There is only one possible escape route left. Can fossil fuels be used without emitting CO_2?

1.6 Coal without carbon: options and limitations

Trying to remove carbon from fossil fuel combustion is a daunting task, because CO_2 is the primary product of combustion, not a secondary one.

In a sense, the simplest way of reducing carbon emissions is to move to fuels with a lower relative carbon content. As illustrated in Table 1.5, a tonne of crude oil contains about 0.85 tonnes of carbon. Coal with a similar energy content contains 25-30% more carbon; gas, 25-30% less. The ratio of carbon to energy content for coal:oil:gas is thus roughly 100:77:56. This variation occurs because oil and gas contain successively more hydrogen, the conversion of which to water contributes to their energy value. The energy used in extracting and processing these fuels, emissions of other gases en route, and non-energy uses, mean that slightly different numbers apply in estimating the emissions of CO_2 from fossil fuel production and consumption statistics, but this does not change the overall picture.[31]

Switching towards natural gas in particular (discussed further in Chapter 5) could certainly help to limit carbon emissions, but clearly there are constraints on this. Coal resources constitute by far the largest and most widespread of fossil fuel resources, and many communities and industries, and some would say nations, have been built around them. Are there any options for reducing CO_2 emissions from coal itself?

---

[31] Volume II; M.J.Grubb, 'On coefficients for determining greenhouse gas emissions from fossil fuel production and consumption', in OECD/IEA, *Energy Technologies for Reducing Emissions of Greenhouse Gases*, Proc. Experts Seminar, Paris, April 1989.

Table 1.5 Carbon content of different fossil fuels

	tC/TJ	tC/Mtoe	Range
Natural gas	13.8	0.61	±1%
Crude oil	19.0	0.84	±2%
Bituminous coals	24.5	1.09	±4%
Anthracites	15.5	1.14	±3%
Oil products			
Gasoline	18.0	0.80	±2%
Kerosene	18.5	0.82	±2%
Diesel/gas oil	19.0	0.84	±2%
Fuel oils	10.0	0.88	±2%

Source:M.J.Grubb, 'On coefficients for determining greenhouse gas emissions from fossil fuel production and consumption'. (See note [31]).

Most efforts have focused on power stations, which account for a substantial fraction of coal use and form a ready and centralised target. The brute force approach is to 'scrub' the CO_2 from the stack gases. This has been investigated extensively, and to say the least it does not appear promising, partly because the financial and energy costs of separating out the CO_2 from the exhaust air are quite high.[32]

[32] G.Marland, 'Technical Fixes for Limiting the Increase of Atmospheric CO_2: A Review', Institute for Energy Analysis, Oak Ridge Associated Universities, Oak Ridge, Tennessee, 1986.

Recently a more promising approach was suggested by researchers at Utrecht.[33] Coal gasification for power generation, in which coal is turned into gases which can then be put into a gas turbine, is a well-known though not fully established technology. The Utrecht researchers pointed out that in the mix of gases produced, the energy in the carbon could be largely transferred to hydrogen using a well-known reaction, to produce CO_2 in the input gas stream at a much higher concentration than appears after it is burnt with air. This makes a process of physical separation possible, with CO_2 extracted at much lower cost and higher efficiency than in earlier processes considered. Initial estimates suggest that the process itself would add 10-20% to the generation costs.

Williams[34] has further pointed out that if one is going to take such trouble to produce hydrogen from coal, burning it in a gas turbine may not be the most sensible thing to do with it. Hydrogen is potentially a valuable fuel, especially for overpolluted urban environments where a fuel which produces only water when burnt would appear as the answer to some prayers. Assuming the hydrogen could be adequately cleansed of contaminants, it would still be more expensive than oil-based fuels in most applications, but it might well be attractive if there were a strong need for cleaner fuels.

However, the real catch to all this is what to do with the vast quantities of CO_2 collected.[35] Some CO_2 could be used to help stimulate more oil from nearly depleted wells, but the total scope for this is very limited. The Utrecht researchers, coincidentally sitting on top of one of the world's major gas fields, suggested that it could be injected into depleted gas fields, which certainly constitute a much larger volume.[36] However, even this would be limited. The volume of gas fields in total

[33] C.A.Hendriks, K.Blok and W.C.Turkenburg, 'The recovery of carbon dioxide from power plants', in Okken et al., *Climate and Energy*.
[34] R.H.Williams, 'Hydrogen from coal with gas and oil well sequestering of the recovered CO_2', Center for Energy and Environmental Studies, Princeton University, Princeton NJ, June 1990.
[35] The ideal solution would be to remove the CO_2 in an inert solid form. The problem is that producing solids to bind carbon from CO_2 may require energy comparable to that released in the first place. Possible lower energy solids are likely to involve minerals which would soon be exhausted if they were used to bind CO_2 from fossil fuels. No serious solidifying process seems to have been suggested.
[36] A.C. van der Harst and A.J.F.M. van Nieuwland, 'Disposal of carbon dioxide in depleted natural gas reservoirs', in Okken et al., *Climate and Energy*.

might be able to hold CO_2 arising from a few decades of global coal use at current levels, but the practical application would be much less than this. Fields need to be almost depleted. Coal is rarely in the same place as depleted gas fields, and shifting either the coal or the CO_2 from one place to another - and then transporting the electricity or hydrogen produced - would not be an easy or cost-free task. Furthermore, the gas industry uses depleted fields for storage, which would become more important if gas use increased greatly. Some CO_2 would also tend to leak back out. There are some other subterranean possibilities but all seem limited.

Disposal of CO_2 in the deep oceans has been widely canvassed. However, it would add further to the costs and, contrary to earlier assumptions which frequently overlooked the dynamics of ocean carbon flows discussed above, would also be of rather limited application.[37] If injected into waters on continental shelves, much of the highly concentrated CO_2 would find its way back to the surface within a few years or decades - perhaps with rather serious consequences for organisms in its path. Pumping it directly to the ocean deeps, where it could stay as liquid and sink to the bottom, would be extremely expensive except perhaps for countries which could operate their systems on coasts near very deep waters or diving ocean currents. Even so, some of the CO_2 would still eventually surface, though much might be absorbed more widely in the deep ocean, and again there might be oceanic environmental impacts.

Much as for other technical fixes for removing or absorbing carbon, therefore, CO_2 removal might be feasible in special cases, and if so it could make some contribution to limiting the growth of atmospheric CO_2. But the problem ultimately is that the huge volume of the global fossil fuel enterprise, operating in a biosphere which is essentially saturated with carbon, simply swamps such measures.

If greenhouse gases really do need to be controlled, then fossil fuels cannot escape the consequences. What then are the options?

---

[37] de Barr and Stoll, 'Storage of carbon dioxide'.

1.7 Technical options for limiting fuel use

The technical options for limiting fossil fuel consumption are many and varied, and vast amounts have been written about them.[38] They differ greatly in their degree of readiness and attractiveness. Volume II summarises some of the main technologies on offer, which divide into two broad categories.

The use of more efficient energy technologies has become recognised as offering the most attractive near-term potential. All societies waste energy, and better technologies which are already available can offer substantial savings at relatively low costs, often in fact with net economic benefits. Such options exist in all energy sectors, and most studies conclude that, if existing technologies could be replaced by the most efficient economic options available, energy use could be reduced by 20-50% in developed and developing countries alike (see Chapter 7).

Furthermore, the currently available technologies in no way exhaust the potential for improved efficiency. From a standpoint of pure thermodynamics, the services demanded by modern societies need not take more than a few per cent of the energy actually consumed today.[39]

Options for reducing the carbon intensity of energy supply also span a wide range. Coal and oil can be used more efficiently, both directly and in power systems for generating and distributing electricity. The same goes for gas, which in many applications can more than halve the carbon emissions associated with traditional coal technologies. Uranium, used either in conventional reactors or one of a variety of possible advanced designs, produces negligible carbon emissions. Finally, there are many and varied forms of renewable energy: hydro, solar heating, solar

---

[38] For example: OECD/IEA, *Energy Technologies for Reducing Emissions of Greenhouse Gases*, Proc. Experts Seminar, Paris, 1989 (Vols 1 & 2); W.Fulkerson et al., *Energy Technology R&D: What Could Make a Difference?*, Oak Ridge National Laboratory, ORNL-6541, Tennessee, US, 1990, Vols 1-3; G.Thurlow (ed.), *Technical Responses to the Greenhouse Effect*, Rooster Books/Watt Committee, Royston, UK, 1990.

[39] A figure of around 2% has been estimated for the US (R.U.Ayres, 'Energy Inefficiencies in the US Economy: a New Case for Conservation', IIASA Research Report RR89/12, International Institute for Applied Systems Analysis, Laxenburg, Austria, 1990), and of 4-5% for Western Europe (N.Nakicenovic, L.Bodda, A.Grubler, P.V.Gilli, 'Technical Progress, Structural Change, and Efficient Energy Use', draft IIASA report, International Institute for Applied Systems Analysis, 1990). The figure varies according to assumptions, but it is clear that societies are a very long way from thermodynamic limits on the efficiency of energy use.

electricity, various advanced forms of waste and biomass use, wind, tidal, wave and assorted other options including the quasi-renewable geothermal sources. Many of the relevant technologies exist, and they are steadily improving.

The total energy resources of each of the major energy options are very large, as reviewed in Volume II and summarised in Chapter 5 of this volume. In terms of resources coal could sustain most projected growth throughout the twenty-first century. Oil is the most constrained fuel, but it is now expected to last several decades at near current levels of production. Gas reserves are comparable with those of oil, but are widely expected to prove larger in the long run, because there has been much less exploration so far. There are also various possibilities for 'unconventional' sources of both oil (tar sands, oil shales) and gas (deep deposits, ice-bound sources).

Limits on uranium reserves might constrain the long-term contribution of nuclear power if applied in conventional reactors, though this is not certain. Application in fast breeder reactors would extend the effective reserves by a factor of up to fifty. The total solar resource is also very large: solar energy reaches the surface of the earth at more than ten thousand times the rate of human energy consumption. Even the weak derivatives such as the winds disperse energy much faster than humans consume it.

Technical options to reduce carbon emissions drastically thus exist, and more can be foreseen. They can also bring additional benefits, in terms of reducing other pollutants and reducing the pressure and dependence upon sometimes volatile fossil fuel markets. Yet this is but the beginning of the story. Many options are still inadequate - too costly, not efficient or reliable enough, or unacceptable for other environmental or political reasons; how can they be improved and made more acceptable? Other options are in principle quite attractive, but they simply do not fit very well into existing infrastructures and institutions; can these be altered to accommodate the technologies, and if so, how? Even for those which, like many energy efficiency options, seem relatively easy and desirable in their own right, there are serious questions as to why, if they are so good, they are not taken up at present, and how this situation might be changed.

Deeper questions underlie these ones. What are the political pressures and constraints upon governments concerned about the greenhouse effect? If governments did want to act upon the issue, what could they actually *do*? What are the pros and cons of the various policy instruments, and how much impact might they actually have on emissions? How much might it cost, and how can this be measured? How would energy markets react to attempts to limit fossil fuel consumption, and what would be the implications for the energy industries and their constituents? To what extent might governments act alone; to what extent is international co-ordination of policy response needed? And how long might such developments take, given the inertia of existing infrastructure and institutions?

These are the much harder questions which underlie the bland statement that technical options exist. It is to these questions that this study is devoted.

Energy Trends and Country Studies

If trends continue unaltered by abatement policies, energy demand and carbon emissions are likely to grow in most countries, quite slowly in most industrialised countries, and very rapidly in the developing world, relative to current levels. The long-term potential for growth in the developing countries is immense, but the currently industrialised countries will account for the majority of carbon emissions for several decades to come. If global emissions of fossil carbon are to be constrained, strong action within industrialised countries will be essential both because of their absolute contribution and as a precursor to action by developing countries.

Detailed studies of the prospects for energy balances, carbon emissions, and abatement policies in a number of countries are summarised. These all support the broad interpretation of energy trends indicated above, but differ widely in their assessment of the practical potential for limiting carbon emissions. Studies of the UK and of Japan suggest that strong abatement policies are feasible, though by no means easy, and that these countries could reduce emissions considerably given time. The constraints are judged to be much greater for the United States and the USSR, where the size of the energy system and historical reliance on cheap energy create a great inertia, and reluctance to countenance measures which would affect consumption and domestic energy industries; in both countries this is compounded by political circumstances.

Studies of China and of India both conclude that reducing emissions from current levels is not possible, but they differ greatly in their assessment of the ease and desirability of abatement policies, and of the impact which they might have on future emissions. Both conclude that abatement may depend heavily on the degree and form of international assistance, though internal factors are also very important. Some of the OECD country studies also suggest such assistance as a less costly route to limiting global emissions than domestic action.

Taken together, the case studies emphasise the extent to which abatement policies and impacts are likely to vary between countries, and suggest that abatement may depend upon broad institutional, socio-political and macroeconomic factors (such as capital availability) much more than on technical issues of performance and cost-effectiveness.

The case study scenarios taken together imply that abatement policies could make a considerable impact on emissions over the next forty years, but not to anything like the extent advocated by many of those concerned about the greenhouse effect. However, in many countries there is a clear need for more data and analysis in several key areas, including: the influences determining future energy demand and the scope for more efficient use; the potential for and obstacles facing non-fossil sources; the costs of carbon abatement; and a more rigorous appraisal of the policy instruments available to governments.

2.1 Energy trends, past and present

Human development has been marked by almost uninterrupted growth in energy use. Consumption rose steadily as civilisations developed around agriculture. Industrialisation led to sharply increasing growth rates; UK consumption rose by a factor of 10 through the nineteenth-century industrial revolution, and other industrial countries followed similar patterns.[1]

The growth has not been smooth. Global demand for commercial fuels from 1860 to 1914 grew by over 4%/yr. Growth slowed to 2-3%/yr following the First World War and during the depression of the 1930s. The economic boom of the post-Second World War years resulted in a resumed growth averaging over 4%/yr up to 1970. There were some signs of a slowdown towards the end of the 1960s, which was greatly strengthened by the direct and indirect effects of the 1973 and 1979 oil price shocks on a world growth dependent upon highly concentrated oil reserves; demand in the developed countries remained almost static during this period. The latter 1980s have seen faster growth again, especially since the oil price collapse of 1986.

The mix of fuels has changed, but not dramatically. In most areas outside the United States, coal dominated energy supplies at least until the Second World War, but the rapid growth from then until 1973 was fuelled by oil. Since 1973, the growth of oil has been drastically curtailed while all other fuels have expanded, with renewed growth in coal demand, a surge in the use of natural gas - previously often regarded as a valueless by-product of oil and flared at the wells - and the completion of many nuclear and hydro schemes. These trends since 1965 are illustrated in Figure 2.1.

Carbon emissions from fossil fuels have grown more slowly than total energy consumption, because of the increased use of gas and non-fossil sources, but this has not prevented them from increasing rapidly. In 1989, world fossil carbon emissions[2] stood at about 6 billion tonnes of carbon

---

[1] For data on early energy consumption trends see D.Schumacher, I.Berkovitch, R.Besketh and J.Stammers, *Energy: Crisis or Opportunity?*, Macmillan, London, 1985; R.Eden, M.Posner, R.Bending, R.Crouch and J.Stanislaw, *Energy Economics*, Cambridge University Press, Cambridge, 1981.

[2] Statistics throughout this book reflect the amount of carbon released from fossil fuel combustion, almost all of which is converted to carbon dioxide. This is kept distinct from non-fossil emissions, mostly from deforestation, for reasons discussed in Chapter 1. The coefficients used in deriving carbon releases from primary fuel data contain

Figure 2.1 Global commercial energy consumption and fossil carbon emissions, 1965-89

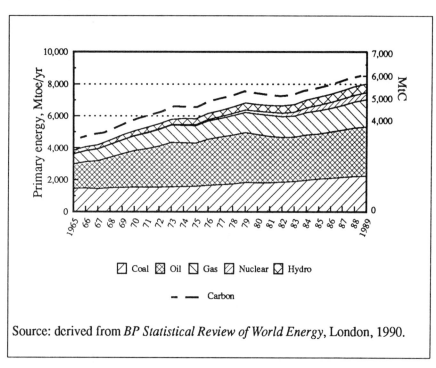

Source: derived from *BP Statistical Review of World Energy*, London, 1990.

(6GtC) - about 10 times the level at the beginning of the century and an average of nearly 1.1 tonnes for each human being.[3]

The speed and nature of the growth in energy demand has varied greatly between regions and economic groups. The European industrial revolution, relying on coal, led demand until the First World War. US demand grew spectacularly from the beginning of the century until the early 1970s, drawing on cheap and plentiful indigenous resources and hardly noticing the creeping dependence on foreign sources until it was

---

allowances for indirect emissions (eg. gas flaring) and unburnt fractions (eg. some petrochemicals), as described in Volume II.

[3] For a description of the historical development of carbon emissions see W.Keeping, I.Mintzer, L.Kristoferson, 'Emission of CO_2 into the atmosphere', in B.Bolin et al. (eds), *The Greenhouse Effect, Climatic Change, and Ecosystems - SCOPE 29*, John Wiley & Sons, Chichester, 1986.

Figure 2.2 Commercial energy consumption by economic group, 1965-89

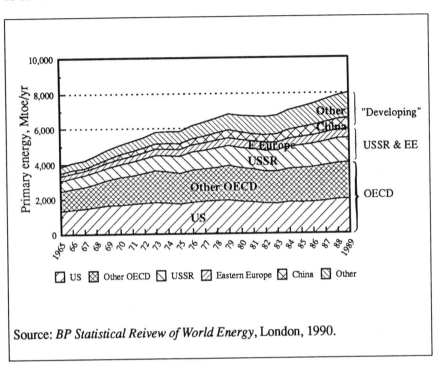

Source: *BP Statistical Reivew of World Energy*, London, 1990.

too late. The impact of the oil price shocks on OECD countries was particularly marked, as illustrated in Figure 2.2; OECD energy demand grew at barely 0.5%/yr over the period 1973-86, and because of the increased role of gas and nuclear power, OECD carbon emissions in 1989 were still below the peak a decade earlier.

Soviet energy consumption grew prodigiously during Stalin's industrialisation, and has continued on that path ever since. Insulated from world markets, Soviet and East European energy demand was scarcely checked by the shocks of the 1970s.

The developing countries (see box, p.38) are relatively new on the energy scene. In 1970 they accounted for only 15% of global demand for commercial energy. Over the intervening twenty years, despite the crippling effect for many of the oil price rises and heavy indebtedness, their commercial energy consumption has nearly doubled and now accounts for 26% of the global total.

Country groups and naming conventions

Reducing the complexity of over 160 sovereign states to a manageable number of economic groups inevitably creates difficulties. This study uses the following terms.

Industrialised countries comprise those which have an extensive industrial base and infrastructure. These are divided between the Soviet and East European countries on the one hand, and developed market economies, roughly synonymous with the member countries of the Organisation for Economic Cooperation and Development, on the other. The term OECD is used for precision where data are concerned.

Developing countries comprise the rest. These obviously span a very wide range, which in addition to the poor countries include some (especially in South-East Asia) which have recently achieved broad industrialisation, many middle-ranking countries of the Near East and Latin America, and the oil-rich countries of the Middle East. These are disaggregated when necessary, but in aggregate the population and potential for future growth in this diverse group are dominated by the poorer countries.

The term 'Centrally Planned Economy' is used to denote the economic system of central planning based on production targets, rather than particular countries, unless otherwise stated.

Despite the unavoidable crudity of these categories, they still provide an effective shorthand for describing many features of international energy trends and other characteristics.

These statistics do not include non-commercial sources of energy, primarily use of biomass - woodfuels and various agricultural and animal wastes. Overall, biomass energy probably accounts for 10-15% of world energy consumption, and contributes perhaps a third of all primary consumption in the developing world.[4] In some developing countries, biomass dominates total consumption, and it is only the urban elite who use commercial sources. Substitution of commercial fuels for traditional ones as countries develop contributes significantly to their fossil fuel growth.[5]

Despite their importance in many countries, non-commercial sources are of limited relevance in considering the prospects for global carbon emissions. Much non-commercial consumption is from renewable sources (waste woods from standing forests, agricultural or animal residues) and since these contain carbon recently absorbed from the atmosphere, there is no net carbon contribution. Expansion of traditional biomass use is limited by the nature of the resource and the inefficiency of its use. Replacing it by fossil fuels would add to net fossil carbon emissions, but this is a relatively minor factor in the potential global growth. Some non-commercial energy is from net deforestation, and thus contributes to net carbon emissions, but this contribution is extremely difficult to measure; the need for firewood is a minor factor in global deforestation, although it is a significant factor in some countries.[6] For these reasons, despite the current importance of non-commercial energy in many developing countries, the discussion in this book concentrates on commercial energy sources.

2.2 Future trends, population and development

Where are these trends heading? Volume II of this study presents some detailed case studies of the prospects for 'business-as-usual' demand in various countries, and the extent to which abatement policies might affect them, which are summarised later in this chapter. Chapter 6 of this

---

[4] The figure is very uncertain. A recent study takes simple mean estimates of average per capita use in rural and urban areas, and concludes that biomass use contributes about 14% of world energy supplies, and 35% in developing countries. J.M.O.Scurlock and D.O.Hall, 'The Contribution of Biomass to Global Energy Use (1987)', *Biomass*, Vol.21, Elsevier, UK, 1990, pp.75-81.

[5] The ratio of commercial energy consumption to GDP tends to rise in the early stages of development. A major study of energy development concludes that this is largely an artifact of substitution for biomass, and that the ratio of total energy use to GDP has often been quite constant in early development. G.Leach, L.Jarass, G.Obermair and L.Hoffman, *Energy and Growth: a Comparison of 13 Industrial and Developing Countries*, Butterworth, London, 1986.

[6] Ibid. See also Chapter 3, note 43, and G.Foley, *The Energy Question*, Penguin Books, London, 1987, pp.202-3.

volume examines in some detail energy consumption patterns and the pressures on them, and Chapter 7 integrates the discussions of trends and policies in developing a view of future prospects. But to set the background, it is useful to start by considering the broad direction of the visible trends.

Most analysts expect energy demand to grow in almost all countries, but with large differences between regions and economic groups. One reason for the difference is the growing perception that per capita energy requirements tend to follow an 'S-shape' curve (Figure 2.3), with demand rising sharply as countries industrialise, and then slackening as basic needs are met and a greater proportion of expenditure goes on services rather than manufactured goods, and manufacturing value itself arises increasingly from information technology and more finished goods

Figure 2.3 Energy consumption and economic development: the 'S-curve'

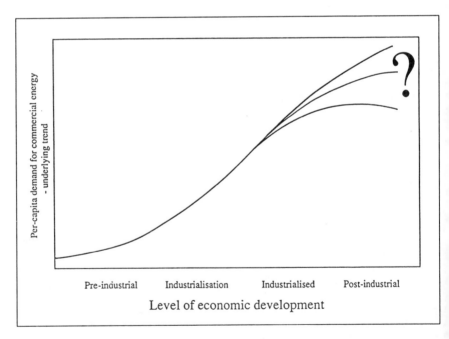

rather than primary production. Such shifts have been characterised by the terms 'from production to pleasure' and 'from bulk to bytes'.[7]

Concurrent with these trends, the ratio of commercial energy requirement to GDP tends to rise in the early stages of industrialisation, peak, and then decline as economies mature.[8] Those maturing later have peaked at successively lower levels, being able to take advantage of intervening technical developments.

As the developed economies move into 'the information age', it is difficult to disentangle the underlying trends from the reactions to the oil price shocks. After the oil price collapse of the late 1980s (to below the levels of 1972 in real terms), demand started to grow sharply again in some OECD countries, but not all.[9] A few analysts believe that the natural underlying trend for developed economies could now be for slowly declining per capita energy consumption, but this is not a widely held view; most believe that, without any other changes, continuing economic growth implies a continuing, albeit relatively slower, rise in the demand for energy. The likely influences are examined in more detail in Chapter 6. In so far as developed economies do stabilise or reduce demand, many argue that it can only be as a transient or policy-driven response, and may also reflect a migration of heavy industry into other countries, which of course does not help to constrain global energy demand.

In Eastern Europe and the USSR, the situation as the new decade opens is highly uncertain. Per capita energy consumption is, on aggregate, somewhere between that of Western Europe and of the United States, but the level of economic development is substantially lower. Continuing economic growth towards the 'mature' phase of the S-curve, combined with continuing population growth, will produce pressures for increasing demand; but there are also clear and large opportunities for improved efficiency, and if energy prices could be brought in line with those in

---

[7] L.Schipper, S.Bartlett, D.Hawui, and E.Vine, 'Energy Use and Lifestyles: A matter of time?', *Annual Review of Energy*, Vol.14, Annual Reviews Inc, Palo Alto, CA, 1989.
[8] U.Columbo and O.Bernardini, 'A Low Energy Growth Scenario and Perspectives for Western Europe', report XVII/398/79, CEC, Brussels, 1979; cited in and extended to a broader range of countries in Leach et al., *Energy and Growth*.
[9] Energy demand in many Western European countries has remained stable, or even fallen, in the late 1980s. It remains to be seen how much impact the price rises surrounding the Gulf crisis of 1990 will have. Such uncertainties and fluctuations are likely to be a continuing feature of world oil supplies.

many OECD countries, this alone would tend to stimulate savings. The Soviet Union is taken as one of the case studies, and the prospects are considered further below.

It is in considering the developing countries that the real nature of the problem becomes apparent. Figure 2.4 illustrates 1989 per capita emissions of fossil carbon by region (with the countries selected for detailed study shown separately). Plotted against population, the area of the blocks indicates total carbon emissions. The developing countries account for nearly four-fifths of global population, but only a quarter of commercial energy consumption and fossil carbon emissions. Many are already either in or entering the high-growth phase of the 'S-curve'. Their populations are still growing rapidly, and are likely to continue doing so for many years because of the existing age structures and the pressures of poverty.

Figure 2.4 Fossil carbon emissions per capita and population, 1989

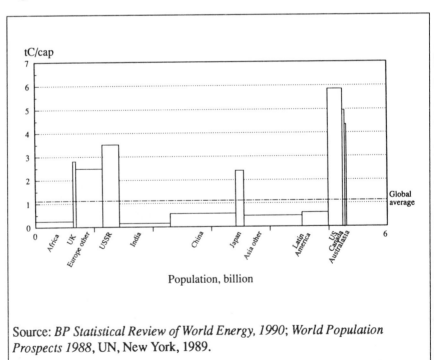

Source: *BP Statistical Review of World Energy, 1990*; *World Population Prospects 1988*, UN, New York, 1989.

Most scenarios foresee demand in developing countries at least doubling from 1990 to 2010, and doubling again to 2030, by which stage they would probably account for at least half of global energy consumption.[10] Because they start from such a low level, and because of the population growth, the per capita energy consumption implied in these figures would still be far below that of the current industrialised countries.

Taking a global and long-term view reveals the real immensity of the problem. Ten billion people is a typical estimate of the levels at which world population might approach stabilisation in the latter half of the twenty-first century. Combining this figure with the requirements for a more than 60% cut in CO_2 emissions from current levels in order to stabilise atmospheric concentrations equates to ultimate per capita emissions of no more than 0.2 tonnes of carbon a year, and probably less. This is one-fifth of the current global average per capita level. It is less than the current per capita fossil carbon emissions from India, and is under one-tenth those of Japan and Denmark, which are respectively widely taken as models of efficiency and of overall 'progressive' energy policies. Current per capita emissions from the US are nearly thirty times this 'stabilisation level'. From this perspective, aiming for long-term stabilisation is an awesome, and many argue quite impossible, challenge.

There is a widespread perception that future population growth is the fundamental cause of this predicament. This is highly simplistic. Economic growth is a much more important cause of increasing carbon emissions than population growth: if the *current* world population reached the level of US per capita carbon emissions, the global total would be increased more than fivefold, to more than fifteen times the global level required for atmospheric stabilisation. The consequences of carbon-intensive economic growth could only be offset by drastic reductions in global population, which could not occur short of global nuclear war or uncontrollable epidemics.

---

[10] Such projections - which assume a substantial improvement in energy efficiency worldwide - are presented, for example, by the former chief economist at Shell, D.Anderson, 'Economics of Energy and the Environment - a discussion of issues', University College, London, April 1990. A World Bank economist has suggested that the contribution of developing countries in tackling the greenhouse effect might amount to reducing annual energy growth from c.6% to c.4% (M.Imran, 'Energy Demand Prospects in Developing Countries', IPCC Energy and Industries Subgroup Meeting on defining targets, London, June 1990).

The scale of the global challenge is alleviated a little if a much more pessimistic view is taken of economic prospects in the developing world. This is sometimes held to be inevitable because it is assumed that the populations projected for the developing world imply densities which simply could not be sustained at the economic levels currently enjoyed in the West. Figure 2.5 illustrates population distribution and growth in terms of the current and projected densities (excluding wilderness areas) by region, with the countries chosen as case studies shown separately. With land area (excluding wilderness) along the bottom axis the area in the blocks indicates total population. Although some areas certainly are heading for very high population densities, for most this is simply not the case. Land area alone is a poor guide to potential productivity, since many other factors are involved, but this does indicate that assumptions of poverty enforced by overcrowding are at best highly oversimplified, if not worse.

The ability to control population growth is distinctly limited; the projected growth to 2030 reflects the implications of existing age structures in the developing countries as much as assumptions of high birth rates. As a final paradox, it is almost universally accepted that the most important factor in bringing birth rates down is economic and social development, to give people the security which is otherwise sought through large families, and to provide some aspirations and opportunities in life beyond those of surviving and raising the next generation. Population growth is an important problem; it strains many environmental resources and is a significant cause of poverty, deforestation, and social instability. But as a policy issue relating to fossil carbon emissions it is far less important than that of ensuring rapid and efficient low-carbon development, and increasing focus on population concerns is in danger of drawing attention away from the more urgent and manageable policy issues.

The long-term importance of energy demand in the developing countries has led some to argue that policies for tackling the greenhouse effect need to concentrate primarily upon them, and that action by the industrialised countries alone is largely irrelevant. This is wrong for several reasons.

First, the industrialised countries still dominate emissions of greenhouse gases. They account for nearly all the CFCs and upwards of 70% of fossil fuel emissions of CO_2 and other gases. Deforestation,

Figure 2.5 Population densities and land area

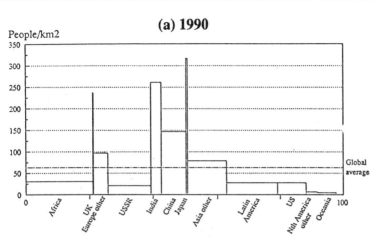

(a) 1990

People/km2

Land area excluding wilderness, (million square kilometres)

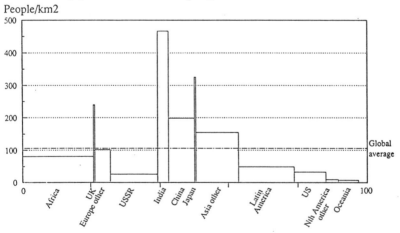

(b) United Nations projections for 2030

People/km2

Land area excluding wilderness, (million square kilometres)

The area of each block is proportional to the total population

Sources: using UN country classifictions, derived from *World Population Prospects1988*, UN, New York; *Statistical Yearbook 1985/86*, UN New York, 1988; *World Resources 1988-89*, World Resources Institute et al, Alexandria, Virginia, 1988.

which is a source of N_2O and methane as well as CO_2, occurs predominantly in developing countries; the developed economies, especially in the 'old world', depleted the forests which occupied potential arable land decades or centuries ago. Recent attempts to quantify emissions of non-CO_2 gases suggest that developing countries contribute about two-thirds of the methane and N_2O,[11] though these figures may be as uncertain as the estimates of CO_2 from deforestation. Average per capita emissions of all gases are considerably higher in the industrialised world.

Changes in the industrialised countries therefore have a large impact on total emissions. Indeed, in 1988 fossil carbon emissions from North America alone rose by about 65MtC, nearly five times the absolute increase in the entire continents of Africa and Latin America combined. Overall, although the *percentage* growth in carbon emissions from industrialised countries in 1988 was half that of developing countries, it was double in *absolute* terms. This was an extreme year but nevertheless sufficient to illustrate that arresting such growth, or even turning it into a decline, would have at least as much impact on global carbon emissions over the next two decades as any dampening of the growth rate in developing countries.

A second reason why the path taken by industrialised countries is critical is because developing countries are trying to follow it. Because global emissions will grow massively if developing countries follow to any substantial degree the carbon-intensive path of development taken by the current industrialised countries, there is much talk of the need for them to 'tunnel through' to a state of more advanced and efficient technology. But if the developed countries cannot demonstrate a decline in emissions, then there may be nothing for the developing countries to tunnel through to.

A third reason why the attitude and the future path of developed economies are important is political. Lecturing the poor about why they should not follow others' path to riches will result in little but resentment unless it is backed up by concrete action. Wealthy countries have led the scientific investigations into the greenhouse effect, and have the greatest resources and capabilities to act upon their concerns. The developing

[11] D.Tirpak, 'Preliminary Estimates of Emissions by Country on a CO_2-Equivalent Basis', paper to the IPCC Workshop on Emissions of Greenhouse Gases, London, 11-13 June 1990.

countries, not surprisingly, want to see evidence that the industrialised world is prepared to act before considering serious steps themselves; this was apparent in the negotiations over CFCs, and it will be more so for the greenhouse effect.

Because of their enormous potential for growth and the costs of altering energy infrastructure once it is in place, early action within the developing countries would indeed be a crucial component of attempts to limit global carbon emissions. But this only strengthens the case for early action in the developed economies, rather than weakening it.

What then may be possible in the way of energy policy developments in response to the greenhouse effect, and how much impact might abatement policies have? These and related questions can to an extent be examined at the level of general economic and political principles. But circumstances vary widely from country to country, and it is this which will determine what is actually feasible or likely in the differing political and economic contexts, and how countries and groups may interact. For this reason, case studies of different countries form a central part of this analysis.

2.3 The country case studies: a general overview

The countries selected are listed, together with key statistics, in Table 2.1. They were chosen to span a wide range of political, economic and geographical situations, whilst including the major current and projected fossil carbon emitters: together, including the European Community, they comprise about three-quarters of current global carbon emissions and economic production, and over half the current global population.[12] Whilst recognising the limitations of this coverage, in particular the absence of any African or Latin American countries, it was considered impossible to manage more studies without losing the key points in generalities, and defeating the purpose of detailed country assessments. Each of the case studies is written by an expert on the country concerned. The full studies are presented in Volume II, and the authors and their affiliations are shown in the box, p.49. The rest of this chapter summarises some of the key points to emerge.

[12] Owing to illness, at the time of going to press only the scenarios and main conclusions of the Indian study, which was commissioned later than the others, had been received. References to this study are therefore limited.

Table 2.1 Country case studies: key statistics (1988)

	Fossil carbon emissions MtC	%global	GDP* $bn	%global	Population m	%global	Carbon per capita
US	1435	23.7	4862	26.3	248.2	4.7	5.85
USSR	1015	16.7	2500	13.5	288.7	5.5	3.58
UK	164	2.7	760	4.1	57	1.1	2.92
EC**	744	12.3	4515	24.4	325	6.2	2.31
China	713	11.8	350	1.9	1112.3	21.2	0.65
Japan	289	4.8	1843	10.0	123.2	2.4	2.35
India	189	3.1	231	1.2	833.4	15.9	0.23
Total with EC:	4385	72	14301	77	2931	56	-
Global	6063	100.0	18500	100.0	5242	100.0	1.17

*GDP at standard exchange rates. These figures change, with large increases for the centrally planned economies and India if estimates are made on a purchasing power parity basis (see M.Grubb, *The Greenhouse Effect:Negotiating Targets*, RIIA, London, 1989.).
**The UK is considered in detail and placed within the broader content of the European Community.

Source: M. Grubb et al., *Energy Policies and the Greenhouse Effect, Vol.II: Country Studies and Technical Options*, Gower, London, forthcoming 1991.

In any work which draws upon case studies, there is a tension between comparability and consistency on the one hand, and the need for freedom of each author's style and assumptions on the other. For this study, the authors were asked to summarise recent energy trends and the indigenous energy resources available, and to present short-term (2000) and long-term (2030) scenarios representing a 'business-as-usual' outlook, and the possible impact of measures to limit fossil carbon emissions both from improved energy efficiency and from fuel switching. These scenarios, classified as in the box p.50, then form a basis for discussing

---

Country case studies and authors

UK/EC	Michael Grubb	Research Fellow, RIIA
	Peter Brackley	Associate Fellow, RIIA; formerly with BP
US	Steve Rayner	Deputy Director, Global Environmental Studies Center, Oak Ridge National Laboratory, Tennessee, US
Japan	Akira Tanabe	Tokyo Electric Power Company; Visiting Research Fellow, RIIA
	Michael Grubb	Research Fellow, RIIA
USSR	Jeremy Russell	Shell UK Ltd, London; Visiting Research Fellow, RIIA
China	Michele Ledic	Birkbeck College, London
India	Ajay Mathur	Tata Energy Research Institute, New Delhi

---

the policy options and issues which are likely to determine the extent to which the country can and will act to limit emissions, and how this will affect the country's international outlook. Authors were asked to concentrate on fossil carbon emissions for the reasons discussed in Chapter 1 but to note the impact of other gases in so far as they impinge on the energy economy.

All the case studies share a few broad assumptions. There are no major long-term disruptions to the world economy. The industrialised countries continue to grow, with GNP increasing at an average of around 2-3%/yr, declining somewhat in the longer term. Most developing countries continue to grow faster than the developed in percentage terms, but few

---

Definition of country study scenarios

Scenarios are defined by the primary consumption of each fuel in a target year. Six scenarios were used:

Short-term scenarios year 2000:

2000A   Business as usual
2000B   Abatement policies

Long-term scenarios year 2030:

2030Ai   Business as usual
2030Aii   Business as usual energy demand, with fuel switching
           to limit carbon emissions
2030Bi   Policies for high energy efficiency
2030Bii   Policies for both high energy efficiency and fuel
           switching to limit carbon emissions

---

catch up within the timeframe considered. There are no fundamental breakthroughs which radically alter patterns of energy development; this does not rule out major technological developments which can be foreseen, for example the possible applications of superconductivity. Even if such breakthroughs did occur most would be unlikely to invalidate many of the broad policy conclusions arising from the studies.

With respect to international energy markets, the current era of relatively cheap international energy (in the absence of environmental taxes) is assumed to last until the early years of the next century, after which markets tighten significantly. Oil is more expensive than coal and gas for the power market, but there is no significant penetration of alternative fuels for transport apart from special cases. The major gas resource areas still have substantial reserves for export even in the year 2030; delivered costs depend upon the ease of access through gas pipelines for regional resources. Liquified Natural Gas remains an option but there are no major technical breakthroughs in gas transportation. International coal remains cheap relative to oil, though environmental requirements do drive total costs up.

Various options are available for trying to construct future energy scenarios. None is very satisfactory. A key division lies between 'bottom-up' analysis, which builds up demand from a detailed examination of energy end-uses, and 'top-down', which projects general trends in demand and judges the macroeconomic influences upon it. Both of these can be applied with differing degrees of formality and sophistication, and various mixes between the two are also possible. Volume II discusses some of the pros and cons of each technique, and concludes that the most appropriate approach depends upon the kind of questions being asked. Overall it is argued that if the required data are available and are used carefully enough, bottom-up analysis usually gives a better insight into the factors driving energy demand and the scope for technical abatement options; but that in practice, adequate data often do not exist, and the complexities can reduce their practical value.

The case studies take various approaches. The UK study develops a completely bottom-up analysis. The US study draws from a range of existing studies, taking a central top-down projection for the base case and a detailed bottom-up analysis for the long-term high efficiency case. Other studies were able to draw on existing projections for the 'business-as-usual' case from which adjustments were made to reflect the possible impact of concerted abatement strategies.

Inevitably, all scenarios, in the longer term especially, depend upon subjective judgements irrespective of the apparent degree of sophistication. Nevertheless, they indicate the authors' judgements as to the likely bounds on future conditions, and the degree and nature of the impact which abatement policies might have, and as such provide a useful focus for discussion and comparison. Figure 2.6 shows the total and per capita carbon emissions in each country in the various scenarios presented.

2.4 The short-term outlook and energy efficiency

In the shorter term - up to 2000 - the opportunities for reducing emissions by deliberately altering the mix of supplies towards lower-carbon fuels are limited, but in principle there could be substantial gains in efficiency. In practice, most authors foresee little opportunity for policy impacts on this timescale. The two exceptions are in the UK and Japanese chapters.

For Japan, this reflects the close-knit nature of the Japanese decision-making process, with close integration between government

Figure 2.6 Fossil carbon emissions in country study scenarios

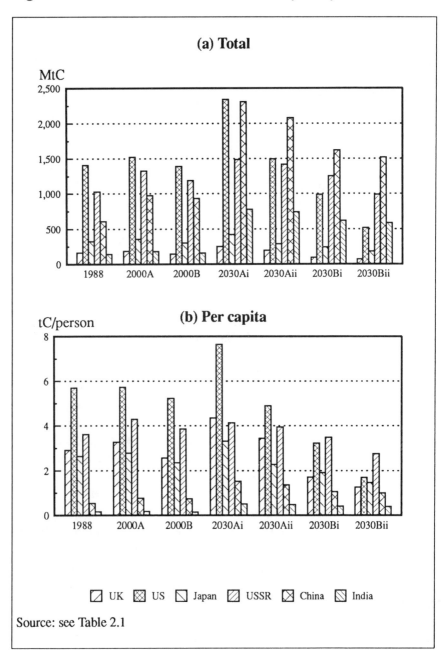

Source: see Table 2.1

and industry, and a tradition of strong intervention in the energy area following the oil price shocks. Whilst noting serious concerns about the possible implications of trying to reduce carbon emissions from levels which are already very low by the standards of most other developed countries, and current doubts about the need, the author concludes that 'Japanese policy could and would change rapidly in the course of developing an international agreement'.

In the UK, the conclusion that rapid changes are possible reflects a number of factors: the relatively fluid situation concerning energy overall, with electricity still in the process of wholesale privatisation and a resulting change in economic criteria and attitudes; the possible impact of the European Community in several areas; and the opportunities provided by inefficiencies in several sectors, most notably the domestic (homes). The UK study draws upon modelling work by the Building Research Establishment to examine how various measures to reduce losses, including time-of-sale insulation and appliance replacement standards, would work through the housing stock.

The political situation in the UK, including relatively centralised government and growing political stakes following the Prime Minister's high-profile endorsement of climate change as a major issue, suggests that such measures are not impossible. However, interventionist policies would undoubtedly face large ideological hurdles; the chapter argues that this may be more important than any direct opposition from industrial or trade union interests. Political obstacles to carbon taxes would also be considerable.

Many EC member countries are pressing ahead of the UK, and the Community as a body may well drive through some measures to limit carbon emissions because of both the 'greening' of the Community (and the way this finds expression through its political dynamics) and a growing perception that limiting carbon emissions may indeed be a vehicle for goals which are perceived as desirable in their own right - improving efficiency and reducing high-cost coal consumption and reliance on imported energy. This dynamic could stimulate savings in some of the more reluctant member countries, but Community-wide measures could not act in such depth as concerted efforts by individual countries.

The US, Soviet and Chinese studies all give a powerful impression of the immense inertia inherent in these large countries and their governments. The political process in the United States, open to a wide variety of conflicting pressures and special interest lobbies, with public resistance to fundamental change a key determinant of policy, ensures that major changes in direction tend to be slow and bitterly fought: 'The democratic and legal mechanisms that distinguish American society will ensure that determined stakeholders have their say'. The general public is concerned about the greenhouse effect, but is far more concerned about its freedom to use cheap energy.

However, in contrast to its 'free market' image, the United States has greater experience of regulatory measures for improving efficiency, with efficiency standards for both vehicles and home appliances and utility regulations increasingly directed at ensuring some investment in conservation. These could be strengthened; they have for the most part brought the US up to levels typical of Western European products. General building regulations could also be reinforced without insurmountable opposition; the US chapter again notes the domestic sector as a prime candidate for relatively short-term action. As a result, the study suggests that stabilisation at current levels would be possible given sufficient pressures.

The winds of change sweeping the Soviet Union create great difficulties for policy analysis. Technically, there are large opportunities for improving efficiency in many sectors. But the causes of inefficiency are very deep-rooted. Like the United States, the USSR has developed in energy abundance which, unlike the US, persists today. The vast Soviet energy infrastructure is strongly supply driven and oriented; quite apart from this, the current economic system cannot cope well with the approaches needed to affect the myriad decentralised decisions required to improve energy efficiency.

Because of its size, the heavy investment it represents, and its crucial role in the Soviet economy including export earnings, the energy sector is expected to be one of the last candidates for radical reform. Price reform might extend to energy, but probably only if it is first successfully accomplished in other areas. Even this would have limited impact without deeper changes, since the costs are of far less importance to industry in centrally planned economies, and many homes do not have energy metering. The task of improving efficiency is thus 'comparable to changing course in a supertanker ... even if it has a highly trained crew ... it takes a long time'.

A number of these themes apply to China as well, with the crucial differences that much infrastructure has yet to be put in place, and that known Chinese energy resources amount to lots of coal and little else. The early stage of infrastructure development in principle offers great scope for savings, but it is far from clear whether these can be realised in practice. The economic reforms attempted since 1978 have run into grave difficulties, and since September 1988 and especially since the events surrounding the Tiananmen Square massacre of June 1989, reform has been much more cautious, and often actually reversed.

The study recognises the large inefficiencies in the Chinese system, but also reflects the complete domination of supply issues, noting cautiously that 'investment in energy efficiency may sometimes require a different sort of investment rather than more investment ... For such developments to occur, however, large changes are needed also in the popular attitudes to the wasteful use of energy and in governmental attitudes.'

Furthermore, given that the system is supply constrained, it is far from clear how much improving efficiency would actually reduce demand in the short term, as opposed to merely freeing supplies for other uses. The author argues that: 'Even large international aid for energy conservation is unlikely to have the required effect in the absence of a drastic reform of energy pricing combined with the adoption of profit maximising objectives for enterprises.'

The Indian conclusions share the Chinese perspective that emissions will inevitably increase, and that international aid will be important in trying to limit them. But the conclusions differ radically in other respects. Power generation, industry, transport and domestic uses (which are dominated by biomass) are all inefficient by international standards (though to a lesser extent than in China). This is related not just to the shortage of capital, but to the overall pressures in a rapidly growing economy:

Energy demand in India has grown, and continues to grow, at a rate faster than that of the increase in energy supply. This has resulted in chronic shortages, as well as in deterioration of quality of supply. The planning process has been forced to focus on a very short-term timeframe - the 'tonight timeframe'. An overriding preoccupation with supply, and measures to rapidly increase supply within the limitations of a resource constrained economy have, therefore, become endemic. The resulting bias towards thermal power, and towards supply expansion in general, is normally at the cost of efficiency upgrading.

Transferring some resources from supply to improvements in efficiency is seen as unambiguously beneficial, but politically and managerially extremely difficult. All of these problems are compounded by the chronic shortage of capital and of hard currency, which are seen as particularly important in limiting efficiency improvements especially in industrial processes, in expanding public transport, and in electricity generation and distribution.

The studies leave a strong impression that, over the next decade, climate change will necessarily be a peripheral issue for the Soviet Union and China, and probably India: they simply have more pressing problems to consider. Taking climate change more seriously in terms of energy efficiency would imply little more than trying harder to do things they should be doing anyway. Altering development paths in countries which are still struggling to meet basic needs and/or which are undergoing profound political changes is hardly an option, though changes which occur as a result of other pressures (including environmental ones in Eastern Europe) may also help to limit emissions. In so far as these countries do consider constraining carbon emissions as a relevant issue, it is likely to be because of the international links - possibly through pressure but more likely through the temptations of foreign assistance with technology, finance, and possibly policy development as well.

Among the OECD countries, the UK/EC and Japanese studies carry distinctly different flavours from that of the US. Europe and Japan seem far more able and likely to move quickly, and relatively much less convinced that it would harm their economic interests, while the United States may be heading for protracted internal debate about first whether and then how to respond, with a potential for what the US author terms 'policy gridlock'.

2.5 Longer-term prospects and fuel switching

These themes extend for decades. All the studies conclude that carbon emissions forty years hence will be significantly affected by current conditions, but to widely varying degrees. The potential impact of abatement policies as expressed through the 2030 abatement scenarios also varies widely. The total and per capita emissions are illustrated in

Figure 2.6, and Figure 2.7 illustrates the relative contribution of the different fuels in the longer-term scenarios.[13]

All the country studies foresee carbon emissions rising in 'business-as-usual' efficiency cases, and only in Japan, with a high nuclear electric scenario, is fuel switching alone sufficient to bring emissions back down below current levels against the projected high demands. The 'high efficiency' scenarios of the OECD countries all depict significant reductions from current levels; the most stringent Soviet scenario also foresees some reduction. For China, there is no question of reductions, but the extent to which emissions grow might be altered significantly.

The UK scenarios are the most optimistic about the possible impact of abatement policies. This is perhaps in part because they were developed from a completely bottom-up analysis of energy demand. Maximum technical efficiency is not assumed in any sector, because of clear political and behavioural constraints as well as ones of timescale (relevant in the building and utility sectors). Nevertheless, large reductions - equivalent to an average improvement in national energy productivity of around 4%/yr - are achieved through the combination of end-use efficiency in each sector, reduced losses in the energy conversion industries, and widespread use of small-scale combined heat and power (see Chapter 4). Together with extensive use of gas and non-fossil electricity sources in the most stringent scenario, these measures serve

---

[13] The contribution from non-fossil energy sources varies according to the accounting method used. They can be included either on the basis of the energy they produce (output basis) or in terms of the total fuel inputs which they displace (input basis). Because of the conversion losses in thermal power generation, these figures can differ by a factor of three. Most statistics use the input basis, obtained by dividing the energy output by a reference efficiency of displaced generation. IEA/OECD statistics usually use 38.5%; BP data use 35%. Some countries with extensive non-fossil generation (eg. Sweden) use the output basis, which makes the non-fossil contribution look much smaller.

The global and long-term scope of this study implies a wide range of systems and possible thermal efficiencies; modern gas plants, for example, can reach 50%. Liquid fuel production from biomass may also involve considerable losses. The output basis is therefore used for all non-fossil energy sources to establish a consistent basis and to avoid the use of arbitrary and perhaps misleading conversion factors. The data for Figure 2.7 and other diagrams has been correspondingly adapted. It must be remembered that on this basis a given amount of non-fossil electricity will be displacing two to three times as much fossil fuel input to electricity.

Figure 2.7 Fuel mix in long term country study scenarios

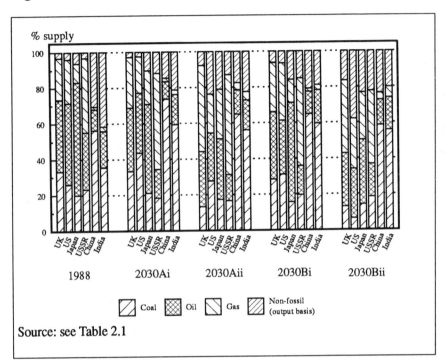

Source: see Table 2.1

to more than halve carbon emissions from the 1989 levels. The study claims that:

> The costs incurred in realising such a scenario would be primarily political rather than economic. Achieving reductions of this magnitude would require extensive government intervention using many novel policy instruments, both market and non-market based. The reductions could probably not be achieved without a concurrent change in consumer attitudes and the focus of non-government organisations, acting more in concert with such government policies.

The Japanese abatement scenarios also depict substantial reductions, with large further gains in efficiency, and with a greater emphasis on the non-fossil component, and potentially a very large role for nuclear power, while acknowledging some of the problems and doubts facing this. The study lays greater emphasis on the technological opportunities and reflects the confidence and imagination of Japanese industry, not only in high technology but also in more mundane possibilities, for example the recovery of waste heat from various industrial processes and Tokyo's subway and sewage systems.

This study also doubts the implications for costs, and shows greater faith in the ability of Japanese society overall to deliver the responses if required. In its spectacular development Japan has had to clear the two formidable hurdles of the environmental challenges of the 1960s and early 1970s followed by the oil shocks:

In clearing these two hurdles, Japan was able to conceive of them not as constraints but as challenges which could be met. The CO_2 challenge is not as easy to meet as the first two. It may take more time and may require more international agreements ... however, this issue also provides industry, consumers and policy-makers with a great opportunity to carry out social renovations which are at the same time desirable in themselves and necessary for future generations ... with commitment within industry and government to the idea of a 'third industrial revolution' or paradigm shift concerning the global warming issue, Japan has promising but as yet uncertain prospects.

The contrast with the other studies is stark. The US abatement scenarios, taken from other technical analyses, do depict substantial reductions from current levels, but unlike the other studies, these are illustrations more of technical than political possibilities. The text warns of immense political difficulties, and suggests in particular that it would be both costly and impractical to make new non-fossil investments, displacing extant fossil industries, to the extent illustrated in the fuel-switching scenario 2030Bii.

The extent of long-term efficiency improvements in the Soviet Union and China are seen to be closely tied to the progress of general economic reforms and energy pricing. However, economic development could also stimulate growth in many energy-consuming activities, especially transport and services. In the Soviet study, modest reductions in carbon emissions, though not in overall energy consumption, are projected for the most stringent abatement case. For China, per capita demand in the high efficiency scenarios remains below the level of all the industrialised country equivalents, though, because of the heavy reliance on coal, per capita emissions are only a little below the lowest OECD 2030 levels. Because of this there remains substantial scope for further increases beyond 2030: 'whatever happens in the way of international assistance, greenhouse gas emissions will continue to increase as far ahead as can be seen'. The Indian study lies between these extremes, seeing abatement policies as possible and perhaps desirable, but very much contingent upon other factors, including external developments to relieve the pressure of capital and hard currency shortages.

2.6 The influence of domestic resources and infrastructure

To some extent these conclusions reflect assumptions of continuity in the underlying political and economic character of the country concerned, with an extension of the kind of implications this has, as discussed with reference to short-term constraints. However, because of the greater opportunities for change and the obvious uncertainties involved, the bounds expressed by the long-term scenarios rely relatively more upon resource conditions and the implications of existing infrastructure. Although, even for those countries with substantial fossil resources, reducing their use could (within bounds) reduce costs and free more of the resources for export, in practice the presence of cheap indigenous resources is seen to lead to attitudes and infrastructures which increase energy consumption, and to create a strong interest group which would undermine attempts to limit fossil fuel consumption, especially as widespread abatement policies would dampen prices and reduce the export market.

In addition, the infrastructural requirements for exploiting reserves involve substantial losses; the Soviet study notes 'a large and growing mismatch between the location of energy resources and the centres of demand', with energy sometimes being transported hundreds or thousands of kilometres for both domestic use and exports. A strong geographical mismatch is also evident in the Chinese analysis, though here it is regarded more as a constraint on exploiting the vast coal reserves; greater regionalisation of energy development is seen as a means of circumventing these constraints, and of encouraging both more efficient use and the use of non-coal resources.

Regional and resource issues are also important in the United States; here, as in China, coal is now seen as a major element of domestic energy security, and as a significant export. Yet the emphasis is very different. The US has a relatively efficient and well developed infrastructure for extracting, transporting and using its coal, which, together with the vast oil and transport infrastructures, represents immense financial and political investments in existing modes of energy production. Of utilities, the author writes that 'replacing this investment under normal conditions will be huge in its own right: speeding up the replacement rate to remove greenhouse gas emissions could be financially intolerable'; similar remarks apply with even more force to changing transport fuels.

As a result, 'this review', states the US author, 'inexorably paints a pessimistic picture. The US economy is as dependent on fossil fuels as a heroin addict is on the needle.' The US long-term abatement scenarios do suggest that substantial reductions might be technically feasible; but the 'democratic and legal mechanisms', as outlined earlier, mean that huge political battles would have to be fought to approach such levels.

The UK too is currently a slight net energy producer, but the study treats this as being of much less impact than for those discussed above. This is partly because oil and gas exploitation is relatively recent, so that the UK has not grown up with a culture and infrastructure based on assumptions of plenty. Also the limited size of the resources means that first oil and later gas production are likely to fall below domestic requirements before 2030. Indeed, the chapter notes that the massive dependence implied by the fuel-switching scenario without high efficiency (2030Aii) might be 'politically unacceptable even if it were economically feasible' because of the import requirements. The coal resource is large, but the high cost of the inherited industry has reduced its attractiveness and political weight: the painful 'rationalisation' of the last few decades has made it more competitive but much less of a political force, and it is still threatened by cheaper imports. Ideological and managerial obstacles to strong abatement policies, as noted above, are judged to be more important than industrial opposition in the UK.

Similar remarks apply to some other major European countries. Tensions within Germany over the high-cost and still quite powerful coal industry could be important, but nevertheless Germany seems committed to action, with declared targets for emission reductions beyond those of almost every other country. Denmark and the Netherlands are already embarking upon radical energy policies to improve energy efficiency and to promote renewable sources, in response to both deep environmental concerns and their lack of domestic oil and coal resources. The study does identify possible tensions within the European Community over the form of responses adopted, with the UK and France more favourable to fuel-switching measures, and most other European countries keener on intervention to promote energy efficiency. However, overall the Community is not rich in low-cost energy resources, and this, combined with the strength of environmental interests, may result in its taking a long-term lead in efforts to limit carbon emissions.

The issues for Japan are similar. With few indigenous resources, reducing fossil fuel use clearly has its attractions if it can be achieved without economic burdens. It also gives Japan greater flexibility in determining its supply mix than countries endowed selectively with fossil resources.

In the scenarios of high efficiency and fuel switching, gas and non-fossil sources supply more than 60% of demand in all three OECD studies and in the USSR. The supply chapter in this volume (Chapter 5) considers the international feasibility of this. China is marked by continuing dependence upon coal, with only very modest reductions from increased use of (speculative) gas and non-fossil sources: the non-fossil input is likely to be constrained by capital infrastructural requirements, or environmental opposition, and the scope for policy-driven increases is very limited. The Indian study notes gas imports as a potentially important contribution to limiting both carbon emissions and other environmental impacts in development, but the practical extent is limited by the shortage of hard currency and domestic capital for developing the infrastructure; again, this leaves heavy reliance on domestic coal resources.

2.7 An international perspective

All the case studies see the international dimension as important, but in different ways and on different timescales. In the UK, the EC relationship is crucial, but in the shorter term there is a strong impression that abatement measures within the Community could proceed irrespective of wider international action. Even in the longer term, the increasing perception that reducing carbon emissions could to an extent be a vehicle for pursuing policies which are desirable in their own right, and the growing political and economic confidence of the Community, means that action may not hinge strongly on international developments.

Japan appears more concerned about its international image: 'Japan did not take the initiatives ... on CFCs and as a result was criticised ... there is a strong concern within government that Japan should not make the same mistake in tackling the CO_2 issue'. Seeing both danger and opportunity in taking action on carbon emissions, and with a growing internal debate, it appears that Japan, currently very reluctant, could change its position quite rapidly, and would be keen to be a part of any international agreement provided that it was of a form which took account of its already high efficiency.

In particular, Japan sees its efficient technology as giving it an edge in a world striving to limit carbon emissions. It foresees a key role for itself in providing efficiency technology to developing countries, and seems prepared to contribute generously towards this; there could be far worse ways of disbursing its balance-of-payments surplus. The chapter highlights a role for Japan as a nation paving the way for the developing countries, by virtue of its high efficiency and technology, and its position as an Asian country rising dramatically from post-war poverty to industrial dominance, and because of its successful and continuing nuclear programme.

The US chapter also lays considerable stress on technology transfer, but with a more negative connotation. In view of the US's large infrastructure investments, 'unlike charity, the best place to start displacing coal may not be at home ... priority should be accorded to saving the developing countries from the energy equivalent of heroin in the first place'. Quite how realistic this is, in view of the persistent budget deficit and the increasingly chequered record on multilateral finance, is open to doubt. Nor is it clear how the developing countries would react to such a suggestion, at least outside a quantitative and binding international agreement.

The US attitude towards an international agreement is seen to be at best cautious. Emissions may be very high by international standards, but most US citizens do not perceive this, or they believe there are good reasons for it. According to the study, 'global equity concerns are barely noticeable on the national political scene. US citizens are infinitely more aware of the federal budget deficit ...' This reluctance to lead efforts to tackle carbon emissions seems likely to persist, but it remains unclear how the US might react to growing pressure from its OECD partners.

The Soviet Union has perhaps the most ambiguous international perspective. For reasons already discussed, it is in no position to make international commitments concerning carbon emissions, but if measures could be enacted they might well be economically beneficial. International attempts to limit emissions could hit Soviet oil but benefit its gas exports. Clearly a developed country in terms of heavy industry and emissions, the USSR could offer some technical assistance on the supply side, and on gas, but would itself clearly benefit from assistance and joint ventures on Soviet soil; it faces a crippling lack of hard currency but could pay for assistance with gas, at least in supplies to Europe and perhaps Japan.

To cap all this, the implications of the greenhouse effect itself are unusually ambiguous. There is a significant element within the Soviet Union which argues that global warming would be beneficial. Warmer and longer summers would extend growing seasons, open northern sea channels, and have many other beneficial effects. On the other hand, much of the Soviet Union's vast infrastructure for extracting and transporting primary resources is based on permafrost, melting of which would be disastrous, the dry southern areas might suffer seriously, and the soil in tundra areas might prove too poor to benefit substantially from rapid warming. A great deal could depend upon the rate at which change occurs.

China, with its vast population already heavily concentrated in limited arable areas towards the coastal regions, and with major river systems prone to flooding, could be hit severely by climatic change, though some inland and northern areas might benefit. Fearful of any international expectations which might inhibit reliance on its coal resources, which are seen as the key to its industrial future, China nevertheless has reason to fear climatic change and is attracted by the lure of technology assistance. By virtue of its population and coal base, China is the single most important country in the long-term future of carbon emissions, but, as with the Soviet Union, its likely attitude towards international efforts to limit emissions remains obscure. Similar factors apply to India.

2.8 Overview and limitations

Set against the targets for carbon emissions proposed by the environmentalist community, the case studies do not present an encouraging picture. The 'business-as-usual' projections clearly support the broad view of international energy developments discussed earlier in this chapter; generalised to other countries, they imply global carbon emissions growing by perhaps 2%/yr over the next decade, and rising to nearly 2.5 times current levels by 2030.

The abatement scenarios do suggest considerable scope for cutting emissions from current levels in the OECD countries, but the US study in particular stresses that this would be difficult. Despite the relative optimism and radicalism of the UK and Japanese studies, compared with many assessments, the overall picture of emissions reduction from the industrialised countries, including the Soviet Union, falls far short of the levels which would be required to offset the inevitable growth in the developing world - let alone to allow global reductions. The Chinese study, despite allowances for large increases in energy efficiency, offers little comfort for those hoping that the enormous potential growth from this country might be substantially constrained.

The conclusions of the case studies suggest that global carbon emissions will continue to rise even if there are considerable abatement efforts. This contrasts sharply with the large reductions required to stabilise atmospheric concentrations. Overall it is hard to escape the conclusion that, if the dominant views of both energy and environmental experts are right, the world may be heading for serious trouble. Not only is a degree of adaptation to climate change over coming decades unavoidable, but forty years ahead, humanity seems almost certain to be altering the atmosphere at an even greater rate than at present.

However, the studies do offer some grounds for optimism. Paradoxically, the two countries with the highest national energy efficiency among the case studies, Japan and the UK, foresee the greatest opportunities for further cost-effective savings. This, and the general discussion in the studies, highlights the extent to which emissions depend upon broad cultural, political and socio-economic factors, rather than being determined directly by geographical and resource conditions. Though clearly these factors are implicated in forming the social attitudes towards energy, as indicated, it is possible that a high level of concern about the greenhouse effect could move other countries more towards the perspectives and possibilities represented by the UK and Japanese studies.

The great uncertainties surrounding the future of the current centrally planned economies may also give greater scope than the studies suggest. The Soviet study in particular highlights the immense difficulties of improving efficiency in existing activities. It is already clear that changes in Eastern Europe will not so much bring about incremental improvements, but rather, major industrial activities may simply close down, to be replaced by the growth of wholly new investments. This could lead to a rapid fall in energy demand - a more extreme and more painful version of what happened in the UK in 1979-82, when sharp industrial contraction reduced total demand by well over 10%. If a similar and much larger-scale phenomenon occurred in the USSR, it could have considerable implications for carbon emissions.

With such short-term uncertainties, it is inevitable that studies reaching forty years ahead are somewhat uncertain and subjective. The case studies reflect the judgement of individuals on a subject which has not been noted for accuracy of predictions in the past, and in which technical and economic developments might substantially alter the picture. The variations between the studies reflect these uncertainties and the different perspectives of the various authors, as well as real differences between countries.

The case studies also reveal more specific limitations in the knowledge base from which the authors were working, which could be addressed in order to improve understanding of the greenhouse problem and options. Though few generalisations apply to all the case studies, taken together, including the experience of the authors in researching their studies, four areas stand out.

First, most governments and analysts know far more about how energy is and could be supplied than about how it is and could be used. Crude sectoral breakdowns of energy use are available for all the countries considered, but the degree of further detail varies considerably. Without such data it is difficult to relate baseline projections to physical end-uses. Furthermore, many of the studies reveal considerable uncertainties about the real extent to which better practice and technologies could save energy, the costs and savings thereof, and the macroeconomic response to improving efficiency.[14] Energy expertise has for too long been identified with supply expertise. It is notable that those studies which were able to use 'bottom-up' analysis of energy demand (see Chapter 7, section 7.1) tended to suggest greater technical scope for abatement than those which could not.

---

[14] Partly in a bid to overcome this limitation, an international and regularly updated compendium of the performance of energy-consuming technologies has been developed at the University of Geneva (B.Giovannini and D.Pain, *Scientific and Technical Arguments for the Optimal Use of Energy*, Centre Universitaire d'Etudes des Problèmes de l'Energie (CUEPE), University of Geneva.

A second area of difficulty is the treatment of non-fossil energy sources, both nuclear and renewable. Due to lack of space if nothing else, none of the studies consider the safety and environmental pros and cons of nuclear power, but there are still wide variations in attitude. The UK study doubts its economic and political feasibility, and argues that renewables offer better prospects for non-fossil power. The US study also doubts the political feasibility of the nuclear option, suggesting that entirely new designs might be required. In discussing options, the other studies clearly identify non-fossil power with nuclear and the existing renewables (hydro, biomass and geothermal), though the Japanese chapter does highlight significant potential for some other renewables.

Whilst recognising the possible political hurdles, these authors tend to regard the nuclear option as essential and inevitable for both economic and environmental reasons, and find it hard to envisage how the energy system would develop if nuclear power were halted by developments akin to those in many other OECD countries. There is a degree of faith that nuclear power will be both economic and acceptable, and a clear if unstated implication that resources devoted to it could not be spent better in other ways, so that constraints on nuclear power would seriously impede attempts to limit carbon emissions.

The truth of this conviction rests heavily on both the costs and the practical potential for further energy efficiency and for renewables. But as with efficiency, the unconventional renewables are also relatively uncharted territory in terms of both resources and technology, at least for mainstream energy policy analysis. Making quantitative assessments of their potential contribution and implications if the technologies improve, particularly if there is a premium on non-fossil sources so that the main competitor is nuclear, proved very difficult.

The UK and Japanese studies go furthest in analysing the possible renewable component. The US study notes a large theoretical potential but doubts the extent to which institutional hurdles could be overcome, even if technical ones could be mastered. But to varying degrees, the view that renewables could make no large contribution on the forty-year timescale considered appears more as a reflection of received wisdom than a conclusion argued from quantitative analysis. Nuclear and renewable technologies are dealt with in more detail in Volume II, and the other issues are considered further in Chapter 5 of this volume.

A third and perhaps inevitable area of uncertainty concerns the economic costs of limiting carbon emissions to the extent considered in the abatement scenarios. The studies recognise that abatement could be difficult, but this is a very different matter. The Soviet study in fact refers to a 'vicious circle' of supply-driven policy which requires ever more capital to increase supplies to provide revenues for its own expansion, and contrasts this with a 'virtuous circle' in which increasing energy efficiency frees supplies for export to an equal degree, with funds which can be used for further efficiency improvements. The Chinese study refers to the high costs of constraining Chinese coal use by more than can be achieved with technical efficiency, and the US study notes the potentially high costs of *replacing* the coal infrastructure; but the costs implied by the scenarios remain unclear. The UK study, as quoted above, is the most explicit in claiming that the costs in limiting carbon emissions would be political rather than economic, basing this upon its end-use analysis of the economic potential for improving efficiency and arguably optimistic assumptions about the application of renewable technology against a background of rising fossil prices.

A fourth area of weakness lies in the assessment of actual policy tools. The US and UK studies consider briefly the possibilities of standards, utility regulation, and energy taxes. The Japanese chapter notes some of these but relies more heavily on the close-knit co-operative relationship between government and industry, and the past history of exhortation and some legislation to limit consumer use. The Soviet and Chinese studies place strong emphasis on price reform backed up by broader economic reform. But with the exception of the US study[15], the authors were unable to draw on any recognised body of analysis examining the range of policy tools which might be used to try and improve energy efficiency or help promote fuel switching, and the limitations and issues raised by each.

These are all important, and interconnected, areas in which further study is required. Without better understanding and analysis of these issues, the wide disputes about energy possibilities and environmental impacts will persist, exacerbating both the domestic and international political tensions which will arise if concerns about the greenhouse effect

---

[15] The US author was a lead author of the US DoE report, *A Compendium of Options for Government Policy to Encourage Private Sector Responses to Potential Climate Change*, US DoE Report to Congress,DOE/EH-0102, Washington DC, October 1989.

do deepen. The case studies provide some answers, but clearly questions remain as to why perspectives differ so widely, and whether societies which have proved so adaptable in the past are really so helpless when it comes to carbon emissions, despite the technical potential for alternatives.

This volume focuses primarily on an assessment of policy instruments, and examines the broad policy and international issues raised by attempting to limit carbon emissions, in much more depth than was possible in the limited space and scope of the country studies. In doing so, many of the other issues and questions raised by the case studies are considered, including the non-fossil debate and other supply issues (Chapter 5), the long-term trends in energy demand, development and the scope for savings (Chapters 6 and 7), and international political themes and other challenges (Chapter 8). Costs and cost assessment run as a constant theme throughout, and the policy analysis starts with a brief review of energy pricing, taxes, and other recurrent economic themes in the energy-environmental debate.

Economics, Prices and Taxes

Much of the debate about energy policy and the greenhouse effect centres around economic themes. Externalities, including the greenhouse effect, imply that energy prices do not reflect the full costs of energy supply and provide a rationale for additional energy taxes, but the real level of environmental costs and hence the 'rational' level is extremely uncertain and likely to remain so. The timescales involved in energy infrastructure and environmental impacts strengthen the need for forward-looking government policies, but also mean that estimates of costs and benefits reflect often arbitrary conventions. The main role of economics is to inform and compare the relative effectiveness and efficiency of different response policies. Because of the scale and importance of energy supply, this role assumes an exceptional importance.

The use of carbon taxes is widely advocated as the most efficient and flexible way of limiting carbon emissions. Yet many governments still subsidise energy, and others remain wary of applying taxes for environmental goals. The arguments advanced for general energy subsidies are very weak. They usually impede rather than aid economic efficiency, and are a much less effective way of providing help to the poor than direct income support and fuel allowances. However, price reform is difficult politically, though some governments have achieved major reforms with careful design and implementation of compensatory measures.

The macroeconomic impacts of carbon taxes are complex, and depend on the economic conditions of the country concerned. In general they will increase non-energy investment and employment, and the available evidence suggests that in most countries modest carbon taxes may aid economic growth as well as reducing carbon emissions. The impact of different levels is impossible to quantify accurately but even large taxes, if phased in, would appear to have a small impact on economic growth, assuming them to be offset by other tax reductions.

Large carbon taxes may be needed to reduce emissions substantially. If applied in isolation from other measures, domestic and international reactions will further reduce their impact on emissions; in the long run, an international agreement would be required to limit migration of industries arising from widely varying tax levels, and taxes on international transport fuels will require special treatment. However, tradeable permits do not appear to be a promising domestic alternative for limiting carbon emissions.

Energy markets deviate widely from the ideal of classical economics in many ways. In addition to subsidies and externalities, there are various market distortions, entry barriers, and a deep-seated division between the economic behaviour of energy consumers as compared with suppliers. These and other imperfections indicate that many factors other than price alone need to be considered. There are also complex trade-offs to be made between economic efficiency and other objectives. Few generalities or ideological absolutes are useful in the energy policy debate.

Introduction

The most common concern about measures for limiting carbon emissions is the belief that they will cost a lot. So, retort others, might climate change; and what evidence is there that abatement would cost a lot? Economic themes lie at the heart of the public debate about energy policies and the greenhouse effect, and economics should have a great deal to say about the choice of policy instruments.

This chapter reviews first the difficulties in trying to establish the degree of emissions abatement which may be economically justified, and the dilemmas posed by the long-term nature of energy investments and impacts including the greenhouse effect. These create substantial economic uncertainties concerning the benefits and costs of responses.

This does not undermine the relevance of pricing in trying to meet environmental goals and to reflect environmental costs. The case studies of countries with low energy prices identify this as a major reason for energy inefficiency, and suggest that price reform should be an important part of any policy response. Many economists suggest a carbon tax as the most economically efficient means of encouraging greater energy efficiency and other changes in responding to the greenhouse effect. The calls for a carbon tax are growing, but as yet most governments remain wary of such measures for both political and economic reasons.

The bulk of this chapter therefore examines the issues involved in energy pricing and carbon taxes, including their likely effectiveness, economic impact, and the political obstacles to them. Tradable permits, as an alternative macroeconomic instrument designed to create incentives to limit emissions across the economy, are also considered.

Energy pricing is important, but its claim to being the most efficient policy response depends heavily on assumptions that energy markets behave in ways which reflect roughly the ideals of classical economics. The final section of the chapter therefore examines the nature of energy markets, and the implications which the extensive imperfections revealed may have for approaches to policy.

The chapter's focus is on understanding the economic issues in market economies. This is partly because of the global trend over the past decade towards market-based mechanisms, but also because such a discussion illuminates issues common to all economic and political systems.

3.1 Externalities and the cost of the greenhouse effect

Externalities are impacts imposed by economic activity which are not reflected in its financial costs. Externalities are endemic in energy supply, stretching from the local impacts of construction, mines, oil spills, gas explosions, etc., through the urban and regional impacts of hydrocarbon, acidic, and radioactive emissions, to the global issue of the greenhouse effect.

Economic theory suggests that the costs of such impacts should be incorporated into the energy price; Pearce and his colleagues provide a recent and influential overview of why this is often the most efficient approach to environmental control, and a review of experience.[1] For some externalities this can be achieved directly by paying for clean-up operations, or direct compensation to victims. More often this is not possible. Taxes on emissions are then the main way of 'internalising' external costs.

In practice, few countries currently levy effective emission charges (though more are now seriously considering such measures). This arises in part because, for many environmental problems, one of the major difficulties is measurement. However, if no other measures are used, this is equivalent to assigning the externalities a value of zero - which in many cases is perhaps the only value known for certain to be wrong.

After a decade of debate about acidification, estimates of the costs still vary widely. Quantifying the greenhouse effect is likely to be far more uncertain. The best-known estimate suggests the total cost of the greenhouse effect over the next century to be a few billion dollars annually in the United States, with an upper limit of a few hundred billion worldwide.[2] But the striking thing about this estimate is its extraordinarily narrow focus; most of the costs were associated with coastal protection.

The scientific uncertainties are not merely those of inadequate data on the rate and pattern of temperature, rainfall and sea level changes. As illustrated in Chapter 8, section 8.1, they concern far broader questions about reaction of the biosphere to an unprecedented combination of

[1] D.Pearce, A.Markandya and E.Barbier, *Blueprint for a Green Economy*, Earthscan, London, 1989.
[2] W.D.Nordhaus, 'The Economics of the Greenhouse Effect', International Energy Workshop, International Institute of Applied Systems Analysis, Laxenburg, Austria, June 1989.

changes. Overall we may be at a stage of ignorance such that further research increases the acknowledged uncertainties rather than narrowing them.[3]

Even if the impacts were known precisely it would still be impossible to value them consistently. What costs should be assigned to encroaching deserts or to forests denuded by climatic and other stresses? Or to loss of life or disease? One discussion asks 'How much does a refugee cost?', and attempts estimates of lost production.[4] People driven from their countries by famine or flood might suggest a rather different value scale, and the possibility of wars over refugees or water resources would add another dimension.

The imponderables in assessing environmental costs have often been circumvented by employing inevitably ambiguous criteria such as the currently favoured philosophy of using 'Best Available Techniques Not Entailing Excessive Cost'. Given the scale of energy industries, and the kinds of pressures discussed in the previous chapter, it is far from clear how much use such an approach would be with respect to the greenhouse effect. An alternative, which may have very different implications from either the cost-benefit or 'BATNEEC' approach, is that of sustainable development. This remains an ambiguous concept; Pearce and his colleagues offer a 'gallery of definitions'. The extensive use of any mineral resources, including fossil fuels, violates some of these definitions; the continued accumulation of CO_2 in the atmosphere violates most of them. The Brundtland Report[5] voiced a fear that energy was the one area in which sustainable development might not be possible, and the case studies in Volume II seem to bear this out.

---

[3] Wynne among others has noted that ignorance creates a false confidence; the acknowledged uncertainties often broaden as wider possibilities are acknowledged (B.Wynne, 'Frameworks of Rationality in Risk Management: Towards the Testing of a Naive Society', J.Brown (ed.), *Environmental Threats: Social Sciences Approaches to Public Risk Perceptions*, Belhaven, London, 1989). The global nature of the greenhouse effect and its interactions with all other parts of the biosphere suggest that the acknowledged uncertainties could continue increasing for a long time.

[4] J.Walter and R.Ayres, *Global Warming: Damages and Costs*, Research Report, International Institute of Applied Systems Analysis, Laxenburg, Austria, forthcoming (draft February 1990). See also Chapter 8, section 8.3.

[5] World Commission on Environment and Development, *Our Common Future*, Oxford University Press, Oxford, 1987.

For some time, decisions concerning the degree of abatement action are likely to be taken more at the level of gut reaction and politics, affected by perceptions of abatement costs and climatic risks. Underlying both of these is the question of how much weight is to be given to costs and benefits in the future. This leads into further areas of economic difficulty which require brief review.

3.2 Rates of return and the discounting conundrum

Costs, in economic theory, carry a clear message. They reflect the resources which have to be devoted to a particular activity or technology, and (excepting inflation) they should not change unless the resources input changes. In reality, costs - and the relative costs of different projects - depend very heavily on how the accounting ground-rules are laid.

It would be hard to find a better illustration of this than the impact of electricity privatisation in the UK. The total asset value of the electricity system was traditionally judged to be around £40bn, but the quoted price in the run-up to privatisation has been variously put at between £20bn and £4bn, depending on the terms of sale. In October 1988 the generating board estimated that electricity from a new nuclear station would cost 2.21p/kWh; within a year, figures of 6-9p/kWh were being circulated.[6] This partly reflected real changes in estimates as prospective buyers added more factors and information, but it also reflected the change in accounting ground-rules. Over the same period, quoted cost estimates for wind energy doubled from 2.5p/kWh, and those for tidal power rose nearly threefold from the original 3.5p/kWh. Estimates for costs from gas turbines rose little. Given that these are investments intended to last decades, and that these are the kinds of numbers used to estimate the costs of competing options for limiting carbon emissions, such variation is disconcerting to say the least.

The example of UK privatisation is an extreme one, and it is likely that quoted costs will settle back a little towards former levels, but the changes point to an important fact. Most of these changes occurred because privatisation changed the ground-rules on which assessments were conducted, as well introducing an element of 'gaming'.[7] Private

[6] An industry view of these changes is given by various articles in *Atom*, No.400, UK Atomic Energy Authority, Harwell, February 1990.
[7] Because non-fossil sources were granted a fixed market share, it became in their interests to exaggerate their costs and hence maximise prices received. Meanwhile

industry usually seeks to get the money invested in a project back more quickly than does a nationalised industry, and is more concerned to aim for a higher 'rate of return' also to hedge against the risks of uncertain investments. That means higher prices - but not equally across all investments. Investments with high capital costs but low running costs, especially if they are built and operate on a long timescale, may be very sensitive to the required rate of return; those with lower capital but higher running costs will be much less so. The perceived risks, the availability of capital, and many other factors can also affect the return sought.

This is especially important in energy because of the long timescales involved, which amplify the effects of differing rates of return. These timescales become even longer when environmental issues, above all the greenhouse effect, are considered. This leads into terrain for which economic theory is ill-equipped, namely that of discounting over long time periods.

Discounting is the economic reflection of the expression that people prefer jam today rather than jam tomorrow. Future costs and benefits are reduced by a fixed percentage (the discount rate) for each year in the future, to derive an equivalent 'present value', after correcting for inflation. This captures the fact that people prefer money now rather than later, and indeed can often invest money now to accumulate interest. Prior to privatisation in the UK, the electricity industry assessed life-cycle costs of investments using a 5% discount rate. The return sought by private investors often corresponds to discount rates of 10% or more.

Small differences in the discount rate become very important over long time periods. The present value of a cost or benefit incurred twenty years ahead is reduced by a third at a 2% discount rate, but by more than two thirds at 6%, and by a factor of 10 at 10%. Discounting at 2% annually reduces costs and benefits incurred fifty years ahead by two-thirds, while a 6% rate reduces them by a factor of 22. A hundred years ahead, the discounting factors at 2% and 6% annually are respectively 8 and 500.

Carbon dioxide and CFCs emitted today will still be having an impact on climate a hundred years from now, so the discounting uncertainties further impede any attempts at a cost-benefit approach to assessing climate impacts. They also have more immediate impacts. The UK case

---

demand projections by the industry plummeted, reducing its attractiveness and the initial sale price, and making it less likely to be saddled with large debts on sell-off.

study notes that the Severn Tidal Barrage, which could supply 5-6% of current UK electricity, would cost billions of pounds to build but could expect to supply pollution-free energy at low operating costs for over a hundred years. Assessed at a 2% discount rate it is a bargain; at a market rate, it is hopelessly uneconomic.

Governments cannot control the financial decisions of industry, though they can alter the signals. But there is a considerable debate about the discount rate appropriate for governments and nationalised industries making investments and evaluations on behalf of society as a whole, for evaluating projects and weighing future benefits and costs. This is a question which has spawned a huge literature without much consensus,[8] but with respect to energy and the greenhouse effect it is so important that it is essential to point to some of the key issues.

Economists use the term 'social discount rate' to reflect the value which societies appear to - or perhaps should, to be consistent with expressed attitudes - place on the future. This is usually judged to be low - a few per cent a year at most. Most people care about the future and do not, when asked, value costs and benefits in the world their grandchildren will inherit at a tiny fraction of the present, which would be the implication of discount rates above 2-3%. The fact that economies expand and technologies develop, and thus become more able to cope with costs, is a reason for discounting; uncertainty about future conditions and preferences may be another. But concerning environmental resources some economists question even this:[9]

> Discounting between generations raises ethical problems. Do future generations deserve less consideration - specifically, a lesser share in the limited resources of the earth - than the present generation? ...
>
> It is thought that people discount the future partly because humans are mortal and cannot personally enjoy benefits that will be received far in the future, and partly because most of us (in the Western world,

[8] A collection of major research studies are published in R.C.Lind et al., *Discounting for Time and Risk in Energy Policy*, Resources for the Future, Washington DC, 1982. A recent relevant review is that of A.Markandya and D.Pearce, 'Environmental Considerations and the Choice of the Discount Rate in Developing Countries', *Environment Department Working Paper no.3*, World Bank, Washington DC, May 1988.
[9] R.Ayres and J.Walter, *Global Warming: Abatement Policies and Costs*, International Institute of Applied Systems Analysis, Research Report, Laxenburg, Austria, forthcoming (draft January 1990).

that is) expect to be richer in the future than we are now ... But the mortality argument does not necessarily apply to the human race, or to societies and nations. And the 'increasing wealth' argument is clearly faulty as regards environmental benefits, in particular. Unlike technologically based wealth, the environment is clearly a limited and deteriorating resource... in environmental terms, our descendants will be considerably poorer than we are today. That being so, we should consider a negative discount rate, at least for valuing endangered environmental assets. But having said this the problem of determining appropriate magnitudes remains essentially unsolved.

The difficulty with actually using very low or even zero or negative rates is that this would create a large gulf between the behaviour of the private and public sectors: innumerable projects would be economic as public but not private investments, and money would be drawn from the private sector and from projects which might yield much higher rates of return. Furthermore, if money can be invested to grow and pay for future costs, it may not make sense to use different rates for different issues.

Consequently, there are continuing pressures for the public sector to adopt rates closer to those sought by private industry, and in practice most governments use discount rates around 4-8%/yr, somewhere between the social discount rate and the assumed or stated private sector rate.[10] Government attitudes have varied with changing perceptions, priorities and pressures. Environmentalists over the decades have been even less consistent than many others. Some have argued for high discount rates because these make hydro and nuclear power developments appear relatively more costly, and generally raise prices and discourage big investments. Others have argued for very low or even

---

[10] A further twist in the discounting tale is provided by the fact that although private investors seek and are widely assumed to get relatively high rates of return, in reality they have often not succeeded. Over the period 1970-87 the pre-tax real rate of return on industry, transport and communications averaged under 2%/yr in Canada, Australia, Finland, France, Sweden and the UK. Only in Japan (manufacturing statistics only available) did the pre-tax rate exceed 10%. After tax, many of the rates would be negative: any investment which after tax kept pace with inflation would have been above average. Real interest rates similarly were often negative, being outpaced by inflation. Such low *ex-post* rates of return would appear to undermine many of the arguments for high public sector discount rates outlined in the text. The author is grateful to Dr Bob Rowthorn for calculating these data, which are derived from the OECD, *Historical Statistics 1960-87*, OECD, Paris, 1989.

zero rates because of indignation at the discounting of future generations, and the practical discounting of environmental damage including the costs of dealing with radioactive wastes and nuclear decommissioning.

Quite apart from the issue of intergenerational equity, there are practical reasons why government rates should be lower than those of industry. One reason why higher rates are sought in the private sector is to hedge against risk: to mix metaphors, private industry is not merely concerned about jam, but about having a bird in the hand today rather than two in the bush tomorrow. Since governments cannot go bust, most economists accept that governments should not pay such a risk premium. Another factor is capital shortage; industry will tend to invest in projects with the highest perceived rate of return and may simply not have the capital to consider more marginal projects. Since governments usually have more access to capital, especially in developed economies, again their discount rates could be lower. Extensive capital shortage in developing countries is one reason why discount rates are frequently much higher, and many argue for government rates, and the return sought on international lending projects, to be close to those sought by markets.[11]

Yet societies need long-term investments for development of infrastructure and some basic resources. Taken to extremes, it is arguable that if discounted cash flow analysis had been invented and applied in the eighteenth century, development of the now developed economies might have been seriously curtailed, because the great infrastructural investments in canals, railways, bridges, and steam technology, on which subsequent expansion was founded, might have been rejected as uneconomic given the prevailing shortage of capital. Capital shortage creates high discount rates, but using high discount rates tends to perpetuate capital shortage, because it encourages investment in projects with high running costs. The possible analogues both with the situation in developing countries and concerning global environmental problems are clear.

Yet if there are capital constraints, investments with low rates of return do draw resources from projects which could pay back more rapidly. In attempting to resolve these dilemmas, some leading economists have argued that the solution lies in separating the impact of capital shortage

---

[11] Markandya and Pearce, *Environmental Considerations and the Choice of Discount Rate*. The World Bank currently uses a 10% discount rate.

from the issues of the discount rate.[12] Government investments should be assessed at a (low) social discount rate to reflect the needs of future societies, but the capital costs of projects should be adjusted to account for the 'opportunity cost' of taking money away from the private sector. This could result in a 'shadow capital cost' for the purposes of investment appraisal of many times the real cost. As a result, major long-term benefits and costs would be captured, but the distortion to current markets would be minimal.

Other attempts to resolve the inherent contradictions in simple discounting have been made,[13] but none seem to have the consistency of this approach, which appears to resolve many of the important theoretical dilemmas - though the exact figures for the social discount rate and shadow capital cost (which is based on the difference between the market and social discount rates) appear uncertain. However, these suggestions seem unknown even amongst most economists, and in practice analysts, governments and financiers seem most unlikely to pay attention to such refinements in their studies and investment decisions.

Inconsistencies and uncertainties in discounting are thus likely to remain extensive. For energy and environmental assessments especially, because of their long timeframe and the capital intensive nature of many non-fossil energy investments in particular, this places a large caveat over discussions of costs. Costs do not reflect an absolute reality, but are based on the shifting sands of ownership, financing, economic circumstance and discounting conventions. The shadowlands of accounting practice can have as much impact on the assessment of greenhouse costs and optimal policies as many other assumptions combined.

---

[12] R.Lind et al., *Discounting for Time and Risk*.
[13] Various proposals for 'dual discounting' have been made. D. Collard (*Faustian Projects and the Social Rate of Discount*, University of Bath Papers in Political Economy, 1979) formulates an approach based on a strong distinction between current and future generations. Collard argues that the value of future money to people existing today, as they get older, is something which is adequately reflected in existing markets. But the value of money to future generations, not alive at the time of the decision, is a matter of ethics. This can be captured by using two discount rates, one near-market rate for the existing generation and another, social rate, for future generations. The total discounting for a given date is a combination of these rates weighted in proportion to the mix of generations. The net result is that short-term investment decisions are more or less unaffected, but longer-term impacts have a much greater weight. The approach is challenging, but inconsistencies still emerge.

For these and other reasons, not only does it seem impossible to estimate the costs of the greenhouse effect, it also seems impossible to provide an unambiguous assessment of the costs of measures to abate it, even if all other uncertainties are removed. This does not, however, mean that economics is of little help. Far from it. The relative costs of different technologies may still vary unambiguously, and, in particular, economics has a very important role to play in examining the relative effectiveness and efficiency of different response policies. Because of the scale and economic importance of energy supply, this role assumes an exceptional significance.

Of all the issues appropriate to the realm of economic analysis, energy pricing stands out as the central theme, and pricing policy as the tool most widely recommended by economists as an effective and efficient way of tackling environmental problems such as the greenhouse effect. To pricing we now turn.

3.3 Energy pricing, subsidies, and welfare

Energy price is important. The trend of global energy consumption, both absolute and per unit of GDP, dropped sharply after the oil price rises of the 1970s, especially in countries which did not insulate their consumers from the increases. The upward trend resumed as the price declined during the 1980s, and rose sharply after the price collapse of 1986. Energy productivity has improved faster in countries with higher energy prices, to a clear and significant degree, as illustrated in Figure 3.1. These and other factors confirm that energy demand can respond quite strongly to price changes, and have convinced many analysts that 'price is more important than we thought'.[14]

Price changes are often an efficient and effective method of altering behaviour in ways which allow the maximum freedom and flexibility, because a single signal can affect myriad complex decisions in broader predictable directions. Energy pricing, and the use of carbon taxes to limit emissions, have thus emerged as a central issue in discussing responses to the greenhouse effect. However, to understand the issues it is important to start from the present reality.

Many countries subsidise energy. It is difficult to judge the scale of subsidies in centrally planned economies, because the overall price structure is not directly tied to resource costs, but they are clearly large;

---

[14] Lee Schipper, unpublished.

Figure 3.1 National energy productivity improvements as a function of retail/border price ratios

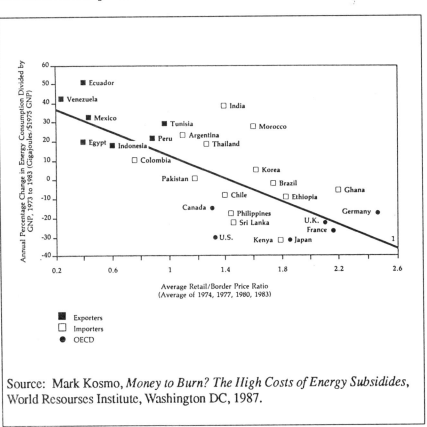

Source: Mark Kosmo, *Money to Burn? The High Costs of Energy Subsidides,* World Resources Institute, Washington DC, 1987.

the Chinese case study, for example, estimates that government coal prices are less than half the production costs. Developing countries often subsidise energy. But even in some OECD countries subsidies are common, though often of more subtle forms; in the United States, total subsidies including tax concessions in 1984 have been estimated to amount to over $40bn.[15]

[15] H.R.Heede, 'A preliminary assessment of Federal Energy Subsidies in FY1984', Testimony to Subcommittee on Energy Conservation and Power, Committee on Energy and Commerce, US House of Representatives, Washington DC, 20 June 1985.

The reasons for subsidies are many and varied. Some are blatantly political: McNeill suggests acidly that 'If governments must subsidize - and no politician that I have met is likely to give up that proven path to power - they should and could subsidize in ecologically sensible ways'.[16] The more public rationales can be broadly divided into economic and social ones.

The economic argument is that subsidising energy prices reduces industrial costs and therefore increases industrial competitiveness. Whilst this is undoubtedly true for the more energy-intensive industries, it is more than offset by the disadvantage to other industries which contribute in one way or another to the subsidy. Subsidies encourage over-consumption of energy, and hence overall lead to excessive expenditure on procuring energy resources. A comprehensive critique of the economic rationales for energy subsidies is given by Kosmo.[17]

A related reason for subsidies concerns energy security and independence. Subsidising domestic sources helps to reduce imports and may ease balance-of-payments problems. It may also increase energy security. Such policies reflect a strong belief that countries should make use of the resources they have, and should help to cushion themselves against the vagaries of the international fuel markets. However, such arguments have generally been given less credit in recent years, reflecting in part an increasing internationalisation of energy economics and a more relaxed perspective on fossil fuel markets.[18] These

---

Even in market economies there is no easy consistent definition of subsidies. The study in question takes a broad definition, as 'shorthand for the full range of Federal incentives and subsidies to the civilian energy sector of the US economy', including a wide variety of tax incentives. A more compact summary and breakdown of this assessment is given by H.R.Heede, R.E.Morgan, and S.Ridley, The Hidden Costs of Energy, Centre for Renewable Resources, Washington DC, October 1985. The scale of US energy subsidies has almost certainly reduced since 1984 with the removal of investment tax incentives and the decline in energy investments, but more recent figures do not appear to have been compiled.

[16] J.MacNeill, 'Sustainable Development: Getting Through the 21st Century', J.D.Rockefeller 150th Anniversary Conference on Philanthropy in the 21st Century, New York, October 1989.

[17] M.Kosmo, *Money to Burn? The High Costs of Energy Subsidies*, World Resources Institute, Washington DC, 1987.

[18] Essays by Clive Jones, David Jones, and Irwin Stelzer (in P.Pearson (ed.), *Energy Policies in an Uncertain World*, Macmillan, London, 1989) all argue that energy security should not be identified with reliance on domestic resources. What matters is not the

subsidies generally do not reduce prices below the internationally traded level, but are more specifically targeted on high-cost domestic industries. The social justifications for general subsidies are perhaps the most serious. Some people cannot afford adequate energy supply without them - something which is not simply confined to the developing world, as noted in the UK case study. Also, the vagaries of energy markets can lead to major industrial and social disruption if left to their own devices. The coal industries which once powered the European industrial revolution could not compete when Middle East oil came on the scene. Government support was judged a social necessity, and far less damaging than allowing industries and the communities built around them simply to collapse.

Such cases represent specific aims, best met through specific subsidies - cold weather payments for the poor, support for the coal industries - rather than through a general policy of subsidising energy. A broader social justification is that energy price increases are *regressive*; irrespective of actual ability to pay, they affect the poor more than the rich, because the poor spend a higher proportion of their income on energy. General energy subsidies are thus a means of redistributing income.

It is a matter of some debate whether in fact this is the case. In developing countries, only the richer city dwellers may use much commercial energy; the rural poor in particular rely largely on locally gathered non-commercial energy. Energy subsidies may thus help the rich more than the poor. In developed economies, it is clear that direct energy expenditure is proportionately much greater for the poor, though this is less pronounced when indirect energy (eg. in transport, and that used in the manufacture of purchased goods) is taken into account. Irrespective of this, it is widely accepted that because general subsidies lead to excessive consumption and waste, and hence harm both the economy and the environment, redistribution can be better achieved through measures other than product subsidies, for example existing tax and income support systems.

Unfortunately there is no guarantee that governments will in practice increase income support to match price rises, and whatever the theory, increasing prices is usually very unpopular. A number of these problems can be overcome by giving closely targeted subsidies - an energy supplement or free minimum fuel allowance for domestic consumers.[19] This can help the poor without distorting the effective price, and was, for example, important in enabling kerosene price reform in Sri Lanka.[20]

The impact of energy pricing on demand has been highlighted by the experience of the last two decades. Energy taxes are therefore a natural focus for policy. When the main aim is to limit carbon emissions, the most efficient tax is one on carbon directly, rather than on particular energy activities.[21] Since carbon emissions come from a large number of disaggregated energy users (eg. houses, cars), it is not practical to tax the emissions themselves, but it is quite possible to tax carbon-based fuels in proportion to their carbon content, i.e. roughly in the ratio 100:77:56 for coal, oil and gas respectively (see Chapter 1, Table1.5). This would provide incentives to reduce waste, and to move to lower-carbon fuels. Since almost all economies rely predominantly on fossil fuels, the macroeconomic effects would be very similar to those of a large general energy excise tax.

Energy taxes are not new, even large ones: the UK Government, for example, has raised about 5% of its total tax revenues from North Sea oil alone over the past decade.[22] However, most such taxes are justified on specific microeconomic grounds, for example to capture some of the

---

location of supplies but their diversity. Domestic sources can also be insecure if they can be easily disrupted by industrial action.

[19] A study by two UK economists argued: 'Energy is a merit good [ie. one essential to survival or participation at a minimum acceptable level in modern societies] ... There is a strong case for intervention on the basis of distributional arguments ... general income tax deductibility and price cuts are among the least effective ... a specific 'energy supplement' is much more desirable on both distributional and efficiency grounds ... it can be designed to meet the informational and other market failures'. (A.W.Dilnot and D.Helm, 'Energy policy, merit goods, and social security', *Fiscal Studies*, 8(3), 1987, reprinted in D.Helm, J.Kay, D.Thompson (eds), *The Market for Energy*, Clarendon Press, Oxford, 1989).

[20] Sri Lanka issued 'kerosene stamps' equivalent to six free litres/month to poorer households as part of its price reform (Kosmo, *Money to Burn*, p.38).

[21] For example, a US study concludes that a general carbon tax would be 2-3 times more effective than a specific gasoline tax in reducing emissions (W.U.Chandler and A.K.Nicholls, *Assessing Carbon Emission Control Strategies: a Carbon Tax or a Gasoline Tax?*, American Council for an Energy Efficient Economy, ACEEE Policy paper no.3, Washington DC, 1990.

[22] Tax revenues from UK oil and gas fields totalled about £65bn over 1980-89 (historic prices). (Source: *Development of the Oil and Gas Resources of the UK*, HMSO, London, 1990). Total tax revenues in the UK were £133bn in fiscal year 1988/9, of which about

large rents available from national resources with costs below the international price (as for oil), or to support pricing at long-run marginal costs. A large literature exists on the theory of such taxation.[23] In discussing carbon and other resource taxes for pollution control, however, the implication is that taxes additional to those traditionally employed are under consideration, for very different reasons, and the economic principles involved would be different.[24] What then would be implications of the central tax relevant to the greenhouse effect - a tax on carbon?

3.4 The macroeconomics of carbon taxes

If general energy subsidies are economically harmful, would a carbon tax aid economic growth? The answer depends on many factors, most noticeably the scale of the tax and the uses to which the revenues are put. A carbon tax could be a politically convenient way of raising funds for specific purposes - for example, energy conservation programmes. A number of European countries are considering such plans, and the approach has been floated for the European Community as a whole, and as a funding mechanism for international institutions concerned with climate change.

Energy is such a large business that a relatively small tax would suffice to raise large sums. A tax adding just 1% to the price of coal would raise around £350m/yr for the European Community, or $2.5bn if applied globally.[25] Yet the price impact of such a tax would be quite negligible - far smaller, for example, than the uncertainties in predicting the spot price of oil a week ahead.

In sharp contrast, most studies suggest that making a significant impact on carbon emissions would require taxes of a different order of magnitude. Some modelling studies talk about having to raise prices several times above current levels to reduce carbon emissions by 20%

---

half was from income taxes (Central Statistical Office, *Statistics September 1989*, London, Table 3.12).

[23] See, for example, a special tax issue of *The Energy Journal*, Vol.6, 1985, the first paper of which is a review of 'Energy taxes and optimal tax theory'.

[24] The most obvious difference is that taxes designed simply to raise revenue seek to minimise impacts on behaviour. Taxes designed for pollution control seek to do exactly the opposite.

[25] M.J.Grubb, *The Greenhouse Effect: Negotiating Targets*, Royal Institute of International Affairs, London, 1989.

in industrial countries alone over the next few decades,[26] let alone achieving the higher reductions discussed by environmentalists.

The response to price changes of both demand and supply, and hence the tax level required to achieve a given impact on emissions, is in fact quite uncertain. One reason for this is the distinction between short-run impacts on behaviour and long-run impacts on technology deployment and development. Sectoral studies of short-run reactions to price suggest that the response is quite small. The overall impact of historical changes suggests that the cumulative impact can be quite large. Cross-country comparisons, as illustrated in Figure 3.1, show a strong relationship between price and the rate of improvements in energy efficiency. On these and other grounds, many people believe that the very high tax levels discussed do not take adequate account of technological opportunities and other long-run impacts.[27] However, the lower tax levels discussed could still be sufficient to double the pithead price of coal.

An important implication of this distinction is that clear long-term commitments to increasing carbon taxes might be at least as important as bringing them in rapidly; this would also help to minimise dislocation costs and losses from interim supply investments.. Unfortunately, politics is rarely able to deliver such long-run commitments with conviction, especially in modern democracies. It will be especially difficult as long as some parties believe that carbon taxes would be economically

---

[26] An IEA study concludes that a tax adding $50/tonne-coal would only reduce OECD carbon emissions by about 11% from projected levels (IEA/OECD, *Policy Measures and Their Impact on CO2 Emissions and Accumulations*, OECD, Paris, December 1989). A UK study of the manufacturing sector suggested that the price of coal might have to more than double by the year 2005 to achieve a 20% carbon reduction (A.Ingham and A.Ulph, *Carbon Taxes and the UK Manufacturing Sector*, Department of Economics Discussion paper no.9004, University of Southampton, 1990). A much-quoted US study suggests that a $250/t tax might be required in the long run to stabilise US emissions at 20% below current levels (A.S.Manne and R.G.Richels, 'CO2 Emission Limits: an Economic Cost Analysis for the USA', *The Energy Journal*, April 1990).

[27] See, for example, critiques of the Manne and Richels results, notably R.H.Williams, 'Low cost strategies for coping with CO2 emission limits', Center for Energy and Environmental Studies, Princeton University, Princeton NJ, 1989; *The Energy Journal*, forthcoming. A UK study suggests that the tax levels examined by Ingham and Ulph could in fact lead to half UK energy being met from renewable sources by 2025 (D.Toke, 'Carbon Taxes and Renewable Energy', Open University Energy and Environmental Research Unit Report, UK, July 1990). See also Chapter 8, section 8.2.

damaging. Vaguer statements would have far less impact than the reality of a substantial short-run carbon tax.

Taxes of the magnitude discussed could certainly be large enough to have a macroeconomic impact. Taking the UK example, a carbon tax sufficient to double the price of coal (which would have a rather smaller impact on final user prices) would generate about 5% of total tax revenues, and 10% of current income tax receipts.[28] Higher levels, or broadening the use of resource and pollution taxes, would of course increase these figures.

However, the nature of the macroeconomic impact is uncertain. Evidence concerning it can come from theory, modelling, or empirical data.

Economic theory. As so often in macroeconomic debates, there are many countervailing arguments about the impact of carbon taxes. If perfect markets existed, any tax would distort the pricing and allocation of the 'factors of production': with an energy tax, labour and/or capital would substitute for energy, drawing labour away from more profitable applications and capital from better investments and/or consumption, resulting in reduced overall economic growth.

However, the position is greatly complicated not just by the specific energy market issues noted in the previous chapter, but also because of many other distortions in the factors of production. Economists, for example, have long pointed to the fact that high income taxes create distortions in the 'labour market', and corporation taxes distort firms' choices. The resulting distortions incur considerable costs.[29] Energy taxes, or more generally resource/pollution taxes, would enable other taxes to be reduced for a given level of government revenue.

Indeed, the primary reliance on income taxes for raising government revenue appears to be something of a historical accident and its dominance is steadily reducing in many countries. Adding resource and pollution taxes could, arguably, simply give a better and broader balance

---

[28] Such a tax would generate about £6.5bn (Grubb, *The Greenhouse Effect: Negotiating Targets*).

[29] A paper from the World Resources Institute states: 'The total efficiency cost of the US tax system has been estimated to be between 4 and 7 per cent of GNP ... estimates place the efficiency loss from marginal increase in tax revenues from the present system at 15 to 45 cents for each dollar collected'. (R.Dower and R.Repetto, *Use of the Federal Tax System to Improve the Environment*, evidence to US House of Representatives Committee on Ways and Means, 6 March 1990).

for the tax base. A report from the Institute of Fiscal Studies[30] states boldly that: 'Nearly all other taxes impose costs on the economy by worsening economic efficiency, whereas environmental taxes improve economic efficiency'.

In so far as taxes stimulate greater adoption of already economically efficient processes, the total human and capital resources devoted to procuring energy inputs will be reduced. In so far as they result in expenditure on items which would not be economic at natural market prices, and stimulate a move to higher-cost energy resources (eg. nuclear or renewables), the overall inputs required would increase. This would to some extent be offset by the impact a tax would have on the development of technologies for greater energy efficiency and for exploiting low-carbon resources, though the overall impact of technical development has been disputed.[31] Dower and Repetto argue that 'The ultimate rearrangement of resources in the economy following the imposition of a properly designed carbon tax should leave the economy better off'.[32]

---

[30] M.Pearson and S.Smith, 'Taxation and Environmental Policy: Some Initial Evidence', *IFS Commentary No.19*, Institute for Fiscal Studies, London, January 1990.
[31] A recent study tried to analyse the impact of energy prices on technology development, by comparing total factor productivity growth in the US economy against energy prices (W.W.Hogan and D.W.Jorgenson, 'Productivity Trends and the Cost of Reducing CO_2 Emissions', Global Environmental Policy Project, Discussion Paper E-90-07, Harvard University, 1990). The summary reported: 'Technology change has been negatively correlated with energy prices and positively correlated with materials prices. Thus ... if energy prices increase, the rate of productivity growth will decrease.' In other words, the study argued that high energy prices dampen technology development, and that consequently other studies underestimated the long term macroeconomic costs of high energy prices.
However, the effortless transition between 'has been' and 'will' in this excerpt belies the fact that the analysis relied entirely on data from 1958 to 1979. It hardly requires statistical analysis to guess the nature of the correlations cited, since the first three-quarters of the period consisted of declining real energy prices and rapid economic growth, while the last six years followed the sudden oil price shock of 1973, with stagflation and a flood of money to OPEC. This is hardly a good basis from which to estimate the impact of gradually rising environmental taxes, which recycle the revenues domestically, on overall technology development; and in any case, six years is far too short a period to reflect much of the impact of higher energy prices on improving energy technology. The report raises an important issue but the conclusions drawn seem entirely unsubstantiated.
[32] Dower and Repetto, *Use of the Federal Tax System*, p.3.

These are some of the general arguments of economic principle concerning the long-term macroeconomic impact of high energy/carbon taxes. In addition, there are more specific issues relating to existing economies, which are usually far from a state of optimal equilibrium (and always will be, since conditions change). Many industrial economies face problems of persistent unemployment, inflation, balance-of-payments problems, and/or 'overheating'. The causes are varied and not fully understood. In the UK, very high interest rates have been used to curb credit-based consumer spending, perceived as a major factor behind inflation and excessive imports, but this can also reduce investment and employment, and create great difficulty for those with large mortgages and other credit liabilities. The damaging domestic and international consequences of the US budget deficit are well-known.

If used initially to raise additional revenue (ie. not offset by other tax reductions), resource/pollution taxes would help reduce deficits and interest rates and stimulate investment, and they might draw consumer spending away from imports, but they would not have some of the beneficial side-effects noted above. However applied, they would also add to inflation if introduced rapidly. But a carbon tax could help ease other problems. Reductions in energy demand would improve the balance of payments at least in energy-importing countries. A tax could be varied in such a way as to counteract international price fluctuations: a decade-long commitment to introduce a tax set to increase average retail energy prices by 4%/yr annually above the rate of inflation, for example, would not only result in a phased but substantial price increase, but would bring unprecedented confidence in energy cost projections and planning. There could however be drawbacks in terms of fluctuating government revenues and lack of market response to international price changes.

The substitution of labour and capital for energy following a price rise would increase employment and investment. A study using a model of the UK manufacturing sector[33] concluded that 'in all cases the effects of higher fuel prices are that both employment and investment rise', albeit largely through a painful process: 'in the short run, output falls, and this induces scrapping of [old] equipment which leads to lower costs and prices, and output being higher in the longer term'. Given the failure of modern economics to provide clear answers to various recurrent

---

[33] Ingham and Ulph, *Carbon Taxes and the UK Manufacturing Sector.*

economic problems, such taxes clearly deserve consideration as a modern instrument of macroeconomic policy - quite apart from the environmental justification.

Given the frequent assertion that unilateral adoption of carbon taxes would be economically damaging, it is surprising that the evidence overall is so ambiguous. Furthermore, if carbon taxes were applied by a number of countries, the reduced demand for oil would also delay the re-emergence of supply shortfalls and cartels in the oil markets, and hence delay, and limit the scale of, future price rises. This is one of the most powerful economic arguments for believing that some measures to limit carbon emissions - taxes and others - will in the long run aid global average economic growth rather than hamper it. However, countries which rely on exports of energy or energy-intensive goods might not share this outlook, and could well lose from taxes or other abatement measures.

To put such arguments in a different perspective, oil is a commodity for which people are prepared to pay well above the production cost, so that there are large economic rents to be earned. Why should importing governments allow all these rents to go to the oil producers, when they could capture a large part of them through carbon taxes, and in so doing, reduce the potential leverage of oil cartels?

Macroeconomic modelling studies. A few studies have now been carried out on the impact of large carbon taxes on economic growth using general computer models of national economies. All the modellers accept that the results are preliminary and uncertain: in particular, the response of markets to offsetting reduced income and corporate taxes is hard to predict (and usually not modelled at all), and none model explicitly the impact of price changes on technology development, or of reduced energy demand on international fuel prices if broadly applied.

Nevertheless, most of the studies conclude that, providing the revenues are retained within the economy, the impact on economic growth would be small, though negative.[34] A number of positive elements discussed

---

[34] A Norwegian modelling study concluded that a rapidly introduced tax to raise fossil prices by 70% might reduce the GNP in 2000 by at most 1% (0.1%/yr) (see Grubb, *The Greenhouse Effect: Negotiating Targets*, note 52). Studies by the Dutch Government suggested that the radical package of measures in their 'sustainable growth' scenario, which includes a three- to four-fold increase in environmental expenditure over 1990-2010, including high energy taxes, would slow down economic growth by less than 0.1%/yr if adopted unilaterally, with negligible and perhaps positive impacts if

---

Macroeconomic impacts of a carbon tax: pros and cons

Con: - Distorts factors of production
- Results in extraction from higher-cost resources
- Inflationary (if introduced rapidly)
- Impact on energy intensive exporters

Pro: - Broader balance of tax base
- Increases employment
- May stimulate technical development
- Lower collection costs
- Reduces/delays exogenous price rises of fossil fuels (if applied widely)
- If revenue-neutral: reduces other taxes and associated distortions;
- If not: reduces budget deficit/increases surplus

---

above are not included; taking these into account could make the overall macroeconomic impact positive in some cases. Anderson[35] presents some simplified illustrative calculations of the impact of a carbon tax on consumer spending, investment, and growth, which 'suggest that even quite momentous changes in energy taxes could be absorbed without severely hampering growth prospects in the long term'.

The only exception to this broad conclusion appears to be that in a study by Yamaji,[36] but this assumes that revenues from a carbon tax are not recycled or offset; naturally, removing trillions of Yen from the economy

---

similar measures were adopted internationally (Ministry of Housing, Physical Planningand Environment, 'Economic aspects of carbon dioxide reductions - a view from the Netherlands,' The Hague, Netherlands, 1990).

[35] D. Anderson, 'Economics of Energy and the Environment', paper presented at an Overseas Development Conference on the Environment, Development and Economic Research, 27-8 March 1990, published in Jim Wynpenny (ed.), *Development Research: The Environmental Challenge*, Overseas Development Institute, London, 1990.

[36] K.Yamaji, 'Case study of Japan', in W.Chandler (ed.), *Carbon Emission Control Strategies*, WWF/Conservation Foundation, Baltimore, US, 1990.

reduces growth rates but this has little to do with a carbon tax directly. The overall problems of cost modelling, and cost estimates, are discussed further in Chapter 8, section 8.2.

Empirical evidence. Given the inevitable limitations of computer models, what can be learned from the actual experience of energy price variations, over time and between countries?

Although some economists dispute whether the oil price shocks were the *main* cause of the worldwide recessions of the 1970s and early 1980s, most accept that they contributed to it. However, it is much more questionable whether this says anything about a carbon tax. The former Secretary-General of the OECD has argued that the oil shocks hurt because:[37]

* The raised expenditure on energy went abroad, instead of being recycled within the importing countries (and a large part of OPEC revenue was not spent in oil-importing countries).

* Many governments attempted to protect consumers against the impact of the price rises, rather than passing the costs through. Demand response was therefore quite slow, and much of the deficit was largely paid for out of profits, thus reducing investment and employment. The problem was therefore not the price rise itself, but faulty adjustment to it.

In addition, the fact that the changes were so sudden caused dislocation, and the technological and investment response took many years to 'catch up' with the price rises. None of these three factors need apply to domestic carbon taxes, though the final point cautions against rapid introduction of large taxes.

For these reasons, cross-country comparisons are probably more relevant. Unfortunately the evidence is highly ambiguous.[38] In general, the impact of domestic energy price changes on economic growth is difficult to separate from other factors: for example, the tendency to have less energy subsidies in more developed economies, which also have lower percentage growth rates, and in countries which

[37] InterAction Council, *Report of High Level Expert Group on Ecology and the Global Economy*, Amsterdam, February 1990, InterAction Council, New York, 1990.

[38] A strong correlation between growth and high energy prices has been noted by Ernst von Weizsäcker (address to InterAction Council, in ibid.), but as yet this is based on only a few countries over a short period. Kosmo (*Money to Burn*) examines a much larger range and reports a slight negative correlation, below the level of statistical significance.

have few indigenous resources, which is probably a more important issue than tax policy especially in the period of oil price shocks. Overall it seems unlikely that convincing evidence either way can be obtained from either time series or inter-country comparisons.

Conclusions. To summarise the discussion, carbon taxes are generally considered to be a logical and efficient approach to limiting carbon emissions, but there are concerns about their impact on economic growth as conventionally defined. Yet there is no clear consensus on this issue on either theoretical or empirical grounds, and if anything the balance of evidence is that some degree of carbon taxation would aid economic growth. There is great uncertainty about the optimal level and, indeed, this may be expected to vary substantially between different countries.

There are so many variables involved that there will probably never be a consensus on the quantitative implications of carbon taxes, but most studies (which are confined to the developed economies) suggest that even high levels would have only a small impact on growth, assuming the revenues from the tax to be recycled domestically. Broad application of domestic carbon taxes would also help to stabilise international fuel prices, and promote the development of more energy-efficient and non-fossil energy technologies.

Finally, it must be stressed that this discussion is based on a very narrow definition of economic growth. If environmental resources are included as part of national accounts, as is increasingly being advocated (see Chapter 8, section 8.3), the degradation of the atmosphere and other resources would detract from growth statistics, and internalising the costs of this through carbon and other resource/pollution taxes would almost inevitably be reflected in increased net growth rates.

Overall, if carbon emissions are to be limited, then price is an efficient tool and the economic case for a substantial carbon tax seems very strong, especially if political consensus can be obtained to phase it in over an extended period, with the signposts visible so that energy and other industries have time to develop investments and technology accordingly. So what are the catches?

3.5 Constraints on carbon taxes in developed economies

Carbon taxes are attractive in theory, but they face a number of practical limitations and obstacles. Even if they were widely adopted at high levels, they would be far from the whole answer, for reasons discussed at the end of this chapter. Indeed it is arguable that a carbon tax might impede other measures to limit emissions, because additional measures would then also reduce government revenues. Taxation of domestic oil production has certainly not meant that governments try to limit it: usually the reverse. Hoel[39] states that if an international agreement forces high domestic carbon taxes, 'it would be in the [economic] interests of each country to make this tax as ineffective as possible', and notes many ways that governments might do this. They could manipulate other taxes, and do nothing about various market failures leading to over-consumption. Carbon taxes applied without any other incentive to limit carbon emissions could therefore be something of a double-edged sword.

International reactions also need to be considered. If adopted unilaterally, high resource taxes could simply encourage relocation of industries rather than more fundamental changes: carbon taxes, offsetting corporate and income taxes, would tend to repel energy-intensive industries abroad and attract light industry. Although energy costs are usually a minor factor determining location in comparison with other issues, to the extent that this occurred it would mean that global emission reductions would be less than they appear from national impacts, and the costs of adjustment could be high.

Special problems are posed by fuel for international transport (marine 'bunkers' and aviation fuels), since ships and aircraft can easily change their country of refuelling. These fuels also create special problems of accounting in estimating national carbon emissions. A separate international agreement might be required to deal with the issues raised.

These observations do not invalidate the earlier economic discussion. However, if carbon taxes develop very unevenly between different countries, these factors could further limit their effectiveness in reducing emissions, and add to the political difficulties. This would become an especially serious problem if the energy-intensive industries move to countries where, for whatever reasons, they operate at lower overall energy efficiency. Relocating industries *can* be an opportunity to improve both general and energy efficiency, because of the new investment, but only if the technical resources are available and incentives exist.

[39] M.Hoel, *Efficient International Agreements for Reducing Emissions of CO_2*, Department of Economics, University of Oslo, December 1989 (draft).

These factors, rather than the oft-cited but probably incorrect notion that carbon taxes would hurt economic growth, suggest a need for some kind of international agreement on the application of carbon taxes in the long term. The difficulties facing such an agreement are considered elsewhere,[40] the most serious problem being that of getting any form of quantitative agreement on domestic tax policies when the circumstances of countries, including current tax structures and resources and political conditions, differ to such an extent.

A general unquantified agreement of principle and intent, and a separate agreement on international transport fuels, might still be possible. However, a weak agreement might do little to encourage or help governments to overcome political opposition to carbon taxes.

The opposition to carbon taxes is bound to be very broad. None of the country case studies foresee them being easy to introduce: several, indeed, see little prospect even of removing existing subsidies. Many governments are instinctively wary of measures which might lead to price rises. Opposition from the coal, oil and electricity industries is likely because the tax would reduce markets and might well cut into profits; in so far as they can pass on the costs to the consumer, they also fear being blamed for this. High carbon taxes could be a devastating blow to coal, trying to fend off competition from gas-fired power generation, and to coal-based electricity utilities competing with gas for direct heating and other applications.

The usual public reaction to price increases would be reinforced by the high-profile social impacts discussed earlier; there are, for example, already signs of divisions between environmental groups and 'right to warmth' groups on carbon taxes in the UK. Trade union interests will generally be opposed on both counts - defence of jobs in existing heavy industry, and defence of workers' living costs. The probable alliance between public, trade unions and industry presents formidable political obstacles: in several developing countries, such forces have been quite sufficient to bring down governments which have attempted to remove energy subsidies, and in nearly all countries they are still far stronger than the forces behind 'green politics'.

Certainly some steps could be taken to mitigate opposition, for example through fuel allowances - entitlements to a given amount of fuel at low

---

[40] Hoel, *Efficient international agreements*; Grubb, *The Greenhouse Effect: Negotiating Targets*.

prices, as discussed earlier.[41] As a way of offsetting the impact of taxes, the revenue could be used directly to fund fuel allowances - a tax-plus-rebate system designed to increase the marginal cost to the consumer without necessarily changing the average cost. Managerially this is quite possible; some countries already have variable tariffs for domestic consumers, and most do for industry. At present, the cost structure is frequently one of declining marginal costs giving an incentive to consume more. A tax-plus-rebate system which reversed this trend would clearly be feasible, and it could well assuage many of the public concerns if that were judged essential. Direct 'energy expenditure' allowances on income-tax thresholds could be a simpler political ploy, making the same point that the consumer need not lose (and could gain) from energy taxes.

None of these refinements would make a carbon tax more attractive to the energy industries; after all, the ultimate purpose would be to reduce the use of carbon-based fuels. It is, however, quite possible that if action is required, many industries would prefer the flexibility of taxes to systems based more on arbitrary standards and targets.

In view of the political obstacles and the probable drawbacks of sudden changes, carbon taxes are unlikely to be brought in very rapidly. But given the broad and growing consensus that macroeconomic instruments should form a major part of any attempts to limit greenhouse gas emissions and the strong arguments in favour of carbon taxes, it seems reasonable to conclude, that, for most OECD countries at least, the main uncertainty is not whether, but when.

3.6 Price reform in developing countries and centrally planned economies

The above discussion focuses on developed market economies. For developing countries the issues are drawn even more sharply. The urban poor especially, existing on subsistence incomes but relying on commercial energy, could be hard hit by energy price rises. Also, raising energy prices could increase pressures for theft (it is estimated, for

---

[41] Section 3.3. For a recent discussion of distributional impacts and measures which can be taken to alleviate them, see P.Johnson, S.McKay, and S.Smith, 'The Distributional Consequences of Environmental Taxes', *IFS Commentary No.23*, Institute for Fiscal Studies, London, July 1990.

example, that up to 20% of power losses in India are from theft[42]), and in some cases corruption. In many developing countries, particularly in Africa and parts of Asia, commercial energy price rises could increase the pressure on dwindling forests, though this is a more complex issue than it seems.[43]

And yet, the economic costs of energy subsidies are all the greater. Subsidies draw government expenditure away from much more important applications. They encourage waste, and make use of indigenous resources much less attractive, thus leading to ever greater dependence upon the fossil fuel imports which have placed such an enormous burden on trade balances, and are a prime cause of the crushing foreign debt. Furthermore, the bulk of subsidies in practice may go to the politically powerful urban elite that consume most of the commercial energy for their cars, air conditioners, etc.[44] It is a truly vicious circle, and trying to break out of it has brought several governments down, though others (such as in Sri Lanka, as noted above) have succeeded by using appropriate measures to ease the transition.

For those that manage price reform, energy taxes are not so fanciful, and indeed have many attractions. Such excise taxes can be much easier to administer than income taxes in developing countries, and with foreign-exchange shortages and debt often being crucial constraints, the added impetus to exploit domestic resources - including possible energy crops - may be very valuable, even if the nominal costs are well above world energy prices. And unlike the situation in industrial countries, the taxes overall would often be progressive; the income raised from the

---

[42] G.Leach, L.Jarass, G.Obermair, L.Hoffmann, *Energy and Growth: A Comparison of Energy in 13 Industrial and Developing Countries*, Butterworth, London, 1986. This study gives a broad analysis of energy trends and policies, including prices, in developing countries. Real prices have been steadily declining, and in many countries subsidies have increased.

[43] The interaction between income and woodfuel and kerosene use and prices is complex. The capital cost of obtaining equipment for using the fuels is at least as important as the fuel prices or effort in gathering wood. In many cases the impact of kerosene price rises on deforestation would be negligible, or easily negated, but the potential conflict is clear (Some discussions are given by G.Leach et al. (ibid.) and P.Stevens, 'The Economic Case for Border Pricing of Energy - the Need to Reconsider', in *Energy Pricing: Regulation Subsidies and Distortions*, SEEDS paper no.38, Surrey Energy Economics Centre, University of Surrey, UK, March 1988).

[44] Stevens (ibid.) bluntly states that 'the equity argument, [for energy subsidies in developing countries] really is a non-starter'.

energy extravagance of the urban elites could be redistributed or used to fund basic education or infrastructural developments. The difficulties may be greater than in industrialised countries, but so are the benefits, and again a long-term if slow trend towards carbon or other energy taxes seems likely.

The issues are different again in centrally planned economies (CPEs). As the case studies of the Soviet Union and China point out, although price reform would clearly help to reduce energy wastage, price is overall a much less important factor than in market economies. It would affect the behaviour of private consumers, but the dominant energy use in state industry might be little affected as long as it runs on the basis of production targets rather than attempts to balance input costs and outputs.

Arguably, industries in CPEs should be able to respond very effectively, because the command structure could be used to dictate a high level of investment in energy efficiency. The problem is not the principle of central command itself, but its practical inefficiency and the fact that it focuses upon production targets. With everything else subordinated to the aim of meeting these targets, and with no means of balancing this against the inputs required or the pollution generated, gross wastage and pollution seem inevitable. Also, the lack of value-related price makes it hard to judge what constitutes 'efficiency' in resource terms.

Including energy-efficiency targets in industrial production would help. However, this would run even more strongly into the fundamental limitations of central planning, namely the unmanageable complexity of directing overall industrial activities efficiently from government, and the lack of motivation and incentives to meet the targets set, especially if the different objectives (eg. gross production and minimum use of resources) conflict.

Increasing recognition of these problems has led many CPEs to try and introduce some market incentives but, as recent events have shown, it is a lengthy, complex and delicate process, which can easily lead to great political instability. With the Soviet Union and China being respectively the second and third largest emitters of CO_2, and with both facing far more pressing problems than reform of the energy sector, the limitations of CPEs based on production targets are likely to have an enduring impact on the international struggle to limit greenhouse gas emissions.

The various drawbacks and political obstacles to carbon taxes do not invalidate the basic rationale for them, but they suggest that faith in carbon taxes as the prime mover in attempts to limit carbon emissions may be sorely misplaced. Are there alternative macroeconomic instruments - those operating right across the economy - which are more appealing?

3.7 Tradeable emission permits for domestic policy

In the United States, tradeable permits have in practice been preferred to taxes for pollution control. These schemes can take many forms, but all have in common the fact that the government decides on the target levels for pollution control and issues permits which companies must obtain in proportion to the amount of the pollutant they generate. Permits can be traded between sources within a company or between companies, without any central direction.

Tradeable permits have many attractions. Like taxes, they leave the market free to choose the best means of limiting pollution. Unlike taxes, they allow the government to control the overall level directly and, if the permits are given out, they do not result in transfer payments from industry to government; an industry only pays at the margin for increases above its initial permit holding, and receives credit for reductions below this. The US systems evolved from existing pollution standards, in an effort to make them more flexible and efficient.[45] Such schemes are estimated to have saved several billion dollars in meeting pollution control targets ranging from water pollution to lead in petrol,[46] and they are a central component of the recent Clean Air Act for controlling sulphur dioxide emissions.

Unfortunately there seem to be major problems in applying emission permits to controlling CO_2. In most existing applications, the permits apply directly to the substance controlled - emission of pollutants by factories, for example - or to substances which are a minor part of larger processes, and which can be removed or replaced without restricting the amount of final product (eg. lead in petrol).

---

[45] Experiences with programmes have been varied, but most have been judged qualified successes. For excellent reviews of US schemes and the lessons learned, see R.Hahn, 'Economic prescriptions for environmental problems', *Journal of Economic Perspectives* 3(2), 1989; and T.Tripp and D.Dudek, 'Institutional guidelines for designing successful transferable rights programs', *Yale Journal on Regulation* 6, 1989.
[46] T.H.Tietenberg, 'Economic instruments for environmental regulation', *Oxford Review of Economic Policy* 6(1), Templeton College, Oxford, 1990.

Comprehensive control of CO_2 at the point of emission faces immense practical problems, because much comes from many small disaggregated units - cars, households, etc. It hardly seems feasible to have emission permits at such levels, to monitor the amount of carbon a person emits in driving a car or turning on the heating, and then make sure that their permit holding is adequate! It would at the very least require some far-reaching applications information technology to monitor, let alone manage, the trades which would inevitably become based on a centralised exchange - a bank with a clearing price. Permit systems might be more manageable for some large industries, especially electricity generation, but even here problems could arise from the timescales for system planning: what if there were not enough permits to meet growing electricity demand from the existing mix of stations?

When faced with such objections, proponents of tradeable permits for national policy often suggest that they would have to apply to the fossil fuel industries, which would obtain permits to cover the amount of carbon in the fuel they trade. However, carbon is not lead: it cannot be removed. Permits applied at any point before final emission (combustion) would simply limit the amount of fuel available.

This would amount to a fossil fuel rationing policy. Without other measures, demand could only be met if the companies forced it down through raised prices. Enormous economic rents would then flow to the fossil fuel companies, which governments would presumably try to capture through windfall profit taxes, or by auctioning the permits initially. This would remove a major part of the attraction of permits for industry. Furthermore, to avoid large price fluctuations arising from the fixed supply in the face of varying demand pressures, a permit banking system would be required to buy back or to sell additional permits at pre-specified prices. The net result would look very much like a carbon tax with several additional layers of complexity and bureaucracy.

It can be seen that for any substance to be controlled usefully through tradeable permits, key criteria must be met. To apply permits at the point of emission, the emissions must be readily quantifiable, and the sources must be of a size and capability sufficient to manage the business of permit trading (eg. SO_2 from power stations). Alternatively, permits can be applied at the point of production or intermediate trade, but in this case the emission being controlled must be determinable from the inputs, and must either form a component which can be removed without restricting the main product (eg. lead in petrol), or there must be substitutes (eg. CFCs). None of these conditions apply to domestic carbon emissions overall, though they might apply to power stations, and it is far from clear how much they could apply to most other greenhouse gas emissions.

Given the many potential attractions of tradeable permit systems, it seems an unfortunate but unavoidable conclusion that they can have little role in domestic control of greenhouse gas emissions, except possibly for certain large users. (This conclusion should not be confused with the possibilities for marketable *efficiency credits* discussed in the next chapter, or with the issues at the international level, where the emitting unit is a country.)

This suggests that carbon taxes may be the only broad macroeconomic instrument available, but this does not mean that price is the only efficient policy instrument. Indeed there may be others which are not only politically more practical, but which unless applied to excess may be more efficient. To understand why, and what these options may be, it is necessary to take a closer look at energy markets.

3.8 Energy markets and policy philosophy

If supply and demand are dominated by classical market behaviour without serious distortion, then, excepting questions of time horizons (discussed above), demand for energy services would be met most efficiently (though not necessarily equitably) by the operation of a free market in energy. If all costs are included, including environmental ones, this would also be the most environmentally benign result consistent with human wants, since maximum economic efficiency means minimum use of resources for meeting given demands.

In practice, few commodities behave in such a textbook fashion, but are affected by a range of market imperfections. Intervention designed to minimise these imperfections may then increase economic efficiency, as well as generating other (eg. environmental and/or social) benefits.

In fact the issue runs much deeper than the choice of policy instruments. Though it is rarely recognised as such, the question 'how well do energy markets work?' ultimately underlies most of the debate about the costs of limiting carbon emissions in the market economies. If energy supply and demand operate as a near-perfect market, then any intervention - even internalisation of environmental costs - is likely to reduce economic growth as conventionally defined. The many statements claiming that a great deal of energy can be saved in a cost-effective way, conversely, reflect a belief that there are important market failures, so that direct intervention can reduce costs as well as emissions, and improve economic efficiency.

The debate is rarely couched in these terms. This is partly because, although market failures are a familiar economic concept, it is still difficult to quantify their impact and implications, and they greatly complicate economic analysis. As a result, many macroeconomic studies yield to the temptation to underplay or even ignore their existence. At the opposite extreme, some 'low energy' enthusiasts are so enamoured of the potential for energy efficiency that they imply that, with minor adjustments, markets could deliver massive savings. It is, of course, politically very convenient so to invoke market forces in support of low energy projections, but, as the case studies all imply, there is little reason to believe that 'business-as-usual' projections will lead to such energy efficiency. On all counts, it is important to understand the nature and limits of energy markets.

Apart from externalities, classical market imperfections include monopolies and other features associated with limited numbers of competitors, various barriers to the entry of new firms and/or technologies, subsidies, and restrictions on capital markets.[47] Many energy activities contain monopoly power to some degree. In the case of pipelines and transmission systems, there is a natural monopoly. More pervasively, the sheer scale of energy developments often limits producers to a small group ('oligopoly'). Monopolies are a common feature in advanced societies, and market economies have generally developed methods for limiting monopolistic behaviour, using specific regulation and general mechanisms such as the Anti-Trust laws in the US, and the UK's Monopolies and Mergers Commission. There is a trend towards ending monopolies in the energy area as far as possible, though this may have mixed implications for the environment.[48]

---

[47] A broader economic overview of energy supply markets is given in the introductory chapter of Helm, et al., *The Market for Energy.*

[48] Traditional monopolistic behaviour involves restricting output to raise the price, thus increasing profit while reducing demand - and environmental impact. Their profitability also means that monopolies may be less averse to incurring indirect expenditure, such as on environmental protection. However, price rises tend to be concentrated on customers who will respond least to them, and in practice the form of

A related and much more important distortion occurs in international fuel markets. These bear little relation to the classical ideal in which price settles at the long-run marginal production cost plus a growing margin to reflect depletion of the resource. For a variety of reasons, most notably the long timescales and heavy capital investments involved, international fuel markets often approximate either to a 'buyers' market', in which the operating capacity exceeds the demand even at quite low prices, or a 'sellers' market', in which operating capacity can be fully used even at quite high prices. In a buyers' market, prices tend to be very low, sometimes barely sufficient for producers to cover operating costs, as for international coal in the late 1980s. In a sellers' market, the price may be very high, well above total production costs. Producer cartels, such as OPEC, which restrict the supply below the total capacity, can artificially create a sellers' market, though these tend to be unstable in the long run because it is in the interests of each individual producer to sell more than its 'quota'.

The long timescales involved in energy developments ensure that oscillations between extremes often span many years. Oil is the major example of such fluctuations, but other fuels tend to follow the oil roller coaster.

All this creates great uncertainty in projecting fuel prices, and means that prices may be only weakly related to production costs. Estimating the long-run average price can be easier than projecting trends over the next few years, but this depends both upon long-run demand and technological developments. Also, the high profits at times of high prices tend to be taxed by governments, which may support industries at times of low prices, but there is no reason why these should cancel out, adding to long-term uncertainties.

Barriers to new entrants in energy markets arise partly because of monopolistic practices, but also reflect the sheer scale of energy operations. A striking testament to this is the fact that almost all of the major oil companies and manufacturers of generating stations have been in existence for more than half a century.

Entry barriers apply equally to technologies. Even large companies are unwilling to invest billions of dollars in research, development and

---

regulation, whether or not state-owned, may lead industries to focus on maximising size and hence political importance and influence. Inevitably, there are also efficiency losses as well as potential gains in breaking up natural monopolies.

demonstration (RD&D) for returns which, however large, are uncertain and likely to be far in the future. Companies do not take responsibility for ensuring adequate and environmentally acceptable long-term supplies, and this is a major justification for government RD&D programmes in the energy sector.

This is but one reason why many energy activities are subsidised. It is usually a minor one. As discussed above, social goals, national security arguments, and the political lobbying power of large companies are more important. This often means that most subsidies go to existing energy operations. Of the US subsidies cited earlier, Brown[49] notes:

> The allocation of these subsidies is awarded neither according to the scale of energy provided nor with reference to the promise of a developing technology ... more than $41bn of the total $44bn 1984 subsidy was provided to mature energy technologies.

This, like the support in centrally planned and some developing country economies, is sufficiently large to distort the analysis of costs and benefits of alternative sources, or of other carbon abatement measures.

If these were the only market distortions, energy would not be an unusual commodity in principle, though the scale of some of them might make it so in practice. However, with respect to energy there is another issue which receives little attention in the general economic literature but which is of profound importance in the context of environmental concerns. All the country studies in this project, and many other analyses, note the existence of many opportunities for energy savings which are much cheaper than investments in supply. Some conservation measures can pay back in a year or two, whereas five to ten years is considered a good return in most industries, and even longer paybacks are common in energy supply investments. A UK Parliamentary enquiry took evidence from a wide range of industry and environmental groups and concluded:[50]

> The most striking feature of our enquiry has been the extent to which improvements in energy efficiency - across all sectors of the economy - are almost universally seen as the most obvious and most effective

[49] Ian Brown, 'Energy subsidies in the US', in *Energy Pricing: Regulation, Subsidies and Distortion*, Surrey Energy Economics Centre Paper No.38, University of Surrey, UK, March 1988.
[50] UK House of Commons Energy Committee, *Energy Policy Implications of the Greenhouse Effect*, Vol.1, July 1989 (paras 102 and 107).

response to the greenhouse effect ... the evidence received overwhelmingly endorses the view that, for a variety of reasons, serious market imperfections persist ... widespread opportunities to invest profitably in cost-effective measures ... are being ignored.

This 'gap' between investment in supply and demand-related technologies is of immense importance. It results in an inefficient use of resources and higher than necessary costs to society, the consumer, and the environment - losses which would not necessarily be reduced by internalising environmental costs or by limiting any of the distortions discussed above. Chapter 4 identifies at least eight reasons for the 'efficiency gap', and considers the various policy measures available for narrowing it.

It is important to stress that none of these factors imply that energy demand is unresponsive to price. But *the fact that price is important does not mean that energy is a commodity in which price allocates resources optimally.* Price changes to incorporate externalities can be an important component of policy responses, but only that: they would not affect the basic logic of the supply/demand imbalance, or many of the other market failures noted.

These themes can be illustrated using the diagrams typical of classical economics. Line S in Figure 3.2 illustrates the way in which the marginal supply cost might vary with the quantity supplied. Line D shows the way demand varies with price. In a 'free market' demand will settle at Q_1, where the lines cross. However, including externalities (or taking account of hidden subsidies) the real cost of supply is higher, at S^*: if these are reflected in the price, the demand is reduced to Q_2. But the line D still represents the demand curve based on consumer behaviour, whereas the supply curve is based on producers' criteria. An optimal allocation - from the point of view of total costs to society - would be obtained only if demand investments were made on the same criteria as supply, which moves the line D to D^* - reducing consumption further, to Q_3.

In more colloquial terms, this is saying that it is all very well putting one's foot on the accelerator but it also makes sense to take off the handbrake. Carbon taxes can accelerate energy savings and other measures to limit carbon emissions, but removing or overcoming market imperfections may be still more efficient, and the best results will be achieved by both in combination. The importance of government

Figure 3.2 Energy supply and demand curves: the impact of externalities and the supply/demand investment imbalance

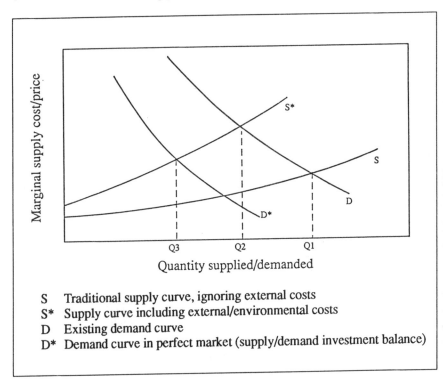

S   Traditional supply curve, ignoring external costs
S* Supply curve including external/environmental costs
D   Existing demand curve
D* Demand curve in perfect market (supply/demand investment balance)

intervention has been illustrated by the response of Japan to the oil price shocks; prices played a role, but more direct policies were given equal or greater status.[51]

This poses something of a dilemma for policy in many countries, where the 1980s have been marked by what might loosely be termed a greater faith in free markets, with a deep suspicion of many forms of government intervention. The energy sector has been no exception to this trend. In many cases this was a reaction to the perceived failure of many earlier government policies in the energy sector. From nuclear and synthetic fuel programmes to the sheltering of domestic oil prices and incentives for exploiting domestic energy reserves, policies failed to deliver their

[51] L.Taylor, *Lessons from Japan,* Association for the Conservation of Energy, London, 1990.

promise, and in some cases proved counterproductive. The strength of market economies is their adaptability, and in the United States in particular many economists have argued that it would have been better to let energy markets adapt.

For all the reasons discussed earlier, including the monopoly nature of many energy industries, their economic and social importance, the volatility of fuel markets, and the long timescales involved in resource exploitation and depletion, infrastructure and environmental impacts, governments cannot avoid a role in managing and regulating energy industries in some form or other. The important questions concern the type of regulations and the criteria on which they are based. A classical example of strident 'free market' analysis of the energy problem concludes:[52]

> Past failures do not mean that government has no role to play in energy markets. That role is to make these markets work better.

But what does it mean 'to make markets work better'? The fundamental argument in favour of free markets is that they can deliver the most efficient use of resources over time. The argument for much intervention is that in practice they do not, and/or that social goals are considered more important. The energy sector, as discussed, is a clear case in point. Markets do not deliver optimal energy efficiency. Can they be made to, and should they? Markets take a short-term view. Should governments compensate for this by supporting long-term energy developments? Markets do not reflect environmental costs. Should taxes be levied to reflect them? And what if the environmental costs cannot be quantified, or if adequate taxes are politically impossible?

In fact, much of the philosophical battle over energy policy has been fought on the vast terrain between *letting* markets work and *making* markets work. It is striking, for example, that in spite of the vitriol poured by some US economists on President Carter's policies of the 1970s, none ever seriously attempted to argue that government measures to promote energy efficiency had, or would, damage overall economic growth.[53]

---

[52] Irwin Stelzer, 'A market-based energy policy: the alternative to past errors', in Pearson, *Energy Policies in an Uncertain World.*
[53] This comment excludes the occasional theoretical economic papers demonstrating that efficiency standards and other measures harm economic development if all

These observations certainly do not provide a *carte blanche* for intervention in pursuit of ill-defined optimality. In general there are at least four major trade-offs to be made.

The first is the traditional tension between economic efficiency and equity. There is no inherent reason why greater efficiency means greater fairness in terms of either wealth or environmental burdens; sometimes the two are directly opposed. Government intervention to 'make' markets work more efficiently may be more equitable than simply letting them alone, but even this is not always the case.

The second trade-off is that between efficiency and freedom; for example, energy efficiency standards restrict the choice of consumer goods. Again this is nothing special to the energy area, and environmental pollution itself inhibits the 'right' to a clean environment. There are many regulations on consumer goods with which consumers are perfectly happy, or indeed demand - safety standards being a case in point. There is little evidence that consumers value the right to waste energy on inefficient goods. But there clearly can be tensions between consumer freedom and efficiency, of which speed limits to reduce oil consumption could be a pointed example.

Third, market failures have to be traded off against those of governments, which can include simple incompetence amplified by internal and external pressures or politics. Well-designed policies may improve greatly on markets and market-based measures. Bad policies can be much worse. In practice, government policies towards energy supply have shown some successes but also spectacular failures. Policies towards energy efficiency seem to have been much more limited, and the main complaint in terms of economic efficiency is that they have not gone nearly far enough towards 'making markets work'.

The fourth point, closely related to this, is the fact that intervention itself carries a cost in terms of the effort and bureaucracy required to formulate, follow, and police the rules. For some measures such 'intervention costs' are trivial in comparison with the benefits; for others, especially if policies are badly designed and focus on minor issues, they may be excessive.

---

participants are making economically rational decisions. To the best of the author's knowledge, it applies to all real world studies with real world figures.

[54] InterAction Council, *Report of High Level Expert Group on Ecology and the Global Economy.*

Energy policy, like many areas of government policy, involves complex trade-offs between conflicting requirements and pressures. Responding to the greenhouse effect will clearly require government action, but the choices will not be simple. Economics is but one component of the energy policy/greenhouse debate, and ideological absolutes do not help the debate. Rather than seeking to advocate goals and to prejudge means, what economics can do is to inform on the relative efficiency, effectiveness and equity of different approaches to reaching them.

3.9 Conclusions

If markets conformed to the classical ideal, economics would be relatively simple. So would policy. Even coping with a problem like the greenhouse effect would, in principle, be straightforward: the most efficient response would simply be to use taxes to internalise the costs of the environmental impact.

In practice the impacts of the greenhouse effect cannot be quantified to any useful degree of accuracy; the timescales involved in supply and impacts are so long that the discount rate used can radically alter economic perspectives; and energy markets are distorted by a wide range of factors. In discussing the importance of economic measures to reflect external costs, a report from the InterAction Council[54] notes that 'prices should not lie'. But what can and should governments do if they do 'lie' due to myriad market imperfections; and, at a more fundamental level, what truths should they tell? Substantial advances in economic analysis and practice are required, as discussed further in Chapter 8.

Energy policy, in its own right and in responding to the greenhouse effect, involves many complex trade-offs, so that it is dangerous to generalise from economic or ideological principles. Carbon taxes can clearly play a major role in limiting emissions and maybe even as a macroeconomic instrument, as part of a broader shift towards resource/pollution taxes; there is little clear evidence that they would be economically damaging in most countries. But they face many obstacles and limitations, and they fail to address key issues arising from the special features of energy demand and supply. The next three chapters consider these more specific issues, starting with a study of the policies available for trying to tap the large economic potential for improving energy efficiency.

Many cost-effective opportunities exist for improving energy efficiency and reducing carbon emissions. They are not taken up because of a wide variety of obstacles, including many deep-rooted market imperfections. Some of these obstacles can be removed, for example by measures to provide information and increase awareness, but more direct intervention is required if most potential savings are to be realised.

Efficiency standards offer a simple approach and are particularly appropriate for the domestic sector, to circumvent some of the high transaction costs involved in millions of small decisions. However, the fact that they restrict consumer and industrial choice limits the likely breadth and depth of their application. More flexible forms of standards can reduce these and other objections, but increase the complexity.

Direct subsidies for conservation measures and efficient goods can be politically easier, but they may be less effective and incur greater costs than efficiency standards. Other forms of fiscal incentive may offer greater scope. There are many options for changing the regulation of utilities to improve energy efficiency and this may have the broadest impact of any single measure. Utility structure and regulation is a critical factor in determining the use of Combined Heat and Power.

Efficiency policies involve some complex trade-offs and interactions. No single approach can deliver much of the total potential, but a suitable combination of policies, forming part of an increased awareness and concern about energy issues, could do much to realise the large scope for cost-effective savings.

Introduction

Improving energy efficiency would be the cornerstone of any attempts to limit carbon emissions. In most developed economies at least, considerable efforts have already been devoted to increasing energy efficiency in the energy conversion industries, which is of particular importance in electricity generation and distribution. Strong market-related pressures mean that carbon taxes would do much to stimulate further supply-side improvements in efficiency.

However, Chapters 2 and 3, in common with numerous other studies, note that there is a large 'efficiency gap' in energy use - opportunities for saving energy at costs well below the costs of new supply, which are not taken up because of various market imperfections. This imbalance between supply and demand investments results in costs to consumers, society, and the environment all being higher than if these opportunities were exploited. Energy pricing alone would do nothing to close this gap.

Estimates of the potential for cost-effective savings are discussed more fully in the country studies and in Chapter 7. Drawing on a range of sources, these indicate that if demand-related investments were made on the same economic basis as supply, energy consumption could be reduced, with profit, by 20-50%; some claim more. There is clearly a large theoretical potential for reducing both carbon emissions *and* the costs of meeting energy needs - if these opportunities can be exploited without incurring other, larger, impacts. This chapter examines the options for trying to 'close the efficiency gap'.

4.1 Causes of the efficiency gap

The first step in considering how to narrow the efficiency gap is to understand why it exists in the first place. At least eight reasons can be identified:[1]

Lack of knowledge, know-how and technical skills. Private households, car drivers, small and medium-sized companies and small public administrations generally know little about the

---

[1] The list given here is synthesised from a number of other discussions, notably: IEA, *Energy Conservation in IEA Countries*, OECD, Paris, 1987; various publications from the American Council for an Energy Efficient Economy, Washington DC; and E.Jochem and E.Gruber, 'Obstacles to rational electricity use and measures to alleviate them', *Energy Policy*, May 1990.

possibilities for energy saving, or lack the skills to implement them. Architects, consulting engineers and installers, who have a large influence on investments by these groups, similarly often have little knowledge of or interest in energy conservation opportunities.

* *Separation of expenditure and benefit.* The person or group owning a building or energy-consuming equipment may not be the user, the classic example being that of tenants who cannot renovate the building they occupy, with landlords who would benefit little from improving the efficiency of their properties. Even when users can make such investments, they may be unable to obtain the full pay-off. Examples include building occupants who may soon move on, or local services which can reclaim overheads but not capital expenditures.

* *Limited capital, often arising from external restrictions on capital budgets.* Poor householders often have more pressing uses for their money than making investments to reduce running costs. In many small businesses, the capital budget is often quite constrained and devoted to business-related investments such as computerisation. This constraint may be exacerbated by the fact that non-labour running costs are often treated as unavoidable peripherals. There is thus little opportunity or incentive to invest in energy conservation to reduce overheads.

Rapid payback requirements. Even when those making the investment have the relevant information and expertise and receive the full benefits, they still tend to demand a much higher rate of return than for supply investments - sometimes differing by an order of magnitude.[2] This alone is estimated to distort energy-saving investments by at least 10 to 15%.[3]

---

[2] One study of the choices made by well-informed consumers in buying refrigerators which differed only in cost and efficiency concluded that only 40% of them bought the more efficient variety if it took more than 3 years to pay back (35% discount rate). Another 40% seemed to apply a discount rate above 60% (ie. requiring payback in well under 2 years). This contrasts with producer criteria on the order of 10% return, or a 10-year payback, while some public utilities have used 5% (A.K.Meier and J.Whittier, 'Consumer discount rates implied by consumer purchases of energy efficient refrigerators', *Energy, the International Journal* 8(12), 1983). The fact that many of the consumers could have obtained credit to cover the extra costs and still make a profit is

* *Lack of interest in peripheral operating costs.* Energy costs are often a small part of personal or business expenditures. People may simply not be interested in them, and cannot be bothered to take steps to save money in this area. Cost-effectiveness is not the only criterion; 'cost relevance' is also required. The attitude may be crudely summarised as one of *'don't know, and don't care'.* This of course contrasts sharply with the attitude in the supply industries where energy is the business.

* *Impact of electricity and gas tariff structures.* Domestic electricity and gas tariffs are usually designed in two parts - a fixed charge, reflecting capital repayment and fixed running costs, and a variable part reflecting variable operating costs. Most energy conservation measures will save the user only the variable part of the tariff, which is often well under half the total charge. Yet most conservation measures do reduce utility fixed charges in the long run since they often reduce the peak loads.[4] Tariff structures therefore further broaden the gap between end-use and supply investment economics. In electricity, similar problems often arise in the buyback rates for private power, for example from small-scale CHP stations, which could contribute greatly to end-use efficiency in some sectors.

* *Tax regimes which discriminate against conservation or otherwise encourage greater use.* For example:

Consumption taxes placed on energy conservation equipment but not fuels, as with VAT in the UK;

Taxes which discriminate against high-cost, high-efficiency equipment, as with German taxes on lightbulbs;

---

one indication that the economic ideal of rational consumers leaves much to be desired in this area.

[3] Jochem and Gruber, 'Obstacles to rational electricity use'.

[4] Part of the fixed charge reflects connection costs, which conservation would usually not affect. The importance of the capacity element will vary greatly according to system and load conditions. The fundamental reason why it is so difficult for conservation to receive its 'capacity credit' is the impracticability of dynamic marginal-cost pricing, in which very high rates at times of peak load on the system would raise the revenues for capital construction. Separation of fixed charges is really a surrogate for this. Utilities also often offer large users declining block tariffs (energy is cheaper the more is consumed) to encourage more consumption, especially in competitive markets.

Tax incentives to increase use, such as company car allowances and mortgage exemptions in many countries.

* *Legal and administrative obstacles.* Finally, there can be a number of legal and administrative obstacles in the path of end-use efficiency, for example rent controls which do not reflect the reduced running costs of buildings after conservation improvements, and capital budget restrictions, as discussed above.

This list reflects market imperfections, hidden costs, and the economic irrationality of some consumers. Economically the distinction is important: if the time and effort involved in obtaining information on the options for reducing running costs are substantial, consumers may be perfectly sensible not to bother. The 'transaction costs' of finding and hiring companies to improve insulation could likewise be very real.

However, in its implications for policy, this distinction may be less clear than it seems. Information costs could be reduced if companies provided better information on their products' efficiency, but other forms of market failures may make them reluctant to do so. Information and transaction costs which are large to each individual household may be very small, relatively, to governments designing and implementing building or other standards which could apply to millions of homes. Although some items in the list clearly fall into one category or another, the dividing lines between market imperfections, hidden costs and consumer irrationality are often hazy.

However it is expressed, the message remains the same. A complex mix of factors, which often compound each other, create a pervasive imbalance between the criteria used for investing in supply and investing in end-use efficiency. Companies dedicated to energy management can play a role in overcoming this, but only a limited one at present (see box).[5] Presuming that, given time, the market alone can deliver optimal energy efficiency is therefore facile. Projections which assume that the full theoretical potential for efficiency can be captured are equally so.

But the economic and environmental potential stands beckoning. What, then, are the policy options for trying to narrow the 'efficiency gap', what

---

[5] French experience emphasises that successful Energy Service Companies offer a broad building management and maintenance contract. See Oliver de la Morinière, 'Energy Service Companies: the French Experience', in T.B.Johannsen, B.Bodlund, and R.H.Williams(eds), *Electricity*, Lund University Press, Lund, Sweden, 1989.

Energy management companies

If there are opportunities for savings, there is money to be made. In economic language, if energy consumers are ignorant of opportunities for savings, or if they apply much higher discount rates than suppliers in making energy investments, then 'energy management companies' should be able to 'arbitrage' on the difference. They can put up all the capital and pass through a portion of the savings, while still making a profit on the criteria of supply companies.

Such is the theory, and many have pointed to it as the ultimate reason why markets should be able to deliver energy efficiency. In practice, such companies have not done well. They can offer surveys for free. They can calculate the savings that could be made, and demonstrate this to the consumer. But they cannot then force the consumer to take up their services. The chances are that consumers either distrust a company telling them that 'everyone wins'; or they really cannot be bothered because only a small saving is involved (and maybe they can pass the operating costs on anyway); or if they are really convinced that it is so easy to save money, they see no reason why they should let someone else take a cut of the profits, and therefore make the investment themselves. Energy management is not such a good business after all.

Where they have done well, it is usually as part of a larger service contract by companies which specialise in the overall operation of buildings, and take this whole area of responsibility from the hands of the occupiers. This is the (broadly successful) model used by some companies in France, and the practice may grow slowly. This has been limited to public and commercial buildings, and cannot easily be applied to private houses.

impacts might they have, and how might governments choose among them?

4.2 Policy criteria and market responses

A broad distinction can be drawn between measures which seek to remove market imperfections and those which seek to counteract their impact. The list above includes imperfections which are created by government legislation and can be removed likewise, the obvious examples being perverse tax incentives and legal obstacles. Providing information is another obvious area in which obstacles can be lessened.

But other obstacles lie deeper, and it is clear that realising much of the theoretical potential would require more active measures to ensure take-up of cost-effective opportunities. Such measures could span a wide range of both fiscal and regulatory options. Though there is often a presumption by economists in favour of fiscal measures, practical constraints are frequently more important, as will emerge in this chapter. In any case the dividing line between economic measures and regulation is quite hazy; a major OECD review notes that 'the confusion about what to regard as economic instruments is substantial'.[6]

This is one reason why the division in this book is drawn between macroeconomic measures (carbon taxes and permits) and microeconomic ones, rather than between economic and regulatory policies. Intervention to improve efficiency is often posed as an alternative to carbon taxes, raising the question of which is preferable. This is a false choice, at least in economic if not political terms. Carbon taxes and other macroeconomic measures seek to internalise environmental costs and more generally to use market price responses to limit emissions. Referring to Figure 3.2, they are measures which aim to shift the supply curve to where it 'should' be. The measures discussed in this chapter are concerned with the demand curve of Figure 3.2, and the extent to which it can be shifted to where it would lie in an ideal market. The measures are therefore complementary, not exclusive, and both would affect the development of technology and behaviour.

However, one concern expressed by many economists is that, unlike higher prices, intervention to improve efficiency will save less energy than expected because of the market reaction: if something is made more efficient, the operating costs are reduced, so people do more with it (an

---

[6] OECD, *Economic Instruments for Environmental Protection*, OECD, Paris, 1989.

effect sometimes called the 'conservation rebound'). Also, people may spend the money they save on other energy-consuming goods or activities, and reduced demand for energy will itself tend to lower prices, stimulating greater use. Indeed, some have argued that such reactions mean that measures to improve efficiency cannot in fact reduce energy demand significantly.[7]

These arguments have been examined in some detail elsewhere.[8] It is clear that the rebound can be very significant in some cases, in particular when energy cost or availability is a constraint on activity. This may be important particularly in some developing countries. In such cases improving energy efficiency is more an instrument of development, allowing greater economic expansion within the constraints of supply, than a measure to reduce demand. Despite this, some of the policy issues are similar.

In developed market economies in particular, energy cost or availability is rarely a serious constraint, and for most applications in these countries it is quite clear that direct rebound effects will be small. For example, people will not use domestic refrigerators or washing machines much more, or necessarily buy much bigger ones, just because they are made more efficient; nor will they choose to swelter if domestic insulation is improved.

In fact, it is precisely these areas, where the energy price has least impact on consumption, that offer the greatest scope for cost-effective, policy-driven savings, because these correspond to the greatest market 'imperfections' as listed above. Thus, although some rebound may occur from measures designed to close the efficiency gap, the impact is likely to be small, usually reducing the 'engineering' estimate of savings from improving efficiency by no more than 5-15% overall. The difficulties for energy efficiency lie not with the way markets respond, but with the way they don't.

---

[7] L.Brookes, 'The greenhouse effect: the fallacies in the energy efficiency solution', *Energy Policy*, March 1990; G.Greenhalgh, 'Energy conservation policies', *Energy Policy*, April 1990.
[8] M.Grubb, 'Energy efficiency and economic fallacies', *Energy Policy*, October 1990, and others in this issue respond to the papers by Brookes and Greenhalgh, also drawing on earlier discussions on similar themes.

A compendium and classification of policy options is given in a report by the US Department of Energy,[9] and Jochem and Gruber give a broad review of options for encouraging electricity conservation. Wilson et al.[10] provide an analysis of experience in some OECD countries. Here, the focus is on the major options available and the issues they raise.

4.3 Information and exhortation

Consumers are ignorant about energy. It is hard not to be. Few people know how efficient the building they live or work in is at keeping hot or cool, or how much it might be improved. The energy consumed by different appliances or processes is rarely known or compared, whether in homes, commercial or service buildings, or in light industry. (Some governments are similarly ignorant about the way energy is used in the economy. Adequate research into energy use is a prerequisite for all the steps discussed in this chapter.)

One of the most obvious and consistent themes in discussions about policies to improve energy efficiency is therefore the provision of information.[11] This has focused primarily upon advertising campaigns about energy use in homes, suggestions for labelling of domestic appliances to indicate their typical energy use (as opposed to power rating), and sometimes building energy surveys and other 'energy audits'.

Some labelling schemes already exist. However, companies are often reluctant to draw consumers' attention to running costs, even if a product is somewhat better than the average, and the schemes are sometimes ignored by manufacturers, or the labelling may be obscure or inadequate. One lesson from schemes to date is that if companies are unenthusiastic, legislation needs to be rather precise about contents, location and size of labelling if it is really to gain the attention of consumers. Even when

[9] US Department of Energy, *A compendium of options for government policy to encourage private sector responses to potential climate change*, Report to Congress, US DOE/EH-0102, October 1989.

[10] D.Wilson, L.Schipper, S.Tyler and S.Bartlett, *Policies and programmes for promoting energy conservation in the residential sector: lessons from five OECD countries*, Applied Science Division, Lawrence Berkerley Laboratory, LBL-27289, California, June 1989.

[11] 'Information programmes are the cornerstone of all members' conservation programmes', (IEA/OECD, *Energy Conservation in IEA Countries*, p120). The study describes and analyses the performance of a wide range of information programmes.

these problems do not exist, it is far from clear how much impact such schemes have.

Part of the problem is undoubtedly lack of consumer interest in calculating cost savings. Schemes which draw attention to the most efficient products - for example, a 'Green Star' scheme in West Germany - seem to have had more impact, because they create a distinct and positive 'green and efficient' image which has more consumer appeal than life-cycle costing.

Ignorance within buildings is at least as important as ignorance when shopping. Leaflets and advertising campaigns can undoubtedly increase awareness. In addition, a number of countries have promoted building energy surveys, often provided free of charge, especially for small business premises. Advanced technologies might help more, especially for electricity consumption, where there seems no reason why advanced meters should not identify and record the electricity use by each appliance on the basis of its power and phase characteristics - though such meters do not yet appear to exist.

However, when energy forms a small part of costs for most people and businesses, the evidence is that they may not act upon the knowledge gained. Whether or not anything is done further in response to building energy surveys, for example, depends heavily upon whether they are followed up by further information and sometimes incentives for adopting energy-saving measures. For industry, the Japanese study notes the importance of legislation forcing companies above a given size to employ energy managers, which creates someone whose job is both to be informed and to push conservation. Apart from this, referring to the list of reasons for the efficiency gap, information alone can, with sufficient effort, limit the 'don't know', but can do little about the 'don't care'.

With periodic bouts of enthusiasm - usually correlated with world oil prices or energy shortages - governments have thus sought to make people more concerned about energy.[12] There is little doubt that such campaigns have had an impact on behaviour. But the impact soon seems to dissipate; people forget the information or impetus they obtain from

---

[12] The most notorious example being President Carter's declaration that energy saving was 'the moral equivalent of war', following the 1979 oil price rise.

TV or leaflets about energy. A detailed study of conservation policies in OECD countries concluded:[13]

> Policies that did things to things have reduced energy use, while those that did things to people have had little effect ... there is little evidence that exhortation causes any permanent energy savings.

Providing information on a sustained basis, as with labelling schemes and legislation for energy managers, is clearly important. Yet overall it seems that the various measures aimed at lubricating energy markets without really touching them are likely to be of limited impact, even when combined with the activities of energy service companies. What then are the options for 'doing things to things'?

4.4 Setting standards

One way of correcting for these market failures is to set standards. Standards, in essence, outlaw behaviour or equipment which is considered unreasonably economically and/or environmentally damaging. They can take many forms, and apply in many sectors.

Standards are obvious instruments for addressing some of the non-CO_2 emissions, which often depend upon technology and operating practice: for example, the integrity and safety of gas distribution systems and appliances, and NO_x, CO and hydrocarbon emissions from cars. Standards for such purposes are a familiar instrument, and as they are peripheral to this book's general theme of energy policy they will not be considered further.

Standards can equally be applied to improve energy efficiency. For such applications they are sometimes criticised as being economically inefficient. However, as long as they are confined to compensating for the obstacles listed above, the reverse is usually true: national standards incur relatively small information/transaction costs, and can bring investments in demand closer to that of an ideal market.[14] Applied

---

[13] L.Schipper, 'Energy conservation policies in the OECD - did they make a difference?', *Energy Policy* 15(6), December 1987.

[14] Analysis by the US Department of Energy, connected with its notorious attempt to make appliance efficiency standards illegal (by setting a Federal 'zero-standards standard'), nevertheless suggested that the overall macroeconomic effects of efficiency standards would be beneficial. The results suggested that 'GNP would increase by billions of dollars, the net foreign trade balance would increase by a billion dollars, and around 100,000 new jobs would be generated.' (See P. Rollin and Jan Beyea, 'US

more generally as a means of controlling environmental impacts, they are usually less efficient than would be internalising the costs through taxes; but even for this, standards can be justified when adequate taxes are politically not possible.

Standards need not necessarily imply legislation. Jochem and Gruber suggest that 'as an alternative to regulations, voluntary agreements by mass producers are an adequate solution'.[15] This clearly has its attractions, as voluntary standards can be brought in more quickly and they reduce the need for an overseeing bureaucracy; but this informality is also their weakness. The effectiveness of, and political attitude towards, voluntary standards is likely to depend strongly upon the relationship between government, industry, and public, and in practice the distinction can be less important than it seems. If standards are met, their legal status is almost irrelevant; if companies persistently fail to meet voluntary standards at the required level, legislation becomes necessary.

Some of the main candidates for standards are buildings, automobiles, and appliances (see box). In principle, such standards are very simple and effective tools, and the general economic rationale is strong. There are, however, a number of complications and objections to be considered.

Cost and performance: how high should standards be set? For many products, efficiency within a certain range bears little relation to cost or performance. Above this range, the capital costs of improving efficiency begin to show above the 'noise' of other design and marketing issues. Though there may be a good economic case for higher standards, because the fuel savings over a few years offset the extra costs, forcing increases in capital expenditure can be politically controversial, particularly if standards are set so high as to force suppliers' criteria of many years' payback on unwilling consumers. Even more sensitive is the fact that in some products there is a trade-off between performance and efficiency.

These issues are clearly demonstrated for both lighting and cars. Compact fluorescent lights are unquestionably economic for most

---

Appliance Efficiency Standards', *Energy Policy* 13(5), 1985). The US Court of Appeals later ruled that the DoE moves 'openly violated Congressional intent', and declared the zero-standards standard illegal. The struggle presents a fascinating insight into some of the pressures and arguments involved in setting efficiency standards.
[15] Jochem and Gruber, 'Obstacles to rational electricity use'.

Standards for efficiency: some prime candidates

• **Building standards.** As emphasised, the potential savings from better heating and/or air conditioning performance are very large. Many of the end-use market failures discussed in section 4.1 are endemic in buildings. Because little or no attention is usually paid to energy costs in building design, governments in many countries have recognised the need for building standards, typically based on overall insulation properties, though other factors such as thermal mass (to smooth the day-night cycle) and passive solar design (to capture the sun's heat) are also important. The standards set, however, vary widely, and some of the country studies note scope for considerable improvements.

With a 'stock turnover' of decades or even hundreds of years, standards for new buildings will only address a small part of the potential. More important for a long time to come is the application of standards to existing stock - either by a nationally sponsored programme of retrofits, or by a system of certification at time of sale (as suggested in the UK case study, and applied in Denmark).

• **Automobile efficiency.** Most people want a car. Few care how efficient it is, within limits, and mpg has slipped to the bottom of the list of selling features. However, there are many opportunities for improvements within the confines of safety and consumer desires, at little extra cost.

Since the achievable efficiency depends upon car and engine size, in practice it is necessary to define standards on an average basis. The US CAFE (Corporate Average Fuel Efficiency) standards have been credited as a major factor in doubling the average efficiency of US cars over 1973-87, saving billions of dollars. Outside the US, such standards would face problems due to the fact that some manufacturers have concentrated on particular car sizes and types, but there are ways around such complexities - if justified - and an international agreement on CAFE standards may be one of the most promising areas for substantial agreements on energy efficiency.

• **Appliance Standards.** Appliances cover a broad range, including refrigerators, boilers, washing machines, dishwashers and various other electrical goods. Opportunities for substantial savings exist; the efficiency of appliances on sale can vary widely, often with little correlation with performance or costs over much of the range. Like cars, most appliances have a fairly rapid turnover, and standards applied to new equipment therefore offer an obvious potential.

applications, but the capital cost is several times that of filament bulbs, and they are bulky and heavier, and do not fit many current fittings - and some people simply do not like them. Similarly, there is little doubt that the efficiency of cars could be doubled or more without increasing life-cycle costs, but the capital cost, appearance, and performance would all be affected (see section 7.3). In practice, such standards as exist err well on the side of caution, for obvious reasons.[16] Standards could do much to eliminate waste, but it seems they are unlikely to close most of the 'efficiency gap'.

One way round this might be to make standards flexible using tradeable efficiency credits. As advanced by the Environmental Defence Fund in discussing refrigeration standards:[17]

> [A manufacturer with] an average energy efficiency better than the product standards could obtain ... credits. These can be statistically translated into CO_2 equivalents using average lifetimes ... A manufacturer whose average fridge did not meet the standard would have to purchase credits ... the end result would be that the average fridge ... would meet the efficiency standard, although the average of any single manufacturer need not.

Standards, freedom, and bureaucracy. There are two common political objections to standards. One is that they interfere with the consumer's freedom. This is undoubtedly true, but then pollution also impinges on the freedom to enjoy a clean or unaltered environment. Furthermore, there is little to suggest that the consumer is particularly concerned about the freedom to waste money on inefficient homes, appliances, vehicles, etc. The 'freedom' argument does not stand up as an absolute one, but is only relative - and industry and consumer groups are quick to register if they think that any important freedoms (such as that of driving powerful cars!) are threatened.

More serious is the problem that standards require bureaucracy: government bureaucracy to decide upon the appropriate levels, and to

---

[16] Rollin and Beyea, 'US Appliance Efficiency Standards' advocated 'short payback' standards, which could recoup costs in the period over which credit loans would have to be repaid. In general the US has had extensive, though unresolved, debates about the merits and levels of vehicle and appliance efficiency standards. Most other countries lack even rudimentary analysis.
[17] J.Tripp and D.Dudek, 'Comments of the Environmental Defence Fund on the IPCC WGIII Economic Measures Paper', EDF, New York, January 1990.

monitor and enforce compliance; and industrial bureaucracy, to follow the standards and ensure that products meet legal requirements. The complaint is not only that this makes life more difficult for industry, but that:[18]

This regulatory burden has left little time or incentive for creativity and human judgement, and no time for concentrating on environmental results. It has created a process-oriented, rather than a result-oriented, approach.

The problems are particularly bad in the United States because of the scope of standards, which are often set differently in different States, and the litigious nature of the whole US system. But the potential difficulty is clear - though it is equally clear that, for the most obvious major applications of efficiency standards, the savings would far exceed any direct bureaucratic costs.[19] Internationally agreed standards would clearly ease some of these and other drawbacks, though as with Federal standards in the US they are most likely to arise from attempts to harmonise independently developed national standards.

Technology development: do standards freeze it or force it? The above quotation illustrates a general concern that standards can codify and freeze technology at existing levels or, at least, that they do not encourage development. In contrast with price-based measures, once companies have met standards, there are no incentives for them to go further. Indeed, it is argued, they may be discouraged from doing so, lest regulators take this as a reason for tightening standards.

This is frequently true if standards specify particular technologies, and will often be so if they focus on performance levels which are well within the scope of existing capabilities, especially if they are used *in place of* market incentives. However, in other cases they could act to force technology development.

This can occur in three ways. One is if standards are set near to the limit of existing technologies in the belief (backed up by analysis of

[18] V.J.Tschinkel, 'The rise and fall of environmental expertise', in J.H.Asubel and H.E.Sladovich (eds), *Technology and Environment*, National Academy Press, Washington DC, 1989.

[19] The impact on industry was the main rationale for the US DoE position cited earlier. Rollin and Beyea, 'US Appliance Efficiency Standards', note that 'the decision therefore comes down to a non-quantifiable choice between the significance of the impacts on a few businesses and the significance of the dollar and energy savings'.

possibilities) that better technologies can be developed. The Montreal Protocol, which committed countries to reducing CFC use when substitutes were far from fully developed, is a clear example (see Chapter 8, section 8.2). Such leaps of faith are extremely rare, for obvious reasons, but goals - if they are serious ones, with commitment and resources behind them - can achieve the same result. The government-industry goals of the 1970s which set Japanese automobiles on the road to being the most efficient in the world are a case in point. In both examples, the impact has probably been much stronger than that of market incentives alone. In this vein Jochem and Gruber (see note 1) suggest *target standards:*

> In most EC countries the current standards represent average practice. Target standards should be set three to five years before the introduction of regulations.

A second option is to use 'rolling standards'. For example, if each year efficiency standards for appliances are reset so as to eliminate the least efficient 10% of existing products, there is a strong incentive for companies continually to develop and to sell more efficient models. There are naturally limits to such an approach, partly because industry could start to 'play the game', by bunching products at the lower efficiency limit, but over a limited period such measures might have a large impact.

The final option is to use marketable efficiency credits as discussed above, which create a permanent incentive for companies to improve irrespective of where the standard is set.

Conclusions. Standards are potentially a powerful tool for helping to narrow the efficiency gap, but they are a far from complete solution. They undoubtedly complicate life for industry which consequently tends to oppose them on principle. However cleverly standards are devised, the resulting incentives leave much to be desired, but the discussion does suggest certain guidelines:

* Standards should focus on areas where they can make a substantial impact: the administrative burden of lesser measures on government and industry may not be worthwhile.

* Standards should focus on results, in terms of energy efficiency, rather than upon specific technologies; this gives the maximum scope for innovation.

* Standards should be developed in close consultation with industry - but industries, if they want to have a major say, need to establish a track record of co-operation in achieving the aims, rather than of obstruction.[20]

* Options for encouraging technology development need more attention, notably:

Rolling standards, which develop over time, and

Target standards, set some years in advance.

* More flexible options also deserve greater attention, notably:

Standards defined in terms of averages rather than absolute limits, and

Tradeable efficiency credits to allow trade-offs within and between firms.

The simplicity and demonstrable effectiveness of standards (when appropriate) gives them considerable political appeal. Standards can be readily applied in both market and centrally planned economies (though management can be problematic, especially in developing countries), and they form one of the most plausible options for early international measures on limiting carbon emissions. Standards are thus likely to grow in importance, particularly as long as no better options for narrowing the efficiency gap are pursued.

Yet for the reasons discussed, they do have significant drawbacks as well, and their overall application and impact is clearly limited. What other options are there?

4.5 Fiscal incentives: targeted subsidies and cost transfer schemes

An alternative approach is simply to subsidise efficiency. The most common example is in home insulation, where many governments have offered insulation grants. Subsidies may have to be a large fraction of

---

[20] The former EC Commissioner for the Environment bitterly criticised the position sometimes adopted by industry in developing standards, and related a case in which the president of a leading car manufacturer advised him that pollution standards being considered by the Commission would ruin the European car industry. After the standards were nonetheless supported, the same person stated his relief that the companies were no longer faced with uncertainty, and now knew the requirements for future cars (S.Clinton-Davis, 9 June 1989). Needless to say, industrial advice from this quarter was given somewhat less weight thereafter.

the unit costs, but the overall costs are usually small in relation to the scale of savings, and can be raised directly from the energy industries.[21] The ultimate subsidy, of course, is simply for the government to pay the full costs, and to manage a national programme of retrofits.[22]

Evidence suggests that simple subsidies need backing up, and can be both more costly and less effective than many other measures.[23] This and concerns about people 'free riding' on subsidies to do things they might have done anyway, tend to make governments reluctant. However, fiscal incentives offer a far broader range of instruments than just subsidies. In the UK, a tax differential between leaded and unleaded gasoline has been widely credited with bringing a rapid move towards lead-free petrol. In the United States, there have been calls for a 'gas guzzler to gas sipper' tax and rebate scheme, in which inefficient cars are taxed and the proceeds used to subsidise more efficient ones.[24] The latter approach could be applied to many goods, and in the general case might be termed a 'cost transfer' scheme. There is no net transfer to governments and no average price increase, but a strong fiscal incentive towards efficiency is nevertheless created.

---

[21] G.Doyle and D.Pearce, 'Low energy strategies for the UK - economics and incentives', *Energy Policy* 7(4), 1979. The authors note that at then existing gas prices, incentives of 65-75% would be needed to promote widespread conservation in the UK in view of consumer discount rates. 'The government would need to raise £2-3bn (1976 prices) over a period of several years to provide a comprehensive cash/grant support system. On the other hand, measures to raise gas prices [which were taken] would almost certainly generate sufficient cash surpluses ...'

[22] The money involved is of course greater than with subsidies, and so are the logistical problems. Yet national energy programmes involving the domestic sector can be managed, as the conversion of home appliances from town gas to natural gas in the UK and other countries indicates.

[23] 'In several cases, grants worked out as costly information campaigns ... financial incentives should be closely linked with information and consultation' (Jochem and Gruber, 'Obstacles to rational electricity use'). The IEA study (IEA/OECD, *Energy Conservation in IEA Countries*) details the patchy response to and economic returns from a wide range of subsidy and grant schemes. Insulation grants in the US have also been widely criticised as relatively costly and ineffective.

[24] This and other measures focused on the United States, but applicable much more broadly, are summarised in P.Craig and M.D.Levine (eds), *Energy Policies to Address Global Climate Change*, Public Service Research and Dissemination Program, University of California, Davis, September 1989, (Executive Summary, with detail in various background papers).

Such cost transfers would seem to have a number of attractions over simple standards. They would still allow consumers to make trade-offs between costs and performance over the full range. Yet on average they might well result in higher efficiencies, because the constraints which tend to keep minimum standards low would be much weaker, and there would be continuing incentives both to produce and to choose more efficient goods right across the spectrum, rather than merely having to satisfy a minimum level. Furthermore, unlike standards, there can be rational grounds for deciding upon the scale of the measures, at least when the primary market failure is the differing discount rates between consumers and producers. The box shows how the transfers can be calculated so that consumers behave as if they had the same payback criteria as industry - which also serves to emphasise the scale of this market imperfection, and the possible impact of 'correcting' it.

One major obstacle to such measures lies in their potential complexity: the regulators need to know a great deal about the costs of the products, and then apply varying tax schedules. This may be a reason why cost transfer schemes do not appear to have been tried, and it probably limits them to products with high capital costs and few ready alternatives other than standards, such as cars.

In other areas, where demands are supplied through utilities, when authorities have become sufficiently concerned about efficiency they have tended to adopt a more direct route to efficiency: the utilities can be forced or enticed into investing in it themselves.

4.6 Utility regulation, competitive bidding, and 'Least Cost Planning'

If utilities can invest in conservation at a cost below their cost of supply, on the surface it seems that they should be able to profit by doing so. The catch, of course, is that although utilities can spend money on conservation, they do not normally receive the benefits, quite the reverse: their customers simply pay lower bills, and if the prices per unit ('the rates') remain unchanged, the loss of revenues outweighs any reduced operating costs. The utilities pay out capital and receive less money back. Unless utilities can receive some of the benefits, it is not a good business at all.

And yet, almost all the obstacles to installing more energy efficient equipment listed in section 4.1 could be overcome if the supply industries

Capital cost transfers for closing the supply/demand payback gap

Suppose that consumers buy equipment as though they require the additional cost of more efficient goods to be paid back within 2 years to make it worthwhile, while suppliers invest and set prices corresponding to payback requirements of 10 years - these do not seem to be untypical numbers.

Let the cost of a product be C, with annual operating cost O. If consumer choices are to correspond to a 10-year payback, this implies that they should choose a good of similar performance but operating cost O-y if its capital cost is less than C+10y. In practice, without intervention they will only do so if its cost is less than C+2y.

Now suppose that a subsidy, proportional to the difference in annual operating costs y, is given to the more efficient product. We need to make C+10y look like C+2y, or more formally, we need a net transfer xy such that:

$$(C + 10y) - xy = C + 2y$$

So x=8. In practice it is only the relative levels that matter; the subsidy could be drawn from the product with higher operating costs. More generally, consumers can be persuaded to choose between two products of differing efficiency in the same way that a producer would if a capital transfer is made from the less efficient to the more efficient product equal to x times the difference in annual operating costs, where x is the difference between the payback requirements of consumers and producers.

This could have a dramatic impact. For example, if one product costs £500 more than another but is £50/yr cheaper to run, and is otherwise identical, consumers using a 2-year payback would never consider it. The 'cost transfer' scheme would reduce the cost difference to £100 - and many might.

did treat conservation as part of their investment goals, and judged the savings for the consumer as if they were returns to the utility. What are the options for achieving this?

Utility involvement to some degree in demand management is nothing new. Information campaigns, rate rebates, loan programmes, and sometimes direct installation have all been applied by utilities encouraging customers to adopt conservation.[25] Sometimes this occurs as a response to government pressure at times of high concern about energy consumption, or in an attempt to prevent supply shortages when there is a danger of insufficient capacity. Sometimes it is pursued by utilities seeking to displace a competing fuel; for example, programmes to insulate buildings can make electric heating more attractive as compared to gas. Because electricity and gas distribution are natural monopolies, these utilities have to be regulated, and in some areas the price regulation takes account of conservation investments, which can greatly change the picture.

Most experience has been gained in the United States, driven in part by the cost and difficulties of constructing new plants. Getting planning permission is increasingly difficult, and the 1979 Public Utilities Regulation and Pricing Act (PURPA) stipulated that utilities could not automatically pass on the costs of new plant; they had to demonstrate to the Regulatory Commission concerned that the investment was reasonably judged to be the cheapest. Some Commissions have interpreted this to mean that options for reducing the peak load, as an alternative to building new plant, must be considered, and many US utilities have been under strong political pressure at least to show that they promote conservation measures to minimise or avoid the need for new plant. Thus during the 1980s, many US utilities have become familiar with the process of comparing supply and demand options.[26]

---

[25] Experience with utility demand-side programmes is summarised in H.S.Geller, 'Implementing electricity conservation programs: progress towards least-cost energy services among US utilities', in Johanssen et al., *Electricity*. Geller emphasises, among other factors, that: efficiency incentives can make a difference; programme design has to be flexible, to cope with the range of consumer circumstances; non-financial factors are important; and utility programmes have not reached maturity in design or application.

[26] Details of a number of programmes are given in I. Brown, *Least Cost Integrated Planning*, Proof of Evidence to Hinkley Point 'C' Planning Enquiry, (COLA/5), Somerset, UK, Association for the Conservation of Energy, London, 1988. This

However, because this concentrates on peak loads rather than on overall energy consumption, it is still some way from full *Least Cost Planning*, which is traditionally defined as:[27]

The 'Least Cost Strategy' ... provides for meeting the need for energy services with the least costly mix of energy supplies and energy efficiency improvements.

This is the definition of most relevance in considering environmental issues, including the greenhouse effect, where the impact depends upon fuel consumption. The principle of LCP is that utilities should compare all demand and supply options on similar criteria, and choose the least expensive.

It is not as simple as it sounds. Because utilities pay towards conservation investments and sell less energy as a result, the price per unit may have to go up. Participants will still benefit, but non-participants will then pay more. It is questionable whether this is a significant objection,[28] but it certainly complicates the whole issue of rate setting and evaluation, especially under some price control systems such as that used for privatised utilities in the UK. The problem may be minimised by basing planning on utility criteria, but this reduces the scope of the conservation measures which can be considered.[29]

---

reasonably establishes the feasibility of comparing supply and demand options in utility planning.

[27] R.W.Sant et al., *Creating Abundance: America's Least Cost Energy Strategy*, McGraw Hill, New York, 1984.

[28] A 'no-losers' criterion has been suggested for demand-side planning, which would greatly limit its scope. The US North-West Power Planning Council has argued that 'incentives should not be diluted simply to protect against rate impacts on those who do not respond', and Brown notes that the results of 'no losers' tests are very sensitive to the difference between the long-term projections of marginal costs and of tariffs, and that furthermore 'to apply the test to conservation only is to apply it in a biased manner', because it could equally rule out some supply investments. It has been argued that the no-losers test is equivalent to optimal efficiency investments (L.E.Ruff, 'Least cost planning and demand-side management: six common fallacies and one simple truth', *Public Utilities Fortnightly*, 28 April 1988, p.27) but this neglects the fundamental impact of differing consumer discount rates.

[29] The utility test simply compares the costs of a programme to the utility - the rebates or other subsidies offered to induce conservation - with the benefits of utility fue and capacity savings. The emphasis is thus upon investments which minimise costs to the utility, rather than on choosing options with the highest returns to society overall; the latter is known as the 'society test'. These and other issues of LCP are reviewed in detail

Another problem is the sheer complexity of the task. All options for supply and demand have to be examined, together with the most suitable implementation strategies, and their costs estimated together with the likely savings over the next several decades. The whole process must be repeated by a Utility Planning Commission, if it is to be effective in regulating prices, and actual performance then needs to be monitored. The problems may be particularly severe if production is separated from distribution and selling, as in many countries other than the United States.

Because of these difficulties, there is growing interest in new approaches to 'marketing' energy efficiency rather than relying on central utility planning, and the concept of *competitive bidding* is gaining popularity. This means that utilities consider bids from external bodies for both new supplies and conservation schemes. As proposed by Lovins,[30] if the conservation bids are cheaper, the utility must buy them, and pay the bidders directly for the electricity saved. The problem is then that the utilities pay twice over - once for the conservation contract, and again through the lost revenues from reduced energy sales. So the net cost to the utility is greater than with conventional LCP, and rates would be even more prone to rise.

One way round the incentive/rate problems of other people paying for conservation is for consumers to continue to pay utilities the amounts they would have had to pay in the absence of the programmes, or at least a portion of them. This would make direct LCP very attractive for utilities, and circumvent the political problems of general rate increases. It could also be applied to competitive bidding: energy management companies submit bids for conservation programmes; the utility pays the successful companies the bid price; the consumers continue to pay unaltered bills; and the company shares its profits with the consumers as an incentive for them to take part.[31] On paper, this 'Cicchetti-Hogan

in R.H.Williams, 'Innovative approaches to marketing electric efficiency', in Johanssen et al., *Electricity*, and by Brown, *Least Cost Integrated Planning*.

[30] A.B.Lovins, 'Saving Gigabucks with Megawatts', *Public Utilities Fortnightly*, 21 March 1985, p.19.

[31] C.Cicchetti and W.Hogan, *Including unbundled demand side options in electric utility bidding programs*, Energy and Environmental Policy Centre Report No.E-88-07 1988, Kennedy School of Government, Harvard University, Cambridge MA, (cited in Williams, 'Innovative Approaches').

proposal would lead to both the least costly solution for society and the lowest utility rates'.[32]

The main drawback is the difficulty of billing under such schemes. Added to the energy consumed is an estimate of how much would have been consumed without the conservation programme. Estimates of aggregate savings have to be made in any such programme, and there is now considerable expertise in doing so, but the problems become much sharper if the customer is paying directly for the 'saved energy'. What happens, for example, if people move and find themselves paying for savings on equipment they do not have or use? Or if they change the use of equipment over time, perhaps in part because it is more efficient?

The difficulties of LCP stem from the fact that three key questions cannot be answered to everyone's satisfaction: who pays for conservation; how are the benefits distributed; and how are they calculated? However, it seems the only approach which can cut through almost all the market obstacles listed at the beginning of this chapter, including those posed by utility tariff structures and opportunities too small and specific to justify national legislation. Despite the inevitable bureaucracy and political wrangles, the use of LCP in one form or another has spread steadily in the US[33] and some other countries, and is being considered in more, because of the great economic and environmental rewards it can bring. It is not a single fixed system, but a continually evolving regulatory framework and set of instruments which differ according to the situation of different utilities. Whether or not full LCP is implemented, the pressures towards it are likely to help bring major changes in the utility business, as discussed further in Chapter 6.

4.7 Combining heat and power

The laws of thermodynamics mean that, in thermal power stations, nearly two-thirds of the energy input is ejected as heat. Combined Heat and Power (CHP, otherwise known as co-generation) seeks to use this heat, greatly improving efficiency compared with separate heat and electricity

---

[32] Williams, 'Innovative Approaches'.
[33] The US Electric Power Research Institute conducted a survey which showed 'LCP development or adoption in at least 43 States', and concluded that 'the trend towards LCP regulation and practice will likely continue.' (EPRI, *Status of Least Cost Planning in the US*, EPRI EM-6133, Final report, December 1988.)

supplies. Some of the case studies note the large potential savings which this could bring.

CHP sits unhappily in the no-man's land between supply and demand issues. It is a means of improving efficiency, but especially if applied in the form of district heating (DH), with waste heat from power stations being supplied through underground heat mains (pipes), the policy issues have much to do with supply and infrastructure management.

Even when the economics are favourable on paper, CHP/DH faces two key obstacles. One is the long payback period and other problems arising from its capital-intensive, infrastructural nature. Laying heat mains in old towns is a major and disruptive undertaking, and consumers need to be enticed - or forced - away from existing heating. The problems are greatly eased if heat mains are laid during the construction of new estates. This poses a large-scale version of the building insulation problem: town planners in many countries have no incentive to consider energy in their plans. In suitable regions it could be an important area for legislation, particularly as heat mains once in place offer great flexibility in the primary supply source.

The second key obstacle to CHP/DH is the lack of incentives (and in some cases prohibition) for electricity utilities to sell heat. It is difficult for large electricity utilities to become involved with the intricacies of local heating system development, marketing projections, heat measurements and billing, etc. They have even less interest in doing so if they hope to capture some of the market with direct electric heating.

Successful CHP/DH requires a much more integrated approach and public finance, which is extremely difficult to achieve at the national level. One study charts the 'vast difference between the countries of Western Europe in the adoption of CHP/DH', and concludes that the centralisation of the electricity industry is a major factor.[34] In practice CHP/DH has been mostly developed in countries with strong local government and municipal utilities, 'whose primary vision of the world is defined by the economic geography of the town rather than the exigencies of a national power system'.[35] Clearly, CHP/DH is largely an institutional rather than an economic issue.

---

[34] W.Rudig, 'Energy conservation and electric utilities', *Energy Policy*, April 1986.
[35] Nigel Lucas, *Western European Energy Policies*, Oxford University Press, Oxford, 1985, p.226. David Toke (*Green Energy - a non-nuclear response to the greenhouse effect*, Merlin Press, London, 1990) quotes Lucas, and advocates that 'responsibility for

Smaller-scale CHP has always been significant in some industries, where medium-scale systems are a natural choice for factories with large heat and electricity loads. The advent of micro-CHP schemes which can readily supply smaller institutions (see Volume II) is of great significance because it expands such potential to a much larger market. The key determinant is the interface between such small-scale CHP and the electricity utility: whether utilities exert pressure against such schemes through lack of co-operation and removal of the 'commitment to supply', or through offering low rates for buying back surplus power. The development of small-scale CHP received an enormous boost in the United States from legislation requiring utilities to buy independent power at marginal cost. Utilities complain that their costs increase because they lose markets but are still expected to provide peak cover - a complaint which is often, but not always, of dubious validity (see the discussion of intermittent power sources in Volume II).

CHP, on whatever scale, is thus primarily an issue of utility regulation and institutional structure - something which emerges very clearly from the official Danish account of their energy policy, which has strongly promoted it.[36] For large schemes, infrastructural funding is also crucial; for smaller applications, some of the general market obstacles to efficiency discussed in section 4.1 are relevant. Like Least Cost Planning, the application of CHP does and will continue to differ greatly between countries, but, especially in smaller scale applications, it seems set to grow in importance as the examples spread, adding further impetus towards the overall restructuring of utility industries.

4.8 Conclusions: economic incentives and regulatory options

The quest for energy efficiency dissolves many common economic presumptions. Responding to environmental constraints can also reduce costs. Regulations can be more efficient than economic incentives. The efficiency gap is an area where the divide between letting and making markets work is a particularly deep and complex one.

---

the distribution of electricity and heat should be given to local energy utilities with either mixed or consumer cooperative ownership' ,(p.111).

[36] IEA, *Energy Policies and Programmes of IEA Countries*, 1988 review, IEA/OECD, Paris, 1989. The review states that district heating networks now serve more than a third of all residences and about 40% of total end-use heat demand in Denmark.

The hallmarks of this area include the diversity of policies which need to be considered, and the complexity of some of the trade-offs. A certain amount can be achieved by addressing explicitly the causes of the efficiency gap, most notably by removing perverse tax and legal incentives and ensuring better information through the use of labelling and other schemes. But this can only tap a small fraction of the potential. Further steps involve more active intervention.

Efficiency standards are most attractive in relation to private consumers, because the relative ease and cheapness with which governments can implement them contrasts forcibly with the high information and transaction costs, high discount rates and other factors involved in millions of separate consumer decisions. Standards for building efficiency (especially if applied at time of sale), appliances, and vehicles, all offer considerable scope for savings. With efficiency standards, as with safety, governments seek to take decisions for the consumer, in their own interests. However, they thereby restrict consumer and industrial freedoms, require bureaucracy to implement and enforce or oversee them, and can inhibit or at least fail to promote technology development. More sophisticated approaches to standards can reduce some of these objections, but are more complex.

Fiscal incentives face other trade-offs. Because they leave decisions to consumers, information costs remain high but they do not restrict consumer freedom. The cost to government is higher, and the impact is likely to be smaller, than with high standards. Cost transfer schemes, which tax inefficient products in a range and pass the proceeds to more efficient ones, reduce or eliminate direct costs to the government and could have a large impact, but the administrative costs could be prohibitive except for expensive goods such as cars.

Utilities supply homes, services and industry, and as such offer a natural channel for efficiency measures. Utilities have to be regulated; with Least Cost Planning legislation in one of its many guises, governments can shift the responsibility for detailed efficiency measures on to those who know more about the business. This can also exploit opportunities which are specific to the utilities (for example, arising from their tariff structure, and CHP), and which are too small or localised to justify national attention. However, because this creates an expanded and somewhat forced market, the need for independent oversight of utility calculations and decisions is increased. Taken to its extreme, Least Cost

Planning might be caricatured as a bureaucratic nightmare yielding immense economic and environmental benefits.

Different measures are appropriate for different problems. Simple standards appeal to the domestic sector because they circumvent the limitations and hidden costs of millions of individual decisions, and cut through complex barriers such as those of split incentives where those who pay for the improved efficiency do not receive the benefits. Fiscal incentives, or at least more flexible standards, may be more appropriate for goods where capital costs and consumer sensitivities are much higher, as with cars. Utility regulation can tap more complex opportunities and promote a broader range of product efficiency than national measures can; it could even replace or exceed national efficiency standards. In particular, utility structure and regulation are crucial to the development of CHP.

Clearly, no single approach can effectively exploit the potential for improved efficiency; combinations are required. Nor, as noted in section 4.2, are such measures in principle alternatives to a carbon tax; though politically there is likely to be some trade-off, logically they are complementary. In addition, there could be important roles for non-governmental actions, which can help to promote greater awareness of wasteful habits and concern about their impacts, and can even create independent schemes for highlighting the good and bad in energy-consuming products and practices. Since energy consumption is the product of individuals' behaviour, the development of awareness and attitudes is an important factor in both behaviour and acceptance of policies. It is hard to better the words of the UK Secretary of State for the Environment:[37]

> In practice, the forces of regulation, price mechanisms and political ethics will intermingle to the point where it will be hard to tell where one ends and another begins. Regulation will adjust the market, the market will respond to the pressures of public opinion which in turn will shape, and be shaped by, the political processes which give rise to regulation.

It is impossible to know in detail the impact which energy efficiency measures might have, because the full complement of policies has never been tried. As with carbon taxes, the key questions about efficiency

---

[37] Christopher Patten, 'Energy and the Environment: a British View', *The World Today* 46(4), April 1990.

policies are not ones of macroeconomic impact - which in this case can clearly be positive - but of the extent of their practical application, given the range of political, institutional and managerial constraints upon them, and of the actual impact they could have on demand, given these constraints and the underlying pressures to increase energy use. These issues are taken further in Chapters 6 and 7. However, even a cursory analysis of the pressures as sketched in Chapter 2 suggests that efficiency policies, for all their potential importance, cannot be expected to stabilise world energy demand in the foreseeable future. They cannot, ultimately, circumvent the thorny issues of supply.

Many technical opportunities exist for reducing carbon emissions by changing the mix of fuels used. Many of the policy tools involved are relatively simple, but the issues raised by trying to change the fuel mix are not.

Global gas use will increase for a variety of economic and environmental reasons, and will thereby help to limit carbon emissions; this would be greatly hastened by a carbon tax. The resources are very large but the long term role of gas will be constrained by the dangers of relying on a limited number of concentrated resource areas.

Oil consumption is very important in the greenhouse effect. However, oil use will be increasingly dominated by transport and petrochemicals, and options for fuel substitution in these sectors are limited. Carbon taxes and other measures related specifically to the greenhouse effect are unlikely to change transport fuels, but if other pressures lead, the greenhouse effect may well affect the choice of substitutes. Governments would have to be heavily involved because of the complex interlocking infrastructure involved in transport.

Coal will be hardest hit by any attempts to limit carbon emissions, particularly in industrialised countries. The industry can adopt various strategies to try and minimise the impact, including the use of higher efficiency coal technologies perhaps in conjunction with CHP. Successful application of methods to reduce or eliminate CO_2 emissions from coal would not necessarily assure a long-term future but would provide a natural bridge for coal industries to diversify into other areas.

The greenhouse effect will give renewed impetus for nuclear power, but it is far from clear whether the industry can capitalise on this. Attempts to expand the use of existing nuclear technologies face formidable political and managerial obstacles and the economic case overall remains uncertain. Attempts to rely on new nuclear technologies and a reformed fuel cycle, which might remove some of the political and economic hurdles, would mean a vast task of technical redevelopment and institutional restructuring. Direct government involvement in any major expansion seems inevitable.

Renewable resources cover a very diverse range. Some are already well developed, but large global contributions would require further technical development. Some involve large-scale capital-intensive projects which would require direct government support, but the biggest opportunities may come from smaller-scale disaggregated sources, whose progress will depend heavily on the structure of utility regulation and the removal of market obstacles not unlike those responsible for the 'efficiency gap'. In combination, the prospects for large-scale contributions from renewables appear promising.

Government funding for RD&D on new sources is very important, and support for deploying them is also justified; the best approaches use a combination of deployment targets and incentives. RD&D and deployment support require strong independent oversight, and reliance on them should be minimised as far as possible by the use of a carbon tax. Development of non-fossil resources in developing countries offers one of the most important potential contributions to limiting global carbon emissions but this can only happen with financial assistance from richer countries.

Introduction

Twenty years ago, the conventional view of energy futures was that large-scale nuclear power would dominate electricity supply in the twenty-first century, and would possibly make inroads into direct heat supply and even transport. Today, most analysts believe that nuclear power has an important role to play but that energy supplies will remain dominated by fossil fuels, with a long-term renaissance for coal because of its large resource base. Combined with the conclusions regarding energy demand discussed earlier, this implies that world carbon emissions must increase, probably roughly in proportion to demand. The long-term trend in the hydrogen-to-carbon ratio of global energy consumption, illustrated in Figure 5.1, must in this view halt as demand outpaces the constraints on oil, gas and nuclear power.

The country study 'business-as-usual' scenarios (Chapter 2) reflect this view. Excepting China, the scenarios in which the supply mix is altered to reduce carbon emissions moderate this picture through a greatly increased role for gas and non-fossil resources, but fossil fuels continue to dominate supply in all cases.

This chapter examines the issues raised by trying to modify the supply mix to minimise emissions of greenhouse gases, with particular attention to the scope for, and obstacles to, nuclear power and renewable energy sources. As in other chapters, the focus is upon carbon emissions, because most measures for other greenhouse gases depend on technical fixes more than fuel changes, and thus have fewer implications for overall energy policy and industries; as outlined in Chapter 1, section 1.4, the leakage of gases other than CO_2 (including methane) does not greatly alter the relative greenhouse impact of the different fuels, barring a few special cases.

One of the main policy levers for changing the fuel mix would be a carbon tax, which was discussed in Chapter 3. Other fuel-specific options emerge in the discussion, and the chapter concludes by examining the options for encouraging the development of new sources, including the area in which many observers place the greatest hopes, but which historically has shown the most notable government failures the world over - energy supply Research, Development and Demonstration.

Figure 5.1 Historic trends in the hydrocarbon ratio of global energy consumption

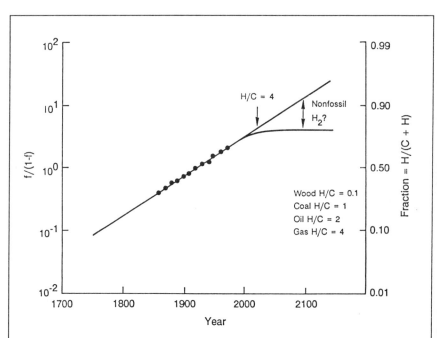

Evolution of the ratio of hydrogen (H) to carbon (C) in the world fuel mix. The figure for wood refers to dry wood suitable for energy production. If the progression is to continue beyond methane, production of large amounts of non-fossil energy is required.

Source: J.E.Ausubel and H.E.Sladovich (eds), *Technology and Environment*, National Academy Press, Washington DC, 1989.

5.1 Drowning in the gas wave?

Gas is the flavour of the decade. It is clear that reserves are much larger than was generally believed possible fifteen years ago. With international pipelines and other infrastructure in place and developing further, gas in many areas is accessible and competitively priced. It is cleaner than conventional coal and oil technologies, and the production and distribution infrastructure faces fewer problems than coal or nuclear power. Recent developments with gas turbines have opened up the huge electricity market.

Gas in most applications gives significant CO_2 savings. Not only does it contain more energy per unit of carbon, but its efficiency of use in many applications is higher than alternatives. As compered with electricity generation from coal stations, modern gas stations halve the CO_2 emitted, and where electricity is used for heating, displacing it by direct gas heating can halve emissions again, to a quarter of that from conventional coal based electric heating. All the country studies see its role growing dramatically as a key component in reducing CO_2 emissions. But gas reserves are not infinite. Is there any danger of drowning in the gas wave?

Current proven global gas reserves total over 120 trillion cubic metres, roughly sixty times the current annual consumption. Proven reserves have doubled in the last decade, and estimated potential resources, which have doubled over the last thirty years, still stand at twice the proven reserves. Some authors believe that there are very large unconventional gas resources which might also be economically exploited.[1]

The UK, Soviet, and Japanese scenarios which concentrate on fuel switching all depict gas demand more than doubling by 2030, from already significant levels, as part of attempts to limit carbon emissions. Some other areas, starting from a lower base, may experience even greater expansion. Professional market analysts are wise enough to avoid such long-term projections (and have little reason to attempt them), but looking two decades ahead, projections by Stern[2] suggest that European gas demand by 2010 could be 60-75% above current levels without placing serious strain on gas resources drawn from within Europe, the Soviet Union, and North Africa. Projections for the United States are less sanguine, with some analysts talking of a gas supply crisis as early as the late 1990s even on current trends.

The implied growth up to 2030 in the fuel-switching scenarios is almost certainly technically feasible in terms of global gas resources, even if combined with still more rapid growth in some other regions, because

---

[1] Volume II gives a fuller discussion of reserves and resources, including unconventional options. The figures in this paragraph are from World Energy Conference, *1989 Survey of Energy Resources*, WEC, London, 1989.
[2] J.P.Stern, *European Gas Markets: Challenge and Opportunity in the 1990s*, Dartmouth/Gower, Aldershot, 1990.

reserves are large and they have a way of expanding to meet demand - but at a price. The price is exacted not just in financial terms, but in the implications of distribution. Gas resources are not evenly distributed. It is in the nature of resource development that countries exploit their own resources first, and then turn abroad. The 2030 gas demand implied in the fuel-switching scenarios would almost certainly be at the expense of heavy dependence on a few key areas - the leading candidates being Siberia, the Middle East and perhaps North Africa, the far American north, and possibly unexplored parts of South and South-East Asia.

The North American resource would be devoted to the United States (and will probably be inadequate for that task alone); most South and South-East Asian resources, and perhaps some of the Soviet, would be devoted to China and the Indian subcontinent. Pipeline networks are vulnerable, and it is far from clear how politically stable some of the main gas resource regions will be over the coming decades.

Consequently, even on a fairly optimistic outlook in terms of both resources and energy efficiency, the gas world of 2030 implied by the fuel-switching scenarios could look suspiciously like the oil world of 1970. On a less optimistic outlook, this could apply rather sooner. Unless major new resources are discovered within the developed market economies, large price rises and volatility, first in the US and later in other areas, seem likely to constrain the long-term role that gas can play.

To summarise, it seems clear that gas is poised to play an important part in limiting CO_2 emissions. But in few areas outside the USSR can it plausibly dominate both the heating and electricity markets for decades, even if demand trends move towards the lower limits discussed in the country studies. Anderson[3] suggests a 'gas bonanza' as being one of the dangers of relying wholly on a carbon tax to combat the greenhouse effect, and particularly if extended over decades it seems hard to dispute this view.

Finally, even if there were no disruptions and resources proved much larger even than in the optimistic forecasts, gas is not a panacea because, emitting more than half the carbon from coal for a given energy content, gas use on the scale foreseen would still result in substantial increases in carbon emissions. And care would also have to be taken to minimise methane emissions. In other words, gas is important, its use will grow,

[3] D.Anderson, 'Economics of Energy and the Environment', University College, London, 1990.

and it will help to limit CO_2 emissions; but if it is promoted as the central solution to the greenhouse effect, there could indeed be a risk of drowning in the gas wave.

5.2 Oil: a problem within the problem?

The country studies in general see relatively little impact on oil from explicit fuel-switching measures. This is for two reasons. One is its intermediate place between coal and gas in terms of carbon intensity. More importantly, most projections see oil use increasingly confined to the stronghold of transport and petrochemicals even in the base case, and foresee little prospect of other fuels making serious inroads into these 'premium markets' even in the strong abatement scenarios. Oil use is projected to grow in the 'business-as-usual' case (with transport growth more than offsetting declines in other markets), and to stabilise or decline from 1988 levels in most of the abatement scenarios of the industrialised countries, with improved transport efficiency and modification of transport patterns.

In identifying oil as the 'energy problem within a problem', the International Institute for Applied Systems Analysis (IIASA)[4] and others have focused upon the constraints of oil resources, and their concentration in the Middle East. In the 1980s analysts have become more sanguine. The price rises of the 1970s have held down demand and led to increased exploration: the ratio of remaining reserves to current production has obstinately remained above 30 years, and in 1987 rose above 40 years following revised estimates of reserves.

However, oil reserves are more concentrated than with gas; two-thirds of the world total, including most recent finds, are in the Middle East. Though increased energy efficiency (particularly in transport) will help to prolong resources and keep prices down, it still seems likely that the Middle East will within a few decades at most again dominate world oil supplies. This is not a comforting outlook, though it is probably not of such over-arching importance as it once seemed, because the world has grown wiser to the dangers of the international oil markets, and is more prepared and will remain more diverse in its use and sources of fuels than in 1973.

[4] J.Andere, W.Haefele, N.Nakicenovic, A.McDonald, *Energy in a Finite World*, Ballinger, Boston MA, 1981.

Oil consumption currently accounts for over two-fifths (42%) of world fossil carbon emissions. Even if consumption can be reduced in industrial countries, the potential growth of transport demand in the developing countries is enormous irrespective of efficiency, and could far outpace reductions in the industrialised world. Just as with security of supply, oil demand is a 'problem within a problem' for carbon emissions.

There are various options for making inroads into the transport arena. Institutionally by far the simplest are those which still rely predominantly on oil products: diesel cars and 'gasohol' mixtures of petrol with alcohol from biomass sources could each reduce carbon emissions by perhaps 10% or more, though they may pose other environmental problems.[5]

Compressed Natural Gas (CNG) and electric vehicles are both technically clear possibilities, and are well proven technologies though still with room for improvement. However, the lower power density of the fuel means that their performance in terms of power and range is unlikely ever to be as good as many petrol- (gasoline) powered cars. In terms of carbon emissions, CNG is at most 20% better than petrol, and electric vehicles charged from thermal power systems may be better or worse depending on the fuel mix in generation and the efficiency of the competing cars. Only more exotic technologies for fuel production and/or use could really make a large impact. These could include various liquid fuels from biomass, electric vehicles charged from nuclear or renewable sources, and hydrogen from various sources.

These fuels are discussed later in this chapter, and all are feasible. However, since oil *production* costs are so low, it will probably always be able to outprice any competitors which threaten its major market. This, and the probable lower performance of many alternatively fuelled vehicles, means that the costs of trying to force societies away from petrol cars could be relatively high. The situation concerning aircraft and heavy goods vehicles, where power density is a still more important factor, is even more difficult.

Consequently, trying to change transport fuels - as opposed to improving transport efficiency - would be a long way down any list of

---

[5] M. Fergusson and C. Holman, *Atmospheric Emissions from the Use of Transport in the United Kingdom, Vol 2: The Effect of Alternative Transport Policies*, WWF/Earth Resources Research, London, June 1990. In total, reductions much greater than 10% using gasohol may be possible if extensive use is made of by-products from alcohol production (D.O.Hall, personal communication).

policy priorities for limiting carbon, were it not for other concerns. But as emphasised in some of the country studies, and discussed further in the next chapter, there is intense concern about transport in many developed economies. Roads are congested; building more faces opposition and seems not to help. Urban atmospheric pollution from vehicles has led to mandatory catalytic converters in the United States, Japan and now the European Community, but even this seems to be insufficient. The US case study chronicles some of the paths being followed, and it seems clear that alternatively fuelled vehicles will play a large part. Where Los Angeles leads, other major conurbations may follow, given time.

Thus, while the greenhouse effect is unlikely to be a driving force in any move away from petrol, it could affect the direction of such a change, and add to pressures for deeper changes in transport policy, as discussed in the next chapter. Taking the greenhouse effect seriously may actually constrain the options for moving away from oil for transport, as it suggests that moves to new fuels should focus primarily on the less developed clean fuels from non-fossil sources.

Changing primary transport fuels is an immense undertaking. It involves not only promoting new vehicle technologies against more familiar, more developed and perhaps inherently better performing rivals. The primary fuel production systems need to be established together with sufficient retail outlets to make the whole system viable for the consumer. Without active government direction, it is likely that, if conditions do force a move out of petrol in some areas, alternative fuels will follow the line of least resistance, which could even increase carbon emissions. One reason for pushing CNG or electric cars, perhaps as secondary vehicles for urban use, though the greenhouse benefits might be marginal, is that they would help to develop the technology and infrastructure required for later moves towards non-fossil sources.

The broad conclusion is that, while oil is a very important factor in the greenhouse effect, the greenhouse effect may not be so important for oil. Oil is cheap to extract and convenient to use, it has a large premium market, and it is only likely to be driven out of its stronghold by powerful forces. Congestion problems will dominate the larger questions of transport structure. Urban pollution will create pressures for alternative fuels. The main impetus the greenhouse effect brings, in parallel with resource concerns, is towards greater efficiency. Greenhouse concerns might well affect the direction of any moves out of oil, but they are unlikely to drive it at least in the short and medium term.

5.3 Managing King Coal

Almost the opposite conclusion applies to coal, particularly in the developed countries. Its dominant role in power generation, retrieved from oil since the early 1970s, could be seriously threatened by the combination of gas and non-fossil sources. Many of its industrial markets do not look much more secure. Excepting metallurgical coal, it relies not upon being a premium fuel, but upon being cheaper than its competitors. Increasing environmental constraints, on mining, sulphur emissions, the land required for transport and storage of fuel and tailings, are all tending to increase the price and the difficulties of coal development in developed economies especially. Clearly in some countries the local availability of coal is crucial: the Chinese case study in particular reveals the extent to which that country's economic development is seen to depend on development of the country's great coal resources. But in several markets, especially in developed countries, displacing coal is an obvious policy step, and most of the country studies reflect this.

Such changes could bring grave difficulties. Contraction of coal industries is painful politically and socially. Furthermore, for many countries coal is the main indigenous fossil resource: switching away from it could increase imports, lessen energy security, worsen balance-of-payments problems, and generally fly in the face of the belief that countries should make use of the resources they have. Though such arguments have generally been given less credit in recent years, as discussed briefly in Chapter 3, they reflect a strong undercurrent.

Faced with this situation, coal industries can adopt various strategies. One, already apparent in some quarters, is to try and stem the tide by emphasising the many uncertainties in the greenhouse effect, and that it may not be as serious as people fear; by pointing to the fact that greenhouse gases come from many sources besides coal, so that coal is but a small component of the total problem especially if sectors are considered individually (eg. electricity); and by highlighting the various possible costs of reducing coal use, including its domestic importance and the long-term danger of further price shocks for oil and gas. All these carry elements of truth but the fact remains that coal would come near the top of any priority list for action on the greenhouse effect, probably following immediately on CFCs, deforestation, and more general efficiency improvements. Given the current evidence, hoping that the problem will go away is hardly an attractive approach nor, given the strength of concerns and other trends, is it likely to be a very successful one.

Technical options offer some scope, especially technologies for improving the efficiency of power generation (such as fluidised beds, coal gasification, and fuel cells, as discussed in Volume II). These might include the replacement of old power stations while taking advantage of the existing transport and storage infrastructure. Another or complementary approach would be for coal to tie its future to large-scale Combined Heat and Power (CHP). Though coal at present has few inherent advantages over gas for CHP, the industry has much more incentive, and the capital, to consider financing CHP development with a long-term contract on the fuel to be used. The carbon emissions per unit of energy delivered would then compete favourably with gas used to supply heating and electricity separately, so a carbon tax and other incentives might favour coal in this context. Some of the practical obstacles to this approach in the past would be removed by the advent of cleaner and smaller-scale coal technologies.

Such measures would help coal to maintain its market shares in the face of competition boosted by concern about carbon emissions. Since this would be achieved by much greater efficiency, it would moderate but not avoid the decline of coal in industrialised countries. Almost by definition, such a decline is unavoidable if their carbon emissions are to be reduced, barring much more speculative options of in situ coal gasification (mines producing methane), and decarbonisation ('coal without CO_2'), as outlined in Chapter 1.

These options are usually considered as 'technical fixes' which could, if successful, maintain long-term and greatly expanded use of coal. Yet it seems probable that the number of pits suitable for in situ gasification, and competitive markets for the gas produced, will be limited, as will the availability of disposal sites for CO_2 (eg. depleted oil and gas wells) which do not involve exorbitant costs. However, such options, if practical, would still help to moderate both carbon emissions and the pressure on coal. More importantly, these processes would broaden coal capital and expertise into other areas; gasification would lead into gas supply and technologies, and the Utrecht/Williams process for extracting the energy from coal as hydrogen could, ironically, make the coal industry the founding father of a future hydrogen economy. Viewed in this light, in situ gasification and decarbonisation techniques would not be a panacea for the future but a bridge to it.

In many countries the political and social costs of declining domestic coal production are being exacerbated by increasing use of low-cost coal imports. The international coal trade is growing, and is expected to expand rapidly when oil markets tighten. Yet traded coal usually involves significantly greater carbon emissions than domestic coal. With a lower energy density than oil, and more difficult handling, the energy used in moving coal around the world is substantial, and adds several per cent to the carbon emitted from combustion. Various other environmental costs, also not reflected in the price, arise from the shipping and transport infrastructure. Furthermore, coal tends to be cheapest when it is extracted either with high local environmental costs, such as from strip mining with unregulated dumping of tailings, or with high social costs, by relying on cheap and oppressed labour forces - or both. On all counts, there is a strong case for thinking again about the desirability of large-scale coal imports.

5.4 Price-demand feedbacks and other limiting factors

Several other factors may constrain the pace or scale of fuel switching. One, of greatest relevance in industrialised countries, is the extent of past investments in both supply and demand technologies, particularly with respect to infrastructure. There may be pressures to use existing capacity, especially that from recent years. Declining markets for a given fuel, obviating the need for new capacity, will certainly make constructing new and more efficient capacity, or promoting competing fuels, more difficult politically and economically.

Another factor is the feedback between price and demand. Fossil fuels are clearly in the rising part of the supply curve: extracting more costs more. Large increase in demand will push prices up, perhaps sharply. Conversely, reducing demand will reduce prices. In principle this could seriously limit the impact of policy measures, because measures to reduce consumption would reduce the fuel price, thus stimulating more consumption.[6] Fortunately for the greenhouse effect, the specific cost structures are such as to minimise the importance of this.

Coal production costs are relatively high, especially in many developed countries, and this will limit the effect especially if imports are constrained. Declining demand will allow concentration on more modern pits, with a reduction in costs, but in many countries much of this effect may be taken by the removal of transitional subsidies rather than through price reductions. Any significant carbon tax is also likely to offset any price falls due to declining markets.

In contrast, production costs on most oilfields are very low; even fields in the deep waters of the North Sea managed to reduce costs to around $12-13/bbl following the 1986 price collapse. Yet the nature of the market is such that price is unlikely to be stable if oil tries to expand far beyond the transport and petrochemicals markets; even if it could sustain this attempt, the price falls required to get back into power generation, for example, would probably be too large to be contemplated. A carbon tax should also ensure that competitive markets continue to find oil unattractive in comparison with gas.

Gas too is relatively cheap to produce, but since fuel switching to limit carbon emissions would be towards gas, price falls are not the issue; rather the question is how price rises might constrain such switching, as discussed in section 5.1. In this case, the price response to improved efficiency will aid further fuel switching for greenhouse and other environmental reasons, rather than opposing it.

This suggests that price-demand feedbacks may not be as important as they appear in limiting fuel switching. However, there is no doubt that reducing oil and coal demand would depress world energy prices below the rapid escalation projected in much of the 1970s and early 1980s, and now returning to favour. Price projections have been so plentiful, so varied, and so often wrong, that it seems unwise to try and quantify this comment.

To summarise, while energy efficiency can limit demand for all fuels, the price-demand feedback will help to limit the scope for economic improvements in efficiency, whilst other factors may be more important in limiting the scope and pace of fuel switching. In several sectors the choice of fuel will be driven by far more powerful forces than those likely

---

[6] This is in addition to the *implicit* fall in energy costs when the efficiency of a technology is improved, which is discussed in Chapter 4, section 4.2.

to be wielded by governments attempting to limit carbon emissions. This applies particularly in the case of transport and petrochemicals, but also the choice of heating fuels may be dictated strongly by local circumstances of economic development, convenience and resource accessibility. Some industrial fuel markets may provide flexibility between coal, oil, and gas. Some renewable sources, for heating or liquid fuels, could also offer scope for displacing fossil fuels in various markets, as discussed below. But by far the most important sector, and the one which dominates most discussions of the options, is electricity supply, which provides the greatest all-round flexibility in fuel switching, including the most widely canvassed but controversial of the non-fossil sources: nuclear power.

5.5 The nuclear debate

On the surface, the answer to the greenhouse effect seems obvious. Scientists have known for over fifty years that if uranium is extracted from rock and placed in a large enough mass, it will generate heat without releasing chemical pollutants or greenhouse gases. The concept has been an operational reality for more than thirty years. Furthermore, if uranium resources prove scarce, more fuel can be 'bred' in fast breeder reactors, to provide an almost infinite supply. That too has been demonstrated. It seems almost too good to be true, and it was hard for anyone of the post-Second World War generation not to be carried away by nuclear euphoria.

The euphoria has long dissipated. Nuclear projections have been scaled down almost since the moment of their first inception with the UK Magnox programme. Few if any nuclear programmes have proved unambiguously economic, and some rank amongst the greatest financial disasters ever. The public and press which once hailed the nuclear saviour now treat it with a suspicion sometimes bordering on the hysterical. In most of the industrial market countries the heady plans for further nuclear development have ground to a halt and, as outlined in the Japanese case study, it is under increasing pressure even in what was once considered one of its safest bastions. The trend of nuclear capacity over 1970-2000, illustrated in Figure 5.2, does not give the image of a healthy technology. What went wrong, and can it be put right?

The first point to note is the sheer ferocity of the nuclear debate. The pro- and anti-camps are divided by a seemingly bottomless chasm. One

Figure 5.2 Nuclear power capacity outside centrally planned economies, 1970-2000

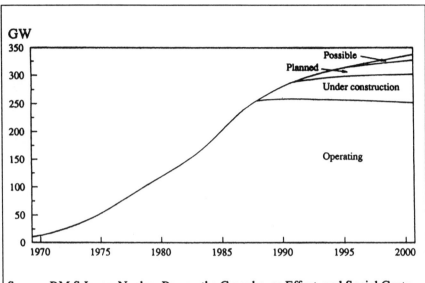

Source: P.M.S.Jones, Nuclear Power, the Greenhouse Effect, and Social Costs of Energy, SEEDS paper no.51, Surrey Energy Economics Centre, Surrey University, May 1990.

side believes that nuclear power, properly handled, has been very cost-effective and can be cheaper still; the other, that it has been and always will be an economic disaster when everything is taken into account. Nuclear power has been and will remain one of the safest forms of power generation - it is one of the most dangerous technologies ever conceived. It already makes a major contribution to electricity supplies and will be an essential component in future attempts to limit CO_2 emissions - it only exists because of the weapons links, it has inhibited other options, and its costs and other factors mean that attempts at expansion will be horrendously expensive and will confound rather than aid attempts to limit CO_2 emissions. What can one say in the face of such contradictory convictions?

It is useful to start with the final claim. Two main reasons are advanced for arguing that nuclear power cannot be an answer to the greenhouse effect. One focuses on the sheer scale involved. Keepin and Kats, in what has become the standard-bearer of the greenhouse anti-nuclear case,[7] examine a range of scenarios against conventional energy demand projections and conclude that a global transition from coal to nuclear generation over the next four decades

> ... would require nuclear plants to be built at the rate of one new plant (1000MW) every one to three days for nearly 40 years, with electricity generation costs averaging between $525bn and $787bn each year. Moreover even these massive programmes ... could not prevent an increase in CO_2 emissions.

This is true enough, and indeed the economic assumptions involved were generous. Yet this logic alone is misleading: it points not to the special costs of nuclear power, but to the extraordinary scale of global resources required to meet rapidly growing electricity demand. As Jones notes, the question posed is not 'can we afford nuclear' but 'can we afford energy?'.[8] Nuclear construction - if and where possible - in place of coal would still help to limit carbon emissions. Keepin and Kats note that even a more feasible six-fold increase in generation would do little to ameliorate global warming against a background of rapid demand growth, but again much the same could be said for many single policy steps, including a carbon tax[9] and renewable energy developments. To paraphrase Burke, the impossibility of doing everything with one option is not a reason for doing nothing.

Keepin and Kats therefore point to the very much greater economic potential for energy efficiency. It could have much more impact, more quickly, and much more cheaply, than a nuclear commitment; the nuclear option is estimated to be up to seven times as expensive per unit of carbon saved, and developing nuclear power therefore carries a large opportunity cost and inhibits more economic options to reduce CO_2 emissions. But again, this is not so much an argument against nuclear power as against any new supply investments while the potential for

---

[7] B.Keepin and G.Kats, 'Greenhouse warming: comparative analysis of nuclear and efficiency abatement strategies', *Energy Policy* 16(6), December 1988.
[8] P.M.S.Jones, *Nuclear Power, the Greenhouse Effect, and Social Costs of Energy*, SEEDS paper no.51, Surrey Energy Economics Centre, Surrey University, May 1990.
[9] An analysis by the International Energy Agency (IEA, *Policy Measures and Their Impact on CO_2 Emissions and Accumulations*, OECD, Paris, December 1989) concludes that increasing nuclear generation throughout the OECD to the level of France - 70% of supplies - could cut projected CO_2 emissions by 19%, as compared with an estimated 11% from a large carbon tax.

economic efficiency is so large. There are ultimately limits on how much efficiency can deliver, and the argument needs to be tied to particular efficiency policies and their costs. Economically, policies such as those discussed in Chapter 4 should be pursued until the marginal cost of squeezing more out of efficiency equates to that of new supply. The country studies suggest that in practice various limits would prevent this. An increased capacity of non-fossil power remains an important component in long-term reductions of CO_2. And despite the opportunity costs, the long lead times involved suggest that it is not practical to wait many years before starting along that path.

What then are the prospects and issues facing a nuclear revival? The problems break down into two major areas. The first lies in the realm of technology and economics; the second concerns safety and public confidence. Though the two are linked, safety concerns have been far from the only factors behind the long story of cost overruns and poor performance in many countries. Boiling water with uranium on a commercial scale turned out to be far more complex than anyone could foresee. It emerged that nuclear power requires an extraordinary degree of centralised commitment combined with very good management to make it work well. A passive public, or an ability to push through developments against popular opposition, emerged later as another key requirement. In many countries these requirements simply could not be met within the prevailing structure of society in general and/or the electricity industry in particular.

Experience in some countries (eg. France, Japan, Sweden) has demonstrated that nuclear power can be a technical success, given the right conditions, though it is still unclear whether it has been or will be economic when all costs are taken into account (see box), especially if private sector criteria are used. The immense scale of commitment and resources in the French case has been such that according to the *Energy Economist* review, 'whatever else is on the agenda in the 1990s, no-one is planning to replicate Electricité de France. It is unlikely that an exercise such as the French nuclear power programme will ever be seen again.'[10]

---

[10] 'World Status: Nuclear Power', *Financial Times Energy Economist*, January 1989. The financing of nuclear programmes is discussed in A.Holmes, *Electricity in Europe - Power and Profit*, Financial Times Business Information, 1990.

Nuclear power economics

It is many years since anyone proclaimed nuclear electricity as 'too cheap to meter'. But many governments and international publications still claim significant cost advantages for nuclear power. Over the years these analyses have become more sophisticated, taking into account country differences, decommissioning costs, and other factors. The most recent review from the International Energy Agency still concludes that nuclear power, assessed at a 5% discount rate, is cheaper than alternatives in most regions.

Such cost estimates remain open to substantial criticism. Key areas of debate on basic data include: the operating costs of nuclear power, which in total seem to be much higher than originally envisaged; the fuel costs including reprocessing, which likewise have escalated sharply; the estimated costs and performance of reactors; and the projected price of coal, assumed to be the main competitor. The dispute extends to much deeper assumptions, including comparisons with other generation options; the financial criteria used, including discount rates; the scale of direct and indirect support from government, which should be included in any overall assessment of the economic desirability; and the level of support and provision for waste, decommissioning and accident insurance which would normally be required of private industry but which in practice private insurers refuse to countenance.

Such debates are well beyond the scope of this book, but even at the strictly financial level it is clear that they are as much about scope and definitions as about numbers. There are few examples of cost estimates having proved pessimistic, and no estimates appear to be available of the total cost of national nuclear programmes, including all forms of government support and contributions to the international nuclear bodies. These seem reasonable grounds for scepticism.

The essential paradoxes of nuclear economics are illustrated by the French programme, widely hailed as the world's most successful. The industry successfully established a nuclear production line which produced reactors faster and cheaper than anywhere else. But with the country's energy industries geared so heavily towards nuclear, the pressures against ceasing construction were formidable even when the extra plants were not needed, and France now has massive overcapacity. The operating costs are lower than conventional plant, so that France can and does sell electricity to undercut all other sources in Europe at an operating profit. Yet in reaching this position, Electricité de France has acquired the largest private debt in the world, one which, according to the Financial Times, there is little chance of it paying off (*Financial Times Energy Economist*, January 1989).

However, the overall economics of nuclear power and other non-fossil sources do depend heavily on the price of competing fuels, and they would improve if fossil fuel prices rose in response to environmental concerns.

Yet even for more modest programmes, public confidence now poses still greater obstacles. Concerns about nuclear safety include not only the fear of major accidents, but of low-level emissions, nuclear waste, weapons proliferation, and various institutional issues. The fear of accidents is probably the greatest single cause of public concern. Though nuclear power carries the potential for massive accidents, in principle enough precautions can be introduced to make such accidents virtually impossible. The questions focus not only on how this affects the economics, but on how reliably humans can apply such precautions in practice. Assessments based on actual history, including 'precursor incidents' of the kind which, if compounded, could contribute to accidents, give higher estimates of accident risk than engineering-based probabilistic risk assessments. A decade which has seen the disasters at Bhopal, Mexico City, Chernobyl, the *Challenger* explosion, the Exxon *Valdez* and various other spills, the Piper Alpha explosion, and a series of major disasters with passenger shipping and aircraft, does not give confidence that humans can manage technology very reliably, whether it is simple and familiar or highly advanced and carefully developed.

The defence of the nuclear industry rests ultimately on the conviction that the risks are small relative to other hazards in modern society, and that the benefits far outweigh the risks. The latter is the rationalist argument; the former, though logically greater evils do not justify lesser ones, carries more political weight.

Certainly, it is difficult to envisage that nuclear incidents (excepting war) will ever cause anything like as many deaths as the carnage on roads, and indeed even after Chernobyl the industry can validly point out that it has caused fewer deaths than most other energy industries including hydro, coal, and gas. Yet several factors serve to ensure that governments and public alike will remain worried. The impact of nuclear accidents, as emphasised by Chernobyl, runs far beyond that which can be accounted in death tolls: people for thousands of miles around were affected, and large areas will remain measurably contaminated for decades. Furthermore, knowing that hundreds of people died in an accident is a very different matter from knowing that, statistically, a similar number, spread throughout a population, may die of radiation-induced cancers, or may pass genetic damage on to their children.

Even more complex factors underlie nuclear waste. The industry believes, probably correctly, that it can handle the problem without significant risk, if it can have access to the best sites and processes. But the best sites remain elusive for a mixture of technical and political reasons, and the waste is steadily accumulating in storage tanks above ground, vulnerable and in some cases leaking.[11]

Still more deep-rooted problems underlie proliferation concerns. Nuclear power is not essential for developing nuclear weapons, but it offers a ready path to obtaining the basic know-how and materials. Major studies conclude that the international safeguards regime cannot be expected with confidence to police for ever the line between energy and weapons, and several countries - outside the Non-Proliferation Treaty but nevertheless with some foreign assistance - are now suspected of having obtained nuclear weapons under the cover of nuclear power.[12]

The task of gaining acceptability for the nuclear industry therefore now seems a huge one. Bitter experience shows the dangers of trying to force through a technology which rouses deep public opposition even in countries where it is politically possible. In most countries, trying to expand current nuclear technology now looks like facing an extremely hard and damaging battle. It would also be a brittle path. The greenhouse effect might conceivably give nuclear power another chance after Chernobyl, but a further major accident, or use of a nuclear weapon derived from nuclear power, would probably spell the end in most countries.

There are two possible escape routes. One is to rely on massive imports from the few areas which, for one reason or another, are able to proceed with nuclear technology. Though this pattern has already emerged in Europe to some extent with the progression of French exports, the drawbacks of taking such an option to extremes are obvious: it creates dependence usually on a single foreign source, which could be

---

[11] Various cases of leaking wastes have been reported at the Sellafield complex in the UK; some cannot be halted, but are contained well within the site. The situation in the US appears to be much more serious, though this is focused more upon weapon-related sites; estimates of clean-up costs have run over $100bn (W.C.Patterson, 'A $130bn nuclear clean-up - and that's just the US military', *Financial Times Energy Economist*, November 1988).

[12] L.S.Spector, *Going Nuclear*, Ballinger, Cambridge MA, 1987.

vulnerable to accidents of technology or politics. In any difficulties, exports would be the first to suffer.[13]

The other path is to turn to alternative and perhaps more attractive nuclear systems. Some parts of the nuclear industry are considering smaller-scale 'passive' reactors, designed so that they cannot melt down even if there is a complete loss of coolant.[14] Development and demonstration will inevitably be a long path, but this might meet many of the concerns, and the smaller scale might in the long run prove better commercially as well. However, others in the industry doubt the wisdom of this route, because it would divert economic and political resources from established technology, and might be seen to carry an implication that existing systems are not safe.

In addition, attention would have to be given to the problems of proliferation and possible terrorist use of nuclear materials. Williams and Feiveson[15] have presented a set of criteria for 'diversion-resistant' nuclear power, and argue that they could be met only by abandoning reprocessing (in which the spent fuel is dissolved and separated into its various constituents, including plutonium) and managing nuclear fuel through safeguarded international centres. Reprocessing is a hangover from the days of hopes for the fast breeder, which have receded. The separated plutonium can be slowly reabsorbed by mixing it back into fuel for conventional nuclear stations, but this cannot consume the volumes of plutonium generated by reprocessing, the handling of which may create a major political headache in the future.[16]

---

[13] This problem was graphically illustrated in November 1988, when the French utility EdF was forced to make emergency coal and electricity imports from Germany during a strike which affected its nuclear operations (*Financial Times Energy Economist*, January 1989).

[14] See, for example, R.Dettmer, 'Safe Integral Reactor: Pacifying the PWR', *IEE Review*, November 1989.

[15] R.H.Williams and H.A.Feiveson, 'How to Expand Nuclear Power Without Proliferation', *Bulletin of the Atomic Scientists*, April 1990.

[16] For example, Japan has signed a contract to reprocess spent fuel at Sellafield in the UK, and to take back the separated plutonium. Yet all physical routes to do this pose grave political problems. Air transport has been made extremely difficult by a ban on the transport of plutonium over key countries. Japan is not supposed to possess an international naval capability which could guard a sea convoy, and permission to pass through the Panama Canal is doubtful. For a fuller discussion of this and related predicaments see F.Berkhout, T.Suzuki, and W.Walker, 'Japan, Europe, and Nuclear Power Problems', *International Affairs*, 66(3), July 1990.

Reprocessing is also the dirty and most troublesome end of the fuel cycle. It persists primarily because of political and institutional inertia, and the desire of the UK and France, which own the major reprocessing facilities, to earn foreign exchange, combined with the desire of others to be rid of their bulk nuclear waste. Though abandoning reprocessing would make good sense it would thus face some political obstacles.

However, these would be trivial compared with the difficulties involved in trying to set up international fuel handling centres. In all, the reformation of the nuclear industry would be a vast task of technology redevelopment and institutional restructuring.

Whether or not nuclear industries attempt to revive along the old path, or to restructure along a new one, the political and other efforts required will be formidable, and the timescales long. If governments do want to help promote a nuclear revival in countries where it has stagnated, what would be required? Many specific steps could be advanced, but two stand out. First, licensing procedures would have to be streamlined, with some promise of minimal political interference, so that utilities could be reasonably assured of being able to construct and run plants without years of acrimonious and litigious debate and changes in regulatory conditions. Second, governments would almost certainly have to accept a role in giving implicit financial support, at least in terms of insurance and probably more directly, with subsidies or as government projects using public sector finance. The first of these is obviously politically delicate; the latter is raised again at the end of this chapter.

Finally, limits on uranium resources suggest that, if nuclear power is to make a substantial global contribution to limiting carbon emissions, there might after several decades have to be a move toward the use of fast breeder reactors. As many have noted, the plutonium economy would face all the problems of conventional nuclear power, writ larger still. Fusion power would probably face less political problems, but technically it remains highly speculative and unpromising, for reasons outlined in Volume II.

The issues can therefore be summarised as follows. Nuclear power, despite its vast theoretical potential, is unpopular, often costly, and in many respects now appears unattractive and insecure as a basis for long-term supply. Attempting to push for a large-scale revival of the technology as it stands would be politically and perhaps financially costly, and is probably impossible in many countries. Some of the problems could be avoided by a large-scale restructuring of the nuclear industry, based on new reactor designs, international safeguards, and an abandonment of reprocessing, but it is not clear if the industry has the will or the resources left for such a strategy. Attempts to expand nuclear power in most countries would probably require major political and financial support from governments, for returns which remain uncertain. The fast breeder economy which might be required for nuclear power to make a large long-term contribution would face still larger obstacles.

Yet all the country studies in Volume II and most other serious analyses, conclude that gas and efficiency alone cannot bring down carbon emissions to anywhere near the levels climatologists say may be necessary. Bluntly, if there is no alternative, then there is no alternative. Or to put it another way, the nuclear debate is ultimately quite inseparable from another debate: that about renewable energy.

5.6 Renewables: the Cinderella options?

Renewable energy is an enigma. Everyone is in favour of it, but few take it seriously. Most agree that renewable energy research deserves more money, but the funding remains small compared with much more speculative technologies such as nuclear fusion. Renewable energy is praised for its environmental advantages, whilst environmental objections are raised increasingly as the major constraint.

There are two main attitudes towards the prospects for and importance of non-hydro renewable energy. One, widely expressed throughout the environmental community, is that in the long run renewable energy will save us all from the unsustainable consequences of relying upon fossil fuels and nuclear power. The Brundtland Commission[17] echoed this in stating that renewable energy 'should form the foundation of the global energy structure during the 21st century'.

The other common attitude is that in the short to medium time horizon relevant to the real world of industrial and political policy formation and investment, non-hydro renewable sources are essentially irrelevant: that for the foreseeable future their contribution will remain marginal. This attitude is reflected in the levels of expenditure, illustrated in Figure 5.3. It is apparent in the institutional imbalance, with the major international institutions devoted to nuclear power having no counterparts for

[17] World Commission on Environment and Development, *Our Common Future*, Oxford University Press, Oxford, 1987.

Figure 5.3 Energy RD&D expenditures

(a) Total IEA direct government RD&D expenditure, 1977-88

Total: US$120bn
(1988 US$)

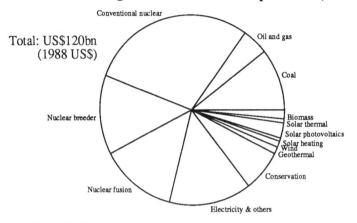

(b) Total UK public energy RD&D expenditure, 1985-86

Total: £565m
(1988 UK£)

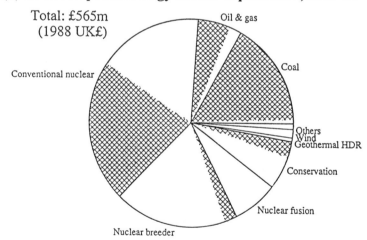

Hatched areas = spending by nationalised industry
Remainder = direct government expenditure
Others: wave, geothermal aquifer, solar, biomass, tide, hydro/general, ETSU services.

Source: IEA, *Energy Policies and Programmes of IEA Countries, 1988 Review*, IEA/OECD, Paris, 1989; Grubb, 'The Cinderella Options', see note 21.

renewable energy.[18] It is evident in the absence of renewable energy from general energy policy developments. Above all, it is demonstrated by mainstream energy forecasts, which project contributions from commercial non-hydro renewable energy still at a few per cent of supply decades into the next century.

Currently, renewables probably account for just over 20% of global energy consumption, composed mostly of hydro (6.7%) and an uncertain but larger amount of traditional biomass use.[19] Biomass is the major energy source for the majority of the world's population, but as used traditionally it is inefficient and labour-intensive, and societies move away from it as they develop. As noted in the country studies there are many constraints on the further development of hydro. Renewable *resources* are large on a global basis, but traditional technologies do not offer practical routes to their exploitation.

'Modernised' renewables form a diverse group of technologies. Some are quite well developed. These include not only hydro (both large dams and, increasingly, small-scale 'microhydro' plants) but the use of various waste products to generate heat and/or electricity; design of houses to capture sunlight for space heating and active solar systems for heating water; and heat and electricity derived from hot subterranean water (geothermal aquifers).[20] A tidal energy scheme has been operating in France for over 25 years. Wind energy has been attractive for water pumping and remote electricity for some time; more recently, it has developed to the point where it is economic for generating grid electricity in many windy locations.

A number of assessments have noted opportunities for cost-effective uses of renewables which are going unexploited. In this there are parallels with the 'efficiency gap', though utility regulation and simple inertia play a greater role, as discussed below. However, even if such obstacles were removed, in most developed economies these renewables could still form only a relatively minor component of supply.

---

[18] The global International Atomic Energy Agency; the IEA's Nuclear Energy Agency; Europe's Euratom. Nearly a fifth of the total text in the treaties forming the European Community is devoted to nuclear energy; there is not a paragraph on renewable energy.

[19] See Chapter 2, note 4.

[20] Geothermal energy is not a renewable resource, since the water and/or heat is extracted much faster than it is replaced by natural process, but it is usually included as such for convenience.

There are widely assumed to be three primary obstacles to larger-scale contributions from renewable sources: technical limitations including those of high cost and other difficulties (eg. reliability); the difficulty of using sources which fluctuate with natural cycles (such as sun, wind, and tides); and limits on the available energy taking into account realistic constraints on siting. In reality, the scale and importance of all these obstacles are questionable.

Avenues for major technical improvements exist in many renewable technologies. A number of these could be of local and perhaps national importance in some countries, and three stand out as having a large global potential if successfully developed: photovoltaics (PV, or solar cells); modernised biomass systems for producing electricity or liquid fuels; and schemes for extracting energy from underground hot dry rocks (HDR geothermal).

These technologies are discussed further in Volume II. The economic prospects for modernised biomass systems based on short rotation forestry now seem good, both for electricity and probably liquid fuels. Overall PV costs would have to reduce by a factor of 2-3 to start making it commercially competitive on grid systems, but there are clear technical avenues suggesting that these targets could be reached during the 1990s. HDR is much more uncertain technically but cannot be ruled out. Also, wind energy is expected to improve further, reducing its costs by 10-40% over the coming decade and making it competitive for power generation especially in a wide range of coastal and upland regions.

The underlying reasons for optimism are simple: the technologies are still developing rapidly; the technical avenues to lower costs in many cases are already visible; substantial cost reductions are inevitable from mass production alone; in detail there are still a wide range of options to be explored; and relatively little has been spent on them to date. This final point is emphasised by Figure 5.3, but even this gives an over-favourable impression: in total, it seems that few if any individual renewable technologies have received more than about one thousandth of the total public expenditure on thermal nuclear power RD&D, with the possible exception of PV.[21] The present author has argued

[21] M.Grubb, 'The Cinderella Options: a Study of Modernised Renewable Energy Technologies, Part I: A Technical Assessment', *Energy Policy* 18(6), Butterworth, July/August 1990.

elsewhere[22] that pessimistic assessments from major global studies in the 1970s were determined by undue technical conservatism; their conclusions amounted to little more than the observation that trying to deploy the then costly and inefficient renewable technologies on a global scale would prove, well, costly and inefficient.

Most of the major renewable technologies produce electricity, the value of which is relatively high and seems unlikely to decline. As the technologies develop further it is quite conceivable that markets will be awaiting them: the economics could become quite favourable, especially if there are substantial carbon taxes and/or public sector discount rates, which tend to favour non-fossil sources, are used.

Technically there are also promising routes into transport, either directly through biofuels or indirectly through electricity; the latter could involve either hydrogen generated from PV in deserts,[23] or electric vehicles charged directly from PV, probably with a combination of cells on cars and recharging/battery exchange points at homes and car parks. These options are unlikely to compete with oil at the prices of the late 1980s; if renewables penetrate transport it will be either as a response to further major oil price shocks or as the winning candidate for environmentally acceptable substitutes.

The second concern, about the variability of many renewable sources, is largely misplaced. Biomass and hydro sources represent stored energy, and geothermal is also relatively constant. Concerning the variable renewables, studies suggest that large integrated power systems could absorb over half their energy from windpower in combination with other variable sources, without either storage or hydro power, and without incurring serious economic penalties.[24] The limits on PV may be either lesser or greater depending on the nature of the system, and in all cases, access to large hydro capacities (which contain natural storage), the

[22] M.Grubb, 'The Cinderella Options: a Study of Modernised Renewable Energy Technologies, Part II: Political and Policy Assessment', *Energy Policy* 18(8), Butterworth, October 1990.

[23] A recent extensive study argued that deriving hydrogen from PV provided a promising long-term option for large-scale global energy supplies (J.O.Ogden and R.H.Williams, *Solar Hydrogen - Moving Beyond Fossil Fuels*, World Resources Institute, Washington DC, 1989).

[24] M.J.Grubb, 'The economic value of wind energy at higher power system penetrations: an analysis of models, sensitivities, and assumptions', *Wind Engineering,* Vol.12, No.1, 1988.

greater diversity afforded by large-scale system interconnection, and the use of modern generation and control systems could increase the extent to which power systems could economically integrate variable power sources.

The third concern is that, although in principle some renewables offer a large resource, practical siting and other constraints will greatly limit their realistic contribution. Without more experience this is a somewhat open question, and it is possible to do no more than to point out the issues and possibilities.

The image of renewables suffers from two caricatures. One is of massive arrays of wind turbines or solar panels, covering tens of miles in a vain attempt to match the output of 1000MW power stations. The other is of the isolated house sprouting a solar panel on the roof with a muck digester and windmill at the bottom of the garden, usually with a battery in the garage to back up supplies.

The reality will be neither. Onshore wind and PV might be deployed in huge arrays in remote deserted areas, but for various reasons wind is usually best deployed in small arrays of a dozen or so machines spread over a few acres of farmland or hillside, generating 1-10MW. Several hundred or even thousand windfarms in a country would be quite visible but, to judge from current Danish and Dutch experience, not necessarily objectionable. Biomass electricity would tend to work best with units of perhaps 5-50MW sited in the centre of the associated forest areas, which a small staff would manage. PV could be deployed mounted on poles in patterns similar to those of windfarms, but they could also usefully be integrated in the surface glazing or tiles of new buildings. This would not necessarily be in an attempt to supply the building concerned with all its needs, but simply as a convenient way of minimising mounting costs and either reducing expenditure on supplies from the grid, or providing a useful source of extra income from sales to the system - or more likely, both, depending on the time of day and building load.

In practice, there seems to be a remarkable absence of serious assessments of the potential for renewables assuming reasonable technology development but taking into account various regional and systemic constraints. The Japanese and UK case studies, which attempted broad assessments, emphasised the uncertainties but concluded that the potential could be of the same order as the projected nuclear/non-fossil contribution in the fuel-switching scenarios,[25] though probably far from the scale of total primary energy requirements in the business-as-usual projections.

To get a better picture of the possible contributions, it is useful to divide renewable sources into three broad types. The energy available from *activity-dependent* renewables depends on the level of human activity, either because this is the source of energy (energy from wastes) or because the contribution is tied directly to particular and restricted uses (solar water and space heating). It seems likely that these together might contribute 5-15% of primary energy supply in developed economies.

Concentrated renewables depend upon natural concentrations of the primary source. Examples include hydro, geothermal energy, and tidal energy (which usually depends upon local estuary resonance effects for viability). These tend to be unequally distributed. In a few countries they can meet all energy, or at least electricity, requirements, and several more might achieve this if HDR geothermal can be developed. Yet unless HDR is spectacularly successful, the future contribution of these renewables is also clearly limited.

Diffuse renewables encompass the primary solar source and diffuse derivatives (biomass, wind, wave, ocean thermal, hygroscopic and saline gradients, etc.) converted into electricity, gas or liquid fuels. The energy is dispersed but in total very large. The major uncertainties are not only technological performance and cost, but also the acceptable density of siting systems to extract the energy. Figure 5.4 illustrates the average energy density which each of the major diffuse renewables might yield if 5% of the land area was involved in renewable energy production (this would not necessarily render the land unavailable for some other uses), and compares this against the density of electricity and total energy demand projected for the long-term (2030) scenarios of the country studies. A range of technical performance for the renewable sources is considered: the lower bound reflects a moderate view of technical development combined with siting in less favourable areas, the upper

---

[25] The Japanese country study notes the potential for electricity-specific renewables as totalling about 10-30% of the projected nuclear contribution, but a large potential for biomass, which if electricity proved the best option, could be of the same order as the high nuclear contribution. The figures assumed siting of photovoltaics restricted to building surfaces, and noted an unquantifiable but probably very large potential for HDR.

Figure 5.4 Renewable energy densities at 5% land coverage: comparison with projected energy and electricity densities

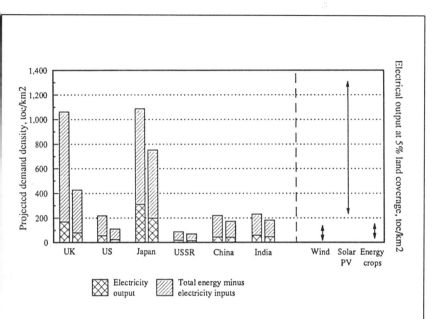

Energy projections: country case studies
1st bar: business as usual (2030Aii)
2nd bar: high efficiency (2030Bii)

Renewables:key assumptions

	Resource density	Conversion efficiency
Wind*	200-800kW/m^2	25-40%
Solar PV	3-8GJ/m^2	7-12%
Energy crops	0.07-0.2GJ/m^2	40-50%

Note: all figures annual averages
*Wind resource density in terms of mean power per unit vertical area.
A 1:100 ratio of rotor to land area is assumed for the diagram.

bound a more optimistic view of technology development combined with siting in some of the best conditions.

Visual and other environmental impacts may be the constraining factor on these and other renewables; sustainability can mean many things but in the energy sector it will certainly not mean invisibility, and environmental groups will have to accommodate this reality if renewables are to make a large contribution. However, at present environmental pressures mostly work in renewables' favour. The 5% siting density used in the figure might be beyond an upper limit in densely populated areas, while in remoter areas, more might be feasible. Clearly the real potential for siting is uncertain, but 5% is a useful indicator. The diagram emphasises that even with the highest demand densities, the potential contribution from renewables, especially PV, could be considerable. With greater energy efficiency, and/or in less densely populated countries, contributions could be very large. In addition, there is a useful geographical spread, with biomass being more productive in humid regions, PV being better in dry areas, and with wind featuring strongly in mid- to high-latitude coastal or mountainous regions.

A rough indication of the global implications may be judged with reference to the discussion of demand and population projections in Chapter 2 (and population density projections shown in Figure 2.4), which suggests that the world may be roughly divided into areas of high energy demand density, comprising Europe and Asia outside the USSR, and low density, comprising all the rest - the Americas, Africa, Oceania, and the USSR. In combination with the technical discussion this suggests that technically:

* The 'confident' renewables of hydro, wastes, geothermal aquifers, solar water heating in sunny areas, solar space heating in colder areas, and wind in very windy ones, can make useful contributions to national supplies in a variety of regions and stages of development, but if traditional biomass use in poor countries is excluded, they can dominate supplies only in a few minor cases.

* Major further development of wind energy would greatly increase the importance of this source but would not change this broad conclusion, except that it might then make large contributions to electricity supply in the Americas, Australasia and the USSR. If offshore deployment of wind or waves proves feasible, these could

make moderate to large contributions to electricity in many coastal countries.

* Successfully modernised biomass could in principle meet a large proportion of primary demand in the low demand density regions of the world, excepting very dry areas, but it is limited on a global scale.

* Photovoltaics could easily meet demand to within the constraints of the energy system, in the low demand density regions. To meet projected demand in the high density regions, PV would have to cover a few per cent of the land area. This would take it beyond any conceivable degree of building surface mounting. The main constraints, however, would be the rapidly deteriorating economics in colder and cloudier climates, and the constraints of power systems.

* Successful development of PV-hydrogen would give the physical potential for an international fuels industry, centred on desert regions, which could feasibly be of the same order as global demand. Clearly, this would require a whole new infrastructure of supply, trade and end-use equipment which would take many decades to develop, and it would be dependent on key desert regions. It could not compete economically with the *extraction* cost of oil and gas resources, but it might enter at the margin if the prices of these fuels increase greatly, or are otherwise constrained, for environmental or energy supply/security reasons.

* Hot Dry Rock geothermal is a largely unknown quantity in terms of both technology and resource potential, but it could be very large in some areas and its geographical availability would be uncorrelated with any of the true renewables.

On these grounds, in combination with a much more detailed technical review, the present author has argued elsewhere that the prospects for large-scale contributions from renewable sources are in fact good.[26] However, it should be emphasised that this view is a very unorthodox one among energy analysts, and is certainly not reflected in the country studies. Non-hydro renewables in almost all mainstream energy projections play a very small role; the World Energy Council suggest that by 2020 they might supply up to 3% of (commercial) world energy demand, and the WEC Renewable Energy Committee is examining three scenarios, of which the highest is 6% by this date. This reflects the

---

[26] Grubb, 'The Cinderella Options: Part I'.

common perception in almost all national energy ministries; projections of large renewable contributions come almost entirely from outside the mainstream energy community.

In a subsequent paper[27] the present author argues that there are clear institutional reasons for this. They amount to the fact that scepticism born of past disappointments and now outdated studies, combined with the pressures of the existing industrial interests and the political imperative towards nuclear power, has led to an entrenched way of looking at energy issues which excludes the possibility of renewables playing a major role. Because non-hydro renewables are deemed unimportant, little attention is paid to them, they receive few resources, and claims for their potential are heavily discounted. Combined with technological conservatism and an attitude towards energy provision which makes it very hard to conceive of large-scale supplies being procured from many diffuse units, this amounts to a vicious circle in which renewables cannot be taken seriously because they are not taken seriously. It is what social scientists would call an entrenched paradigm. In the author's view, this paradigm can no longer be plausibly defended against the existing and continuing technical developments in renewable energy.

Whether or not technical optimism is justified, the possibility of some major renewables becoming competitive clearly cannot be rejected with confidence. Three things seem clear. One is that renewables will be more significant than most energy specialists currently believe. Second, if current trends continue, the commercialisation and penetration of renewable technologies will be relatively slow, and most are unlikely to emerge on a large scale until expanding conventional supplies start running up against further price rises and/or various environmental and logistical constraints. These might include the political reactions to dramatic climatic events at some point in the future, resulting in rapid and drastic measures to penalise carbon and promote alternatives - the 1970s syndrome of crash programmes. This would be an unnecessarily costly, painful and relatively ineffective way of bringing alternatives in. Third, renewables face some serious non-technical obstacles which will have to be addressed if this prospect is to be avoided, and their potential is to be realised.

It was noted above that several cost-effective options for renewables remain unexploited. This is reminiscent of the 'efficiency gap' discussed

[27] Grubb, 'The Cinderella Options: Part II'.

in Chapter 4, and some of the reasons are similar. Architects may be unaware of the potential for solar energy for heating - and/or for reducing the need for cooling - through building design. They may also have little interest. The wide variation in the take-up of solar water heaters between countries of similar climate - 60% of buildings in Israel use them, for example - is very largely a function of government policy using the kind of tools discussed in Chapter 4.

In addition, there are various legal impediments. In the UK for example, micro-hydro schemes which have an energy cost half that of conventional power are rendered uneconomic by the charges levied for 'use' of the water; regulations in the United States have similarly rendered micro-hydro development almost impossible, and some other renewables face other idiosyncratic obstacles.[28] These include, in some countries, large-scale existing support for conventional sources; in the US, the first plea of the renewable energy community is not for subsidies but for a 'level playing field'.[29]

However, probably the most important factor affecting the development of renewables is the question of utility regulation. Many renewables share the characteristics of localised CHP, in that they require detailed local understanding of conditions, and may be associated directly with other developments, for example, biomass from agricultural or forestry wastes, or for using marginal farmlands; wind developments on hill slopes used for cattle farming; and perhaps PV integrated into the design of commercial buildings. It is very difficult if not impossible for large centralised utilities to manage such developments even if they want to. They would have to be developed by independent producers, selling excess power to the grid. The ability to do this, and the terms on which it is done, will therefore be crucial in determining renewable energy developments. This is a matter of utility regulation.

The parallels in all this with measures to address the 'efficiency gap' are clear. Both involve more attention to the conditions under which relatively small-scale, decentralised decisions are made, and the consequent failures of markets at this level. In addition, there are more

---

[28] Climate Institute et al., *Report of the Forum on Renewable Energy and Climate Change*, Washington DC, June 1989 (various papers).
[29] Ibid; also M.Brower, *Cool Energy - The Renewable Solution to Global Warming*, Union of Concerned Scientists, Cambridge MA, 1990.

specific issues. For example, a credit for absorbing carbon, in conjunction with a way of reflecting the costs of agricultural subsidies in many countries, could well tip the balance in favour of developing energy crops.[30]

In parallel with these and other developments, major institutional reforms would be required to correct the current imbalance in energy institutions, to protect and promote the needs of renewable energy sources both at the national and international level.

Changing the market for renewables in this way could have a large impact for those renewables which are quite well developed and predominantly small-scale. Yet as already noted, renewables form a diverse group which include poorly developed technologies and large-scale, capital-intensive forms. These factors raise a number of issues which are held in common with conventional supply developments, with which this chapter concludes.

5.7 Research, Development and Demonstration

The first cry of supporters of renewable energy - and most other energy sources - is for more government expenditure on Research, Development and Demonstration (RD&D).

The basic justification for RD&D expenditure in a market economy is simple enough. Companies work on too short a timescale to invest in long-term technology; they are unwilling to undertake the scale of investments and uncertainties involved; and they would often not be able to obtain the full returns on RD&D because the basic industrial processes cannot (and should not) be patented. A common theme of official assessments has been that the world is not technically equipped to limit carbon emissions.[31] The natural corollary is that the case for increased RD&D is strong.

---

[30] The author questioned elsewhere whether national biomass changes could be measured well enough to enable them to be included in any international system of carbon trade-offs (M.J.Grubb, *The Greenhouse Effect: Negotiating Targets*, Royal Institute of International Affairs, London, 1989). However, estimating carbon cumulation at specific monitored sites to an acceptable accuracy, for the purposes of domestic subsidies, is an entirely different matter, and would appear to be quite feasible.

[31] For example, a résumé of studies by the International Energy Agency concluded that 'in the long term, we will have to rely on new technology, not yet forecastable' ('Impact of Global Warming', *Petroleum Economist*, March 1990, pp.83-84). A major study by the US Oak Ridge National Laboratory concluded that 'Non-fossil energy

However, energy RD&D expenditure has a poor track record. Governments have devoted enormous resources to nuclear power, but in many countries the returns now seem likely to be far less than originally envisaged, and fusion and fast breeder reactor research may never bear useful fruit (see Volume II). President Carter's response to the 1979 oil price shock devoted large sums to the development of technologies for synthetic fuels from coal; it is now clear that these are unlikely to be of commercial interest without spectacular oil price rises, and furthermore synfuels have the dubious distinction of involving carbon emissions far higher even than direct use of coal. Even renewable energy expenditure has, some critics say, been wrongly focused and has yielded little; for example, wind energy programmes focused on very large machines, yet the successful commercial designs evolved from small-scale technologies under the influence of tax credits.

It is by definition impossible to ensure success from RD&D, but nevertheless this record seems a poor basis from which to recommend new programmes without establishing the nature of the problems.

There are inherent institutional problems in managing RD&D. One is that expenditure is most likely to go to projects backed by lobbies with political experience and influence, but these may not offer the best options. Another is that those with the best knowledge of a technology are usually those involved with the programme, who therefore have a vested interest in seeing that the RD&D programmes continue. It is also politically difficult to terminate programmes, which may be seen to involve the admission of mistakes.

All this points to the need for strong independent oversight of RD&D programmes, with a mandate to obtain all available details on the technology and assessments provided by those involved. Assessments also need to be grounded in some consistent framework, which has often been remarkably absent. Yet quite powerful techniques do exist, including probabilistic techniques for assessing pay-offs under a wide

---

sources individually and collectively are not yet ready to substitute massively for fossil fuels, and providing better technologies will require long lead times. Correcting this inadequacy will probably require an additional R&D investment of about $1bn per year.' (W.Fulkerson et al., *Energy Technology R&D: What Could Make a Difference?*, ORNL-6541/V1, May 1989).

range of possible future conditions.[32] Such techniques cannot give 'the answer', but they can at least encourage a broader approach to thinking about RD&D. A further option is to try and involve resources from private industry, even if only as minor partners, so long as it does not compromise the availability of the primary results; corporations are unlikely to stay with a project if they conclude that it really has no significant prospects.

Finally, because of the nature of the uncertainties in technology development, there has to be a degree of balance across a wide range of technical avenues. As Figure 5.3 makes clear, this has not been a feature of government energy RD&D, which has been dominated by support for nuclear power first, and fossil fuels second. With the caveats noted, the case for greatly increased expenditure on renewables and energy efficiency RD&D, together with a range of other technologies relevant to the greenhouse effect, is a powerful one.

Clearly, there is a strong case for managing large RD&D programmes internationally, to minimise duplication, and this could be one of the first areas of international agreements on the greenhouse effect. However, RD&D covers only the initial stages of bringing technologies to large-scale deployment. The later stages, which may also cost more and are less appropriate for international co-operation, also require consideration.

5.8 Supporting the deployment of new sources

The rationales for supporting the deployment of new energy sources are simple. New sources face many obstacles, including simple barriers of scale and more direct wielding of market power by established interests. As noted above, existing sources may themselves be heavily subsidised. Furthermore, although (as discussed in Chapter 3) there are strong reasons why taxes on polluting activities are a better way of reflecting environmental costs than subsidies to clean ones, so long as it remains politically impossible to impose a carbon tax of the level required to stimulate deployment of new technologies, more direct and specific support is an obvious surrogate.

---

[32] C.W.Hope, 'Assessing Renewable Energy Research and Development', *Energy* 7(4), Pergamon Press, 1982, pp.319-333; M.Grubb, 'The Potential for Wind Energy in Britain', *Energy Policy* 12(6), Butterworth, December 1988.

Two major forms of encouragement can be considered. One is to define *target levels* of deployment for specific technologies. The other is to offer *subsidies.*

Guaranteed deployment targets ensure that a market for a new technology exists and can thus ensure investment in it, almost irrespective of costs. This has both advantages and disadvantages: it can promote technologies which are seriously uneconomic, but does at least ensure that some attempt is made, and the total costs are limited by the size of the target. In some forms, the real costs involved may also remain obscure.

Deployment subsidies, unless very large, place a far greater emphasis on technologies which are nearly economic, and are thus less good at stimulating more speculative or risky technologies. They are less likely to shield 'white elephants', but if policies rely solely on moderate subsidies this may result in the technological equivalent of throwing out the baby with the bathwater. Also, paradoxically, the total costs of a subsidies programme may be more uncertain than with deployment targets; a very large response can result in a large payout.

Perhaps the best approach lies in a combination of the two, as, for example, used in Denmark and the Netherlands for promoting wind energy. A set of deployment targets sufficient to stimulate the development of a serious industry were set, and the governments specified utility sub-targets and also offered subsidies for private developments which were judged sufficient to ensure that the near-term targets were met. The costs of the programme, and the incentive to efficiency, remain clear, but the stimulus has still been strong enough to create new industries. Denmark is now established as the world's leading manufacturer of wind turbines, and domestic subsidies have been withdrawn on the grounds that the industry can now compete unaided, given the relatively strong winds and high electricity prices; in the Netherlands, with different conditions, they remain a necessary part of reaching the targets.

However, like RD&D, many programmes of subsidies and targets have less favourable outcomes. Often, similar factors are involved to those which make control of RD&D difficult. In countries with strong lobbying structures, subsidies tend to go to the industries which can lobby hardest, but which rarely correspond to the real needs. In addition, they tend to be easier to offer than to withdraw, leading to what might be termed the 'banana' problem, after the parallel drawn by Nordhaus with a youngster's grammatical difficulties: 'I know how to spell it but I don't know when to stop'.[33]

As for RD&D, there are no magical solutions to this, other than to define the reasons for support very clearly and to place greater emphasis on some form of independent oversight of deployment-incentive schemes. This problem as a whole reinforces the rationale for using macroeconomic measures - a carbon tax in the context of the greenhouse effect - as far as possible, in order to minimise justifications for wide-ranging subsidies for technologies vaguely related to the overall objective of limiting carbon emissions.

However, there remains an important respect in which government support may be required irrespective of the development of a technology and the scale of any carbon tax, namely funding for long-term and capital-intensive projects. Most non-fossil energy technologies are capital-intensive relative to fossil developments: expensive to build but cheap to run. As noted in Chapter 3, most private industry operates on timescales much shorter than can be justified for decisions affecting society overall, especially concerning an issue like the greenhouse effect. The problem of this 'payback gap' is endemic, but reaches extreme proportions in two cases.

One is the funding of capital-intensive goods in developing countries, of which many renewables are examples *par excellence*. The Indian case study notes this as a fundamental obstacle. Given the acute shortage of capital in most developing countries, it is plain that the vision of solving the greenhouse effect by fuelling development with renewables will remain a mirage unless capital is made specially available to install these sources in countries where the primary concern is with procuring enough energy for the next week, rather than for the next century. Since developing country governments are also often under intense pressure concerning the resources they have, they are hardly likely to promote technology with a ten-year payback when far less capital-intensive options - such as strip mining or oil imports - are available. Even if the economics appear favourable in the spreadsheet calculations of Western economists, nothing is likely to happen in the field without large-scale

---

[33] W.Nordhaus, 'The Energy Crisis and Macroeconomic Policy', *The Energy Journal*, 1(1) 1980.

foreign assistance. This issue extends beyond that of supply choices, and is taken further in Chapter 6, section 6.5.

The second issue in which the payback gap reaches extreme proportions concerns very long-term projects. Obvious examples include not only genuine infrastructure funding, but energy sources which are slow and expensive to build but which may run for decades at low cost. This provides the main rationale for government ownership or at least support for nuclear power, but an even more striking case is that of tidal power. For the UK, where large tidal schemes could produce perhaps 15% of current electricity generation, the country study notes:

> Politically the most difficult source is tidal power. No combination of fossil fuel taxes and incentives could make the largest schemes commercially attractive because the timescales are too long and the schemes too large. Yet the benefits, in terms of providing large volumes of low-cost, pollution-free power for many decades, could be very high. Treated as a long-term development of national infrastructure, the large tidal schemes would be hard to beat; as a commercial decision for short-term payback they are non-starters.

More traditional infrastructure funding raises similar issues, and these can again be tied to the greenhouse effect. Development of large-scale interconnection of power systems, perhaps based on superconducting technologies, would enable greater exploitation of non-fossil sources - nuclear power from countries able to develop it, renewables from regions rich in special reserves (eg. geothermal or hydro), or simply enable greater system diversity for exploiting the variable renewables of PV, wind, etc. International pipeline systems would also have to be extended to exploit the large gas resource areas, and perhaps later to form the basis for an international hydrogen market. However, because these are more familiar kinds of decisions, and concern facilitating exchange between large existing industries for whom the gain is obvious, developing such infrastructure is likely to pose far fewer political difficulties than many of the other policies discussed in this section.

5.9 Conclusions

The history of energy supply has been marked by a succession of dominant energy sources and the transitions between them: first wood, which gave way to the coal age, and then oil, the dominance of which arguably was stunted prematurely by the actions of OPEC in the 1970s.

Some have suggested that gas will be the foundation of the next energy age.

The discussion in this chapter lends some support to this view, but the picture is more complex. Given time, gas might well become the single largest energy source for a considerable period, and its development might well be hastened to help limit carbon emissions. But overall it seems that the hallmark of future energy supplies will be their diversity.

Whatever steps are taken, coal is bound to remain important in some countries. Oil, because it is so cheap to produce and because of its special markets, will also remain important on a global scale. Nuclear power is firmly established in some countries and may expand further, but it cannot now follow the path to being the long-term foundation of global energy which was once mapped out for it, and it may even contract. A variety of modernised renewable sources could emerge on the scene to fulfil various roles, on various timescales.

Renewable sources cannot provide a painless solution to the greenhouse effect: many factors constrain their possible contribution over the coming decades, and even in the long term their role is likely to be bounded for some sectors and some very densely populated countries, and they will also have environmental impacts. However, along with energy efficiency and natural gas, renewables may help to form a path out of the growing energy/environmental impasse, with a continuing major but not so dominant role for other fossil and nuclear sources.

The progress of all the sources, but especially the fledgling renewables, will depend heavily upon the policies adopted by governments towards the specific issues which different supply options raise, and the general issues underlying the overall development and exploitation of unconventional energy technologies. The future of energy supply is not predetermined, but it will depend strongly on the policies adopted by governments, and on how technologies and markets react to these and other changing conditions.

Carbon emissions from OECD countries have become increasingly dominated by two energy services: oil for transport, and electricity production for use in other sectors. Together these account for nearly 60% of OECD fossil carbon emissions, and the underlying demand for these energy services will continue to grow. Industrial demand, including its electricity consumption, remains important in the OECD, and industry is the largest single source of fossil carbon emissions from non-OECD countries, where expansion of all sectors seems inevitable.

Achieving goals of efficient further electrification with minimal carbon emissions will depend upon radical changes in the structure of the electricity industry, with the focus of utilities moving from production to co-ordination of inputs, and from supply to more general energy services including efficient end-uses. These changes could be driven by a range of pressures of which overall environmental concerns will be one. There could be similar implications for gas utilities, and the two will probably become more closely related. In the long run many energy industries may become more integrated energy service companies with different specialisations. These changes could themselves go a long way towards limiting the growth of electricity and gas, and the associated emissions, especially for domestic and service applications.

Transport is in a mess in many countries. The pressures of congestion, urban pollution, opposition to road building and various other factors mean that transport demands cannot be met by exclusive focus on the private car. Policies are beginning to change in ways which will tend to promote the evolution of more integrated systems including high speed trains and rapid urban transit, with private car use becoming reserved more for local, regional and suburban journeys. These policies and structural developments may simultaneously allow transport demands to be addressed with lower overall intensity of energy use, and they will also provide better opportunities for non-fossil fuelled vehicles, though these are still unlikely to become significant without explicit government involvement. The timescales for these changes will inevitably be long.

Industrial demand in the developed economies shows an important trend towards reduced use of materials, which has been a factor in declining industrial energy demand. There are grounds for believing that this is a long-term trend which, together with more recycling and other use of waste products, will constrain industrial demand. Despite this, long-term continuing reductions are unlikely, barring deeper changes in attitudes towards materials consumption.

Developing countries carry a much lesser burden of past inefficient and carbon-intensive infrastructure, and if in development they can 'tunnel through' to advanced technologies, policies and systems, this could radically change the outlook for global carbon emissions. In reality the prospects for this are extremely poor. Domestic policy changes could greatly improve energy efficiency, with economic benefit, but are politically and managerially extremely difficult because of the broader obstacles of poverty, supply shortages, and the lack of hard currency. External factors, notably, indebtedness and often the impact of foreign industrial interests, compound these difficulties. If these problems can be addressed, large efficiency improvements may be possible. Additional improvements, and large-scale use of non-fossil sources, would depend upon well managed and extensive international resource and technology transfers.

Introduction

Most of the literature on energy and the greenhouse effect concentrates on technical options for improving the efficiency of use and on alternative sources of energy. The previous chapters have examined the policy issues involved in these. Underlying these options are the questions of what drives growth in energy demand and the choice of energy services, whether or not these pressures might be altered, and how this affects the overall outlook.

These questions cannot be dodged. The way in which energy-dependent activities develop will determine the areas on which any abatement policies should focus, and the effort which might be involved in constraining demand. It will also determine the kind of targets which are feasible. If the underlying pressures are for continuing and rapid growth in energy demand even in developed economies, as many expect, even a stabilisation target for CO_2 emissions could be a very serious undertaking. If the pressures for growth are easing, substantive cuts become much more feasible. In aggregate, this is the question of how the 'S-curve' depicted in Chapter 2 develops, and this also helps to determine long-run possibilities for developing countries.

This chapter briefly examines trends and characteristics of energy end-uses, to identify the sectors which are likely to be of greatest importance over the coming decades. The potential developments in these sectors, and the options for affecting them, are then considered. The chapter concludes by examining some of the issues concerning energy development in developing countries.

6.1 Energy demand trends

Figure 6.1 shows the development of energy consumption in OECD countries over the decade 1979-88, broken down into different sectors, with the inputs to electricity also illustrated. Figure 6.2 shows similar information for the non-OECD world. These graphs illustrate many important features of energy demand, structure, and trends.

Total OECD consumption in 1988 was divided in three roughly equal parts between industry, transport, and other uses, the latter consisting mostly of domestic use and public and commercial services. The trends in these sectors and their implications vary greatly.

Aggregate energy consumption in OECD industry declined over the period 1979-88. A sharp fall in oil use in the four years following the

Figure 6.1 OECD final energy consumption trends, 1979-88

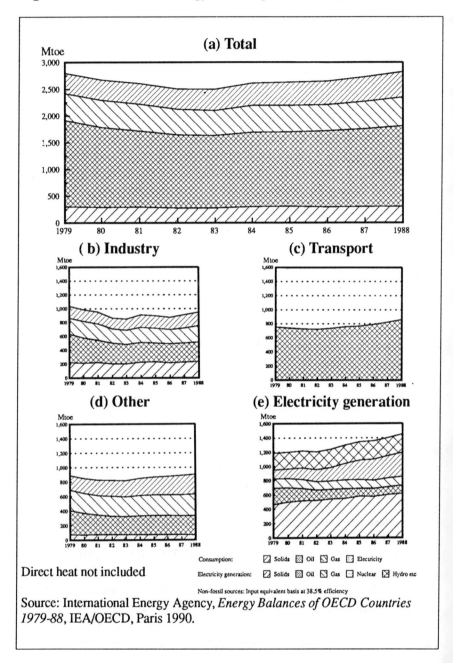

Direct heat not included

Consumption: Solids Oil Gas Electricity

Electricity generation: Solids Oil Gas Nuclear Hydro etc

Non-fossil sources: Input equivalent basis at 38.5% efficiency

Source: International Energy Agency, *Energy Balances of OECD Countries 1979-88*, IEA/OECD, Paris 1990.

Figure 6.2 Non-OECD final energy consumption trends, 1971-85

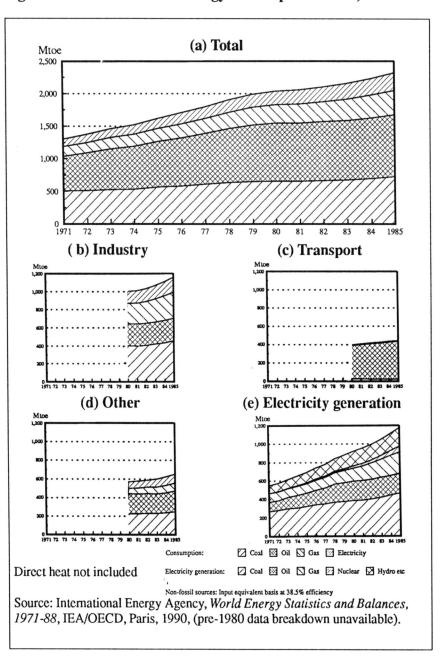

Direct heat not included

Non-fossil sources: Input equivalent basis at 38.5% efficiency

Source: International Energy Agency, *World Energy Statistics and Balances, 1971-88*, IEA/OECD, Paris, 1990, (pre-1980 data breakdown unavailable).

1979 price shock led to a 10% fall in direct carbon emissions[1] despite continuing GDP growth. However, the decline halted in 1983 and industrial demand and emissions started to increase again following the oil price collapse of 1986.

Energy use in OECD transport is dominated by roads (82% in 1988), with air (12.7%) also significant. Energy consumption in both was stable for the five years following 1979, but with improvements in efficiency ceasing after the mid-1980s, consumption has grown rapidly, especially in air transport, with an average 5%/yr increase since then. With transport demand being based almost entirely on oil, carbon emissions have followed total demand and in 1988 stood at 29% of the OECD total.

Other end-uses consist mostly of domestic consumption (58%) and general services (33%) - local government and public facilities, private financial services, etc. Though there are significant energy differences between these, they do share many characteristics. In both, consumption occurs almost entirely in buildings, where low-grade heating and cooling feature strongly. Other uses consist largely of electricity for information technologies and various appliances.

This, combined with the fact that people inhabit the same place as the energy-using equipment, has led to strong pressures to make energy in domestic and service sectors as convenient and pollution-free as possible, which in turn has led to the sectors being dominated by gas and electricity. As a result, *direct* carbon emissions from these sectors are relatively small (18% combined) and have declined steadily; the indirect contribution from the electricity used is almost as large, and is still growing.

Electricity is important in all sectors other than transport, and has continued to grow despite the overall decline in final consumption. Though its contribution to energy end-uses is fairly small (17%), the conversion losses in thermal power generation mean that it equates to about 30% of primary energy consumption, depending on the convention

---

[1] Carbon emissions are derived from OECD energy data using coefficients which are adjusted for the energy used in producing and delivering fossil fuels to end-uses. These differ from those used for estimating emissions from primary energy consumption (Volume II); (M.Grubb, 'On Coefficients for Determining Greenhouse Gas Emissions from Fossil Fuels', in OECD/IEA, *Energy Technologies for Reducing Emissions of Greenhouse Gases*, Seminar Proceedings, OECD, Paris, April 1989). In the figures cited, emissions from electricity production are considered separately.

used for counting non-fossil sources.[2] Electricity generation is now the major coal user in OECD countries, and largely because of this, despite the non-fossil input, power generation contributed 31% of 1988 OECD carbon emissions.

Overall consumption in the OECD over the decade 1979-88 was quite static. Total final consumption declined by about 10% in the four years following the 1979 oil price shock, and recovered to its former level by 1988. The decline occurred almost entirely in oil in non-premium industrial and domestic markets; growth focused mostly on electricity and transport.

These trends reflect the underlying shifts outlined in Chapter 2. Decline in industrial demand has followed from the often painful 'bulk to bytes' decline of heavy manufacturing. The rise of transport and consumption in services and domestic appliances follows the trends of 'production to pleasure'. The growth in electricity reflects both.

The situation and trends in non-OECD countries are very different. Obviously, the non-OECD category comprises a wide variety of countries. Despite this, they do share important features in terms of the structure of demand, and in aggregate the contrast with the OECD countries is striking. Direct carbon emissions from all end-use sectors grew at 4-5%/yr from 1971 to 1979; this increase fell to an average 2-3%/yr over 1980-85. Complete sectoral data are not available after 1985, but over 1986-9 there was a strong divergence between the countries of Eastern Europe and the Soviet Union, where primary energy consumption rose by about 1%/yr, and developing countries, where demand resumed a strong growth exceeding 5%/yr.

Non-OECD demand remains heavily dominated by industry, which in 1985 accounted directly for about a third of all non-OECD fossil carbon emissions; industry also consumes much of the electricity, which emits nearly another third. This reflects the basic needs of industrial development, producing materials for buildings, transport infrastructure, heavy machines, etc. Only a small fraction of the total population in this group are in countries where this process is well advanced.

Aggregate transport demand is small compared with the OECD but in terms of carbon emissions accounts for about 15% of the total. In many of the richer developing countries especially, private cars have been amongst the most visible fruits of development, and they are choking the

---

[2] See note 13 in Chapter 2.

cities as in many OECD countries. Yet in countries such as India and China and others which contain the bulk of the global population, with only one car per several hundred people, the potential for growth is immense.

Direct carbon emissions from domestic and general services account for about 17% of non-OECD fossil carbon emissions. In rural households especially, biomass energy is very important, but this is not included in the present study for reasons discussed in Chapters 1 and 2; moves away from biomass have contributed to the steady growth of fossil fuels in this sector.

Electrification remains one of the primary goals of, and tools for, development. Unlike fossil fuel in other sectors, electricity generation sustained its growth of around 5%/yr through the oil price shocks. Electricity accounts for about a third of non-OECD fossil carbon emissions, a slightly higher fraction than in OECD countries, but in end-use terms it is lower because of less efficient generation and distribution. Electrification is projected to require trillions of dollars over the next few decades, and at present much of the capacity is projected to be coal-powered stations. If this does occur it will be one of the major areas for growth in carbon emissions.

Of all these various components, the domestic and services sectors pose the fewest fundamental problems for limiting emissions in both industrialised and developing countries, and not only because direct emissions are relatively low. These are also the sectors where the 'efficiency gap' is most prominent. The technical opportunities for savings appear to be particularly large in these sectors, partly for this reason and also because the low-grade heating which dominates demand need not, intrinsically, take much energy. The UK case study in particular notes the large potential for reducing domestic heating demand.

The strong pressures for growth and heavy reliance on high-carbon fuels in electricity, transport and (especially in developing countries) industrial demand suggest that these all pose more deep-rooted problems for any attempts to reduce carbon emissions. Worldwide, each of the sectors *alone* already emits more CO_2 than the lower range of levels required to stabilise atmospheric concentrations, and all are growing rapidly.

Previous chapters have discussed the policy issues and options for improving efficiency and increasing the use of low-carbon and non-carbon fuels. How might such measures in practice interact with the trends in these sectors, and are there further, more sector-specific developments which might occur, and could be encouraged, to limit demand and encourage lower carbon emissions? The rest of this chapter examines these questions, focusing on each of the major energy services in turn. The sectorial analyses focus on the paths which OECD countries may be forging and the chapter concludes with a broader discussion of energy in developing countries, and whether they are likely to follow these paths.

6.2 Electricity and utility prospects

The future of electricity remains assured, but the organisation does not.[3]

It is some seventy years since Lenin wrote that 'Communism equals Soviet power plus the electrification of the whole country'.[4] Lenin may now be turning in his grave, but electricity remains in burgeoning health. Unlike other fuels, electricity has kept pace with economic growth in the OECD, and far outstripped it in most other areas of the world. Electrification in developing countries is one of the major goals of development, and one of the major consumers of capital. Is all this a cause for celebration or disquiet?

At the point of end-use, electricity is a very desirable fuel. It is clean, convenient, and efficient, and its growth in many applications has had as much to do with these attractions as with costs. And yet, in production, it is a major source of environmental impact. Whether it is the loss of land and forest from hydro plants, fear of radioactive contamination and accidents in nuclear power, or the acid and other emissions from coal-fired power stations, electricity generation has aroused some of the strongest environmental protests ever seen.

In addition, critics point to the large waste in thermal power generation, where typically two-thirds of the energy in the fuel is lost between input

---

[3] Mans Lohnroth, 'The Coming Reformation of the Electric Utility Industry', in T.B.Johanssen, B.Bodlund, and R.H.Williams (eds), *Electricity*, Lund University Press, Lund, Sweden, 1989.
[4] Report of the Eighth All-Russian Congress of Soviets on the Work of the Council of People's Commissars, 22 December 1920. *Oxford Dictionary of Quotations*, Oxford University Press, Oxford, 1979, p. 313.

and final use. Many commentators have highlighted the importance of 'matching input energy quality to end-use', and they have often concentrated their attacks on the failure of electricity to do this. Olivier,[5] for example, made the confinement of electricity to the estimated 7% or so 'premium' uses such as lighting and motors a central part of his low-energy strategy. Concern over the greenhouse effect has given renewed impetus to the view that electricity is an environmental 'bad'.

In sharp contrast, others sympathetic to the industry have argued that increasing electrification will reduce CO_2 emissions, because of its much greater efficiency in some applications. Examples include: vapour recompression and reverse osmosis techniques for drying, evaporation and distillation; some high temperature processes; and microwave heating for cooking and surface warming. The Electric Power Research Institute concluded that 'replacement of fossil fuel with efficient electrical technologies would result in net savings of [nearly 10Mtoe] by the year 2000 ... the energy use would be 46% less'.[6] Smith[7] has estimated that 'a 15% reduction in UK CO_2 levels could be achieved by setting realistic targets for conversion ... to electricity'.

There are several points to be made about this apparent contradiction. One is that it is impossible to generalise. The greater efficiency offered by electric technologies in some applications indisputably outweighs the losses in production. Conversely, electric space heating is usually no more efficient than gas, and hence involves several times greater carbon emissions when the production losses are included.

Secondly, a great deal hinges upon the assumed generation technology. For example, combined cycle gas turbines result in less than half the CO_2 emissions of thermal coal stations. Many of the optimistic claims for CO_2

[5] D. Olivier et al., *Energy Efficient Futures*, Earth Resources Research, London, 1983. For an advanced general discussion of energy 'quality' and the theoretical savings obtainable from matching input to output quality see F.M.J.A.Diepstraten and W.van Gool, 'Prospects for Carbon Dioxide Emission Reduction', *Climate and Energy; the feasibility of controlling CO2 emmisions*, Kluwer Academic Publishers, Dordrecht, The Netherlands, 1989.
[6] The savings are reported as 363 trillion Btu. Electric Power Research Institute, *Efficient Electricity Use: Estimates of Maximum Savings*, EPRI CU-6746, March 1990.
[7] J.C.Smith, 'Council enters green debate', *IEE News*, No.40, London, 1990 (Summary of unpublished conference presentation 'Energy and the Environment: the Role of Electricity').

savings from increased electricity use assume such generation. Yet in operation, marginal changes in electricity demand will usually be met from coal- or oil-plants, and probably fairly inefficient ones, so it is usually incorrect to estimate emissions on the basis of such new plants even if there are some on the system. On the other hand, if new units are built *only* to prevent potential supply shortfalls, it may be valid to use their characteristics in estimating the emissions from increased electricity use. Often it is impossible to assign specific generation to specific end-uses.

The third point is that this is not an issue which can realistically be resolved through desire or diktat. Trying to compare the end-use efficiency of hundreds of different processes with the possible marginal generation efficiencies, and then to decide which are to be encouraged or discouraged in a bid to limit carbon emissions, would be a task of hopeless complexity. It would also be largely pointless, unless followed up by highly controversial attempts to interfere directly with consumer choices of preferred fuel. A carbon tax, in contrast, would automatically penalise the processes which were less efficient overall in the combination of production and end-use losses.[8] Policies such as those discussed in previous chapters may well improve the efficiency of electricity uses, but they cannot easily be directed to affect the fuel choice.

A major exception to this is the use of electricity for low-grade heating.[9] This is rarely more efficient than gas and usually reflects various market failures including capital constraints, high consumer discount rates, and sometimes predatory pricing by the electricity industry. Apart from this, the question of whether electricity is an environmental 'good or bad' relative to other fuels is both meaningless, because of its aggregation, and irrelevant: the major option would seem to be simply to find out by using a carbon tax.

The trend towards electricity as societies get richer appears to be very deep-rooted. In all countries, its market share is still expanding, and it is

---

[8] In a comparison of industrial electricity trends and choices, Kahane concludes that 'One external factor has been generally important: the price of electricity relative to other fuels' (A.Kahane, 'Technological Change and Industrial Electricity Use - Towards Better Generalisations', in Johanssen et al., *Electricity*).

[9] For example space or water heating. The remarks do not necessarily apply to quartz linear heaters which heat surfaces rather than air.

far from clear whether external measures such as efficiency standards and a carbon tax will reverse this trend. As noted above, electricity generation is already a major contributor to carbon emissions. It is also the sector most amenable to changes in the input fuel used, though some of the options are highly controversial. Electricity and options for producing it seem assured of a central place in the greenhouse debate. However, while the future of the electricity industry is assured, the greenhouse effect and other environmental pressures may have radical implications for its structure.

Until very recently, electricity supply in almost all countries has been organised through utilities owning both grid and power stations and charged with the task of producing and transmitting electricity. This arose so that the development and operation of the system between production and transmission could be co-ordinated, and to take advantage of economies of scale in both the power stations themselves and in the centralisation of their operation.

However, in industrialised countries at least, the conditions have changed fundamentally. Systems are well developed, with adequate supply and transmission established. The technology of the steam turbine has been pushed to its limits and the maximum efficiencies of scale have been achieved, if not exceeded; the difficulties of building and operating very large plants reliably appear to have more than offset any further technical gains from scale. Technology has meanwhile progressed in the opposite direction: modern gas turbines and new means of generation from coal (such as fluidised beds and fuel cells) can exceed the performance of modern steam turbines at a fifth of the scale, while sophisticated information and control technologies open the possibility of operating systems efficiently in a decentralised manner.

In this melting pot, environmental pressures could serve as a catalyst of radical changes in the way the electricity business is organised. The discussions of the previous two chapters have pointed to at least four major factors which cannot be adequately addressed with the existing structures:

* Direct constraints on, or increased costs of, new centralised capacity, creating a direct incentive to take measures to limit the growth of peak demand

* More formal procedures of Least Cost Planning regulation which require direct utility involvement in comparing the costs of supply expansion with end-use efficiency improvements

* Combined heat and power, which depends almost entirely on the nature of utility organisation and regulation

* Renewable energy sources, which by their nature are often best developed and operated by non-utility interests.

Furthermore, the rise of natural gas and gas-using technologies has created a more serious competitor for the clean, convenient end-uses in which electricity once had a monopoly, again increasing pressures for greater involvement in end-uses.

Taken together, these various factors suggest two major changes in the structure of electricity utilities, as noted in a broad-ranging review by Lohnroth.[10] The first is a shift from utility *production* to *co-ordination* of different producers. This has occurred to a limited degree in several countries, with legislation to allow independent electricity production, often also setting terms on which utilities must buy independent power, as led by the US Public Utilities Regulation and Pricing Act of 1979. This process has been taken to an extreme with the privatisation and division of the industry in the UK. Although the form in which this has been done may well be far from optimal, so that many of the lessons learned are likely to be negative ones, the principle that electricity generation can and should be opened up to independent generators seems unstoppable, though the pace and detail of change may vary greatly between countries.

Once this has been effectively achieved, the way will be opened for greatly increased use of CHP and disaggregated renewable sources. Recent studies have suggested that this could even extend to the household level: advanced technology may make it possible to provide electricity economically from domestic gas boilers, while for renewables, one review suggests that 'development of the grid-connected photovoltaic roof market [in very sunny climates] will probably occur in the mid-1990s'.[11]

---

[10] Lohnroth, 'The Coming Reformation of the Electric Utility Industry'.
[11] David E.Carlson, 'Low Cost Power from Thin-Film Photovoltaics', in Johanssen et al., *Electricity*.

The main technical obstacle to such developments is the interface between small-scale sources and the electricity meter. Lonnroth notes that

Compared with the level of electrical sophistication in today's households, the electricity meter stands out as a relic of early 20th century technology. As a component in electricity control systems - and not only in financial flows - the potential of intelligent metering has barely been tapped.

The potential is enormous. Modern electronics can interface small power sources of varying output with a grid system at low costs, and register flows in either direction. Intelligent meters have also been demonstrated which can register the use of electricity within households on different circuits, transmitting the information back to the utility for billing, and receive signals for controlling interruptible appliances, such as refrigeration circuits, if the system needs the flexibility; lower tariffs can be offered in return. Such flexibility would also increase the capacity of systems to absorb economically larger inputs from variable renewable power sources.

Such developments would also be implicated in the second change, namely that from a *supply-oriented* industry to a systems-wide, *service-oriented* one. As pressures for balancing the costs of expanding supply against the costs of increasing end-use efficiency increase, 'efficient production and inefficient use will increasingly become an anomaly'.[12] In other words, utilities will be forced to behave increasingly as, or to accept as intermediaries, energy management companies involved in the choice of end-use technologies and, perhaps, their operation and development. Indeed commercial buildings, industries and some agricultural operations might increasingly become 'mini-utilities' with heat and power sources matched to the local requirements and/or resources available, and with sophisticated interfaces for selling to or buying from national utilities according to the conditions.

At the level of policy, such changes would depend respectively on legislation for liberalising access to utility systems, and on forms of 'Least Cost Planning'. Because the changes are so profound, and cut across existing interests, where such legislation has been attempted it has generally been strongly resisted by utilities - as with PURPA in the US,

[12] Lohnroth, 'The Coming Reformation of the Electric Utility Industry'.

and attempts to liberalise access in the process of UK privatisation. This is likely to be a continuing theme, but ultimately there is no reason why the structures which emerge should be less satisfactory or less profitable businesses.

Although this discussion is focused on electricity, similar although less profound changes could occur in gas utilities. The second shift - towards a broader service orientation rather than just supply - is already in some evidence, and could be driven by similar pressures. The first shift, from production to co-ordination, is much more limited and questionable for gas because gas sources are naturally very concentrated. But even here there are issues of 'common carriage' (use of gas pipelines by companies which do not own them) to be resolved, and increasing exploitation of gas from coal mines and a few miscellaneous sources might create pressures for broadening access to independent gas producers as well, though issues of gas quality would need careful attention.

The electricity and gas industries are already learning about each other because of the rise of gas turbines for power generation. At the point of end-use, electricity and gas may become increasingly intertwined for the reasons noted above - competition for the same markets, and gas-fired CHP. Indeed it is possible to envisage these industries divided along quite different lines, with companies emerging to manage overall energy services perhaps even at the household level, and interfacing with regional gas, electricity or even direct heat co-ordinating industries.

Looking further ahead, the emergence of a hydrogen economy would set the seal on these changes. With electrolysis and the fuel cell, hydrogen and electricity are almost interchangeable. Modern gas pipelines can be adapted for hydrogen transmission, if the pumps and valves are replaced, with about 70% of the throughput of natural gas.[13] Furthermore, successful application of the Utrecht/Williams process for hydrogen from coal (see Chapter 1) would bring the coal industry into the picture, even if production of methane from mines did not. To an even greater extent, the current clear divisions of energy industries by fuel could dissolve into broad-ranging energy service and co-ordination companies.

It is impossible to tell how far these changes might go, or where they will lead, in part because there has as yet been little incentive to develop

---

[13] R.H.Williams, 'Hydrogen from Coal with Gas and Oil Well Sequestering of the Recovered CO_2', Center for Energy and Environmental Studies, Princeton University, Princeton NJ, June 1990 (draft).

most of the technologies which could take advantage of the opportunities offered. However, it is clear that the implications for the efficiency of meeting electricity and heating requirements, especially in the domestic sector but also in many areas of industry, could be profound.

6.3 Transport prospects and policies

Despite all the criticisms levelled in some countries, and the likely changes to come, electricity remains one of the great success stories of the twentieth century. Some would say the same about transport, and rapid continuing growth in vehicle mileage seems a sign of this. But despite - or arguably because of - the extraordinary mobility afforded by the motor car and air transport, serious problems with transport are apparent in many countries, and they seem set to worsen. What are the pressures on future transport demands, and what implications might they have for transport emissions and possibilities for abatement?

As noted above, transport currently accounts for about 29% of carbon emissions in the OECD, and about 15% in the rest of the world. There is an apparently unbounded thirst for growth in both. In the UK, Department of Transport projections based on growing vehicle ownership and use suggest an increase of 85-130% in vehicle miles by 2025.[14] Projections in the United States, which has the highest level of car ownership and use in the world, nevertheless foresee a doubling of highway transport by 2020 (see US case study, Volume II). Many doubt whether such projections are realistic given existing congestion and travel times, but as one UK commentator noted 'we had a good laugh at the 1984 forecasts ... after a quick look at the current congestion we thought that people must eventually end their love affair with the car ... and were we wrong!'[15]

There must be limits but in terms of total mileage they do not seem to have been reached yet. If the road-building and aircraft focus of transport policies continues as in the past, a doubling of car use and perhaps a trebling of aircraft miles in the OECD over the next few decades cannot easily be ruled out. If based on current technology, this alone would more than offset any conceivable improvements in emissions from the utilities sector, and transport could rise to half of OECD carbon emissions. Is this

[14] Department of Transport, *Roads for Prosperity*, HMSO, London, 1989.
[15] Quoted in *Financial Times Energy Economist*, February 1990.

a realistic prospect, and is it likely that much can or will be done about it?

Undoubtedly there is an important role for technical improvements. In the United States in particular, new vehicles are much more efficient than the average on the road, and cars with efficiency double that of average new models have been demonstrated.[16] Aircraft efficiency could also be doubled, partly through the use of propfan engines.[17] Various alternative fuels to reduce emissions are technically possible, as discussed in Chapter 5.

However, in practice attempts to exploit the technical options for road transport, at least without much deeper changes in transport structures and/or attitudes, would be difficult. Improvements in car efficiency can have a much greater impact on the user than similar improvements in heating and many appliances and other processes.[18]

Significant improvements are certainly possible without sacrificing performance, but the penalties of large changes on performance and cost suggest that improvements sufficient to offset the projected growth in use would not be possible without radical and unpopular measures, which might well be politically impossible. Alternative fuels which could greatly reduce carbon emissions in open competition with oil-based cars for current uses also appear very unpromising, and certainly are some time away, for reasons discussed in Chapter 5.

Many other measures, such as application and enforcement of speed limits and computer traffic management, are possible. One modelling study, starting from official traffic projections, suggests that strong measures to introduce more efficient cars combined with various traffic management options might stabilise carbon emissions from cars in the UK, but road emissions including those from commercial vehicles would

---

16] A widely quoted example is that of the Volvo LCP 2000 (R.Mellde, 'Volvo LCP 2000 Light Component Project', Paper No. 850570, Society of Automobile Engineers, Warrendale, PA, 1986).

17] UK Department of Energy, *Background papers relevant to the 1986 Appraisal of UK Energy Research, Development and Demonstration*, ETSU-R-43, HMSO, London, 1987.

18] Very high efficiency cars tend to be smaller, with lower power and/or range, and they may be less safe in impact. Motor manufacturers in the US have successfully resisted attempts to raise standards for some years, partly by drawing on public fears concerning such implications.

still increase; and the large political difficulties even of this are acknowledged.[19]

Unlike electricity, the prospects for 'technical fixes' to reduce transport emissions seem therefore to be poor. However, transport displays a second important difference from electricity supply: transport policies are in a mess.

This does not seem apparent to all, particularly to many car owners who when roads are clear can enjoy a personal mobility undreamed of in earlier generations. However, the problem lies not with the individual car but with the totality of the transport system.

One area of concern is the overall health and environmental impacts of transport, which are startling. Road accidents kill on the order of 100,000 people annually in the OECD.[20] Many more receive serious injuries. Roads cut through old communities or through previously serene countryside, and together with airports occupy large tracts of land. OECD statistics suggest that 110 million people were seriously affected by road noise in 1985,[21] and aircraft add to this impact. Pollutants emitted from cars contribute to chest and other ailments; even the stress and lack of exercise arising from long journeys - in time if not in distance - is an identifiable health hazard. Cars contribute indirectly to oil spills at sea and on land, and the ozone formed from car exhausts contributes to crop and forest damage and - along with the CO_2 - to the greenhouse effect.

All this might be more acceptable if modern transport systems succeeded well in their basic aim of enabling people to enjoy greater mobility, but in fact even this seems highly debatable. Large and growing investments in roads have not prevented large and growing congestion; some argue that they have merely encouraged it. It is over fifteen years since Illich[22] calculated that in fact the average speed of travel in US cars, when all the time spent sitting in them and in earning the money to

[19] M.Fergusson and C.Holman, *Atmospheric Emissions from the Use of Transport in the United Kingdom. Volume 2: The Effect of Alternative Transport Policies*, WWF/Earth Resources Research, London, June 1990. The statement is derived from Figures 7.1 and 7.2 of the report, which the authors acknowledge include a fairly extreme uptake of very efficient vehicles.
[20] OECD, *Statistical Report on Road Accidents in 1987*, OECD, Paris, 1987.
[21] OECD, *Compendium of Environmental Data*, OECD, Paris, 1987, cites 110 million people as being subject to road noise above 65dB.
[22] I.Illich, *Tools for Conviviality*, Fontana, London, 1979 (reprint of 1973 edition).

buy and run them was taken into account, was no greater than a fast walk. Few would suggest that this situation has greatly improved.

Perhaps worse is the impact on those who do not or cannot own a car. A generation ago, teenagers, the elderly and the infirm could often enjoy their own independent mobility through widespread and cheap public transport. In countries now dominated by the private car, they must usually depend upon the help of others to get around, unless they are rich enough to rely on taxis.[23] And for many, car owners or not, short journeys for shopping or social purposes which would once have been a pleasant short walk or cycle ride have become a far from pleasant struggle across fast and noisy roads.

None of this suggests that cars are intrinsically a bad thing: the problems arise because of an imbalance in the whole process of transport development. Institutionally it is easy to see some reasons for this. As Button[24] notes,

Transport users who are responsible for adverse environmental impacts often form clearly identifiable groups, and it is relative easy for them to organize and lobby for their case. In contrast, those affected by environmental degradation are dispersed; some may not even be born yet.

The imbalance thus arises because many of the negative impacts of transport developments are not given adequate weight. The economists' solution is therefore simple in theory: the 'external' costs need to be included in transport pricing and assessments. Unfortunately, in practice this is far from simple, either technically or politically.

Various attempts have been made to tackle the problem of urban congestion (and pollution) by more direct measures. In the United States, efforts have focused on measures to make more efficient use of cars and road space, for example with legislation requiring firms to run 'ride sharing' schemes for employees, and taxis to accept more than one passenger if they are going in the same direction, and on road planning to increase the flow of traffic (see US case study). But these are attempts

---

[23] The DoT projections assume a 'saturation level' of 55% car ownership, which was widely criticised as being too high - a striking recognition that a significant fraction of the population could never become full members of the car economy, however far it extended.

[24] K.Button, 'Environmental Externalities and Transport Policy', *Oxford Review of Economic Policy*, 6(2), Templeton College, Oxford, Summer 1990.

to cope with the problems of excess rather than any deeper attempt to reflect external costs.

In many European cities there are tighter restrictions on the use of cars, including growing pedestrian areas, and increasing emphasis on providing bus and cycle lanes and urban public transport. These represent more serious attempts to get to grips with some of the urban impacts of motoring, and are perhaps the first hesitant steps towards real application of the principle of factoring in external costs. This principle has been known for decades, but in most countries it has had very little impact on policy. However, three factors seem to be combining in developed economies which might radically change this situation.

First, public attitudes appear to be changing, with steadily increasing concern about the negative impacts of modern transport indicated above.[25] Second, the march of technology has opened up major new opportunities for putting principle into practice, as outlined below. Third (as suggested by Goodwin[26]) there are signs of a consensus evolving among transport planners themselves, based around two broad principles: first, that there is no possibility of increasing road supply effectively to meet the forecast increases in traffic; and second, that transport policies need to be integrated, so that different options are compared on a similar basis. To these might be added a growing acceptance that the 'polluter pays principle' might apply in some form to transport.

The implications of these seemingly innocuous principles could be momentous. The first indicates that policies need to pay as much attention to demand management as to increasing road supply. As noted above, there have been various attempts at this, usually forced upon local government with some reluctance, but the issues of avoiding wastage, such as duplicated taxi and commuter journeys and discriminating between important and trivial journeys, are likely to assume ever increasing importance.

---

[25] For example, *The Observer* colour magazine in the UK ran a special edition on 'The Transport Crisis' which amounted to a broad-ranging attack highlighting all the negative aspects of the car economy, and suggesting that 'we cannot keep pretending that nothing is wrong. We must start the new decade with a new approach.' (*Observer*, London, 8 April 1990).

[26] P.B.Goodwin, 'Demographic Impacts, Social Consequences, and the Transport Debate', *Oxford Review of Economic Policy*, 6(2), Templeton College, Oxford, Summer 1990.

Second, it is apparent that different transport modes have never been treated equally. Public transport has 'unchallenged advantages in providing movement for large numbers of people with less use of scarce resources, including land-take, fuel and environmental costs',[27] yet it is widely expected to pursue financial targets, whereas roads are usually funded by governments and assessed using a cost-benefit framework which may be wholly inconsistent with the criteria used for public transport.[28] Furthermore, public transport often has declining average costs; adding a new user costs less than the average cost of the system. The principle of marginal cost pricing may suggest intrinsic economic grounds for subsidising public transport in such cases. On congested roads, the reverse may be true. Quite apart from this, the failure to reflect the various external impacts of car use (including congestion) in the price of private transport provides a *de facto* rationale for subsiding public transport, to prevent discrimination in favour of more harmful activities.

However, such subsidies are a 'second-best' solution, in part because there are always pressures to minimise the overall loss involved by reducing the scale or quality of the subsidised activity. Thus perhaps the most important implication concerns the more direct use of the price mechanism. Newbery[29] presents strong reasons for taking this as the preferred solution to congestion.

In fact it has always been an anomaly that, in many countries, funds for road building are raised through a tax on vehicle ownership rather than use; putting the tax on petrol, to reflect the actual use of vehicles, would make more sense. However, it has recently become more widely accepted - if rarely applied as yet - that a better solution to congestion problems is explicit road pricing, with levels varying according to how heavily different roads are used, in order to discourage use of crowded roads and to provide funds for new ones. Until recently this was barred by the relatively cumbersome nature of toll booths, but the advent of electronic systems for charging cars automatically for the use of roads is

---

[27] Ibid.

[28] S.Glaister, D.Starkie, D.Thompson, 'The Assessment: Economic Policy for Transport', *Oxford Review of Economic Policy* 6(2), Templeton College, Oxford, Summer 1990.

[29] D.M.Newbery, 'Pricing and Congestion: the Economic Principles Relevant to Pricing Roads', *Oxford Review of Economic Policy*, 6(2), Templeton College, Oxford, Summer 1990.

removing this constraint.[30] Newbery estimates that, in fact, urban road pricing adequate to control congestion in the UK is technically quite practical and that it would raise roughly as much as the current fixed 'road tax' on vehicle ownership.

If they did largely displace fixed vehicle charges, such measures would make *owning* cars much cheaper, but make urban car journeys much more expensive, so that users would be much more discriminating in their choice of whether, where and how to travel. Money raised could be split between road-building, other traffic management and urban transport; the overall costs of travel could go down while the quality improved. In addition to being more efficient this could also be more equitable, since those currently excluded by cost from the realm of private cars might be able to afford one, reserved for special journeys, while those excluded by youth, age, or disability would in the long run benefit from the impetus given to public transport.

Broadening pricing to include other external costs - the wide-ranging health and environmental impacts - could have similar qualitative impacts.[31] Many might be best expressed in road pricing, others in fuel taxes. By making concealed costs visible, both would tend to discourage driving, and promote public transport alternatives; the latter would also tend to promote improved efficiency and less polluting fuels, though, as indicated in Chapter 5, such charges might have to be very high to make the alternatives attractive for general-purpose driving, and even if they were, they would face large hurdles of infrastructure development.

How likely are such changes, how fast might they come in, and what impacts might they have? The first question is hard to answer. Transport reform could be one of the rare cases where almost 'everyone wins'. All would benefit from reduced congestion and better public transport. The shift from taxes on vehicle ownership to taxes on use would make cars cheaper, so motor manufacturers may not lose either. Non-car owners

[30] P.Hills and P.Blythe, 'Paying Your Way', *IEE Review*, London, November 1989.
[31] A major objection raised is that prices would have to be increased by a very large amount to have a great impact on driving habits or technology. However, the US case study notes that, despite intensive study, 'the long-term relationship between fuel price and fuel use in the US is not understood', and Button suggests that full environmental costs could be large in comparison with current driving costs, suggesting a several-fold increase in costs if they were fully internalised, which most accept would have a big impact on driving (Button, 'Environmental Externalities'). Needless to say this raises on a grand scale the political problems discussed in the text.

obviously would benefit, as would car owners with less than average mileage. The only adverse economic impacts would be on heavy drivers, especially in towns, and fuel companies.

Nevertheless, serious reforms could be extremely difficult, and not just because of industrial opposition. The most visible feature would be that car drivers would be paying for the use of roads which were previously free, and they and/or all taxpayers might be paying more to support apparently loss-making public transport (though if road prices were high, public transport could become more profitable). Increasing frustration with congestion and concern about environmental impacts might make changes possible, but progress is likely to be slow, and much will depend on public attitudes and understanding. The process is furthest advanced in the Netherlands, with quite radical measures planned in the National Environmental Policy Plan,[32] though pricing still plays a relatively small role. The examples may spread, but in many countries the political obstacles may be considerable. The experience of gasoline taxes in the United States, which remain very low despite almost universal recognition of the economic and environmental benefits which increases would bring, is a sobering indication of some political realities.

However, assuming that more sense does evolve in transport policy, how might this change the picture for transport and emission projections? In the short term, a move from vehicle to road pricing in combination with other measures to tackle congestion would help to improve traffic flow in towns and reduce wastage, but more people might own cars and outside towns the cost of using them might change little. Evidence suggests that prices would have to increase substantially to move many people to use current public transport, and in any case this shift would be limited by the fact that public transport too is often overcrowded at peak times; even a large increase in the use of existing public transport capacity might have little impact on overall vehicle mileage. In combination with more efficient vehicles, feasible pricing and other measures might conceivably keep transport fuel use constant, but even this is far from clear.

Nevertheless, as with other areas in energy, long-term responses could be much greater than short-term reactions. Steady increases in the costs of driving and in support for public transport would lead to major

[32] Ministry of Housing, Physical Planning and Environment, *National Environmental Policy Plan - to Choose or to Lose*, MHPPE, The Hague, 1989.

improvements in the speed and overall desirability of public transport, using technologies which are still on the drawing board or not yet thought of. The long-term effect could be not so much to price people out of petrol cars as to create conditions in which they could be attracted to other forms of transport.

National networks of hire cars, always available at airports, already exist; it would not take much to extend this practice to mainline train terminals. Again, information technology could greatly ease the practicalities.

Furthermore, there is an important link between the structure of the transport problem and the technologies available for alternatively fuelled vehicles (AFVs), especially electric cars but also those running on gas and hydrogen. The main difficultly with these is their more limited range and in some cases the lower top speed and longer refuelling/recharging times. Most AFVs could be quite suitable for local driving but are limited for longer trips. However, it is in the longer trips that high speed trains (and aircraft) already offer increasingly strong competition, with great scope for further improvements.

Thus, given the kinds of incentives and policies discussed in this section, it is not difficult to foresee a future transport infrastructure evolving around four overlapping tiers. Aircraft would naturally be used for the longest journeys, but high speed trains for most intercity travel, up to several hundred kilometres, would play an increasingly important role. Rapid urban transit systems, combined with walking and cycling facilities, would feature in larger towns and city centres. Cars, with widespread and efficient facilities for self-drive or taxi hire or in some cases transported on trains, would be reserved more for local and suburban driving, and would act as the lubrication for the whole system.

It is impossible to judge how far such measures might go, or on what timescales, but they are clearly to be measured in decades. However, many of the structural changes would tend to develop naturally from the kind of policies discussed and, combined with other forms of traffic management and more direct policies for improving vehicle efficiency, it seems quite conceivable that such developments could enable steadily increasing mobility without increases in carbon emissions, and perhaps with a slow decline even if petrol cars remained dominant.

Furthermore, if environmental concerns were a driving factor, reflected in high petrol prices and other incentives, it would be relatively easy to integrate AFVs into this structure. This is because cars would be used predominantly for shorter journeys, and because many would be owned by hire companies who could switch fuels more easily. Nevertheless, a strong government role would probably still be needed to introduce many alternative fuels because of the overlapping infrastructural issues noted in Chapter 5. Given time, however, success in this direction could lead to very large reductions in carbon emissions from the kind of journeys currently dominated by the private car.

This discussion has focused on private ground transport, which attracts the greatest attention and accounts for the greatest emissions. Goods transport by road is also expanding fast, and the options seem more limited than for private transport, because of the greater difficulty of journeys which shift from one transport mode to another. Non-fossil fuels other than some biomass-derived liquids are also more problematic because of the greater importance of high power and high density fuels to give a reasonable range and performance under heavy loads.

Aircraft use and emissions are growing faster (relatively) than road transport in the OECD. Shorter flights might well be displaced by the rise of efficient high speed train services, but there are no alternatives for intercontinental travel, though, as noted, there is scope for improving efficiency. Non-fossil fuels would be limited for the same reasons as with goods vehicles, though, again, some biofuels could be feasible.

However, at present the prime task is explore possibilities for transport which can cope with the demands made of it by private users, and to consider the possible implications and options for carbon emissions. Transport poses perhaps the most difficult problems of any sector for reducing carbon emissions, but in the long run they do not seem to be as insurmountable as many believe. Furthermore, reductions would not require draconian measures focused on carbon, which in fact seems likely to remain a comparatively minor issue in transport policy: most of the critical changes could arise as a natural consequence of coming to grips with the many problems facing transport today.

6.4 Industrial demand and dematerialisation

Industry is the backbone of economic development. Industrial activities both precede and underpin electricity and transport, and almost all other services used in modern society. In extracting, processing, and reforming materials to meet the demands of industrialised societies, industry consumes prodigious amounts of energy.

Figure 6.1 appears to suggest that industrial demand may be the least of concerns, as in the OECD it fell substantially following the oil price shocks. A review of manufacturing energy in seven OECD countries notes that, while industrial production rose by an average of 2%/yr over 1973-85, the average energy use fell by 2.1%/yr.[33] The Japanese case study charts an even more impressive record of industrial energy productivity, and notes further opportunities.

These trends cannot automatically be extrapolated. As the sector most responsive to price rises, industries exploited opportunities for savings which had previously been ignored, especially in the lighter industries which had largely neglected energy efficiency much in the way of domestic consumers. The decline in price reversed this trend.

More opportunities for savings exist, and improvements in industrial efficiency still offer important potential. In general, industrial markets are more responsive than domestic consumers to price signals, but barriers of information, and some other features of the 'efficiency gap' also apply to industry, especially for investments peripheral to the main business. Combinations of carbon taxes and information campaigns, with some other measured in special cases, could have a considerable impact.

But there are clear limits, especially in the raw materials sector which accounts for some 70% of manufacturing energy in the OECD-7.[34] Unlike the demands of domestic consumers for low-grade heating and cooling, many industrial processes require substantial energy for fundamental physical reasons - to extract and pulverise rocks and extract ores, to overcome physical and chemical bonds in concentrating and reforming materials, and to process them into the shapes and characteristics required.

This sets physical limits to how much energy can be saved by improving technical efficiency. Furthermore, for some processes, the physical limits are rising, as lower-grade ores have to be exploited, and

---

[33] R.B.Howarth, L.Schipper, R.A.Duerr, *Manufacturing Oil and Energy Use in Seven OECD Countries: A Review of Recent Trends*, Lawrence Berkeley Laboratory, LBL-27887, October 1989. The countries were the US, Japan, the UK, Germany, France, Sweden and Norway.
[34] Ibid.

in some cases pollution control adds to the energy requirements of processing effluents. Even without this, if industrial demand in developing countries follows the path of the industrialised, this alone would add greatly to global carbon emissions. Without recourse to the almost boundless technical improvements theoretically possible for much domestic and services demand, and the infrastructural limits which may eventually be forced upon transport, industrial demand is thus an area of crucial interest.

There are, however, reasons for believing that the pressures for increasing industrial demand are not as deep-rooted as this implies. A relatively modest factor lies in the overall shift from industry towards services in some developed economies.[35] A more important factor is the great range of energy and carbon intensities of industrial processes. Figure 6.3 shows the carbon intensity - emissions per unit of value added - for various industrial categories in the UK.[36] Metals top the league, resulting in over 3.5 tonnes of carbon per £1000 value added. The carbon intensities of mechanical and electrical engineering, vehicle manufacture and services are less than a tenth of this, while air transport, minerals, chemicals and other manufacturing (itself spanning a wide range) result in about 1 tonne per £1000.

This demonstrates that the energy demand for a given total industrial output depends heavily on the structure of that output, and consequently, that industrial energy and GNP may be only loosely related. Industrial demand can in principle be greatly reduced by shifts between industries, where possible. For example, if £100m of production shifts from metals to some of the possible modern replacement materials, carbon emissions might be reduced by up to 250,000 tonnes. Furthermore, industrial demand is quite concentrated: the US case study notes, that 65% of

---

[35] For an extensive study of this phenomenon as it has occurred in the UK, and its relationship with employment and trade, see R.E.Rowthorn and J.R.Wells, *De-industrialisation and Foreign Trade*, Cambridge University Press, Cambridge, 1987. There are clear limits to how far the shift towards services can go, and how much energy it can save.

[36] Similar graphs, of energy intensity versus manufacturing value added, are presented for the US, Sweden and Brazil in J.Goldemberg, T.B.Johanssen, A.K.Reddy, and R.H.Williams, *Energy for a Sustainable World*, World Resources Institute, Washington DC, September 1987, pp.45-7

Figure 6.3 Fossil carbon intensity in the UK economy by sector, 1987

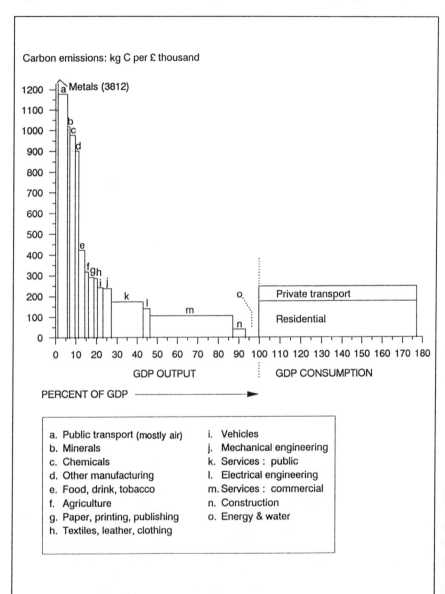

Source: G.Leach, *Cutting Carbon Dioxide Emissions from Poland and the United Kingdom*, Stockholm Environment Institute, Stockholm, 1990.

industrial demand arises from 8 energy-intensive industries,[37] and this is itself helpful because it means that conservation policies can affect large blocks of demand by concentrating on a limited number of industrial processes.

The scope for direct government intervention to bring about such shifts is extremely limited, partly because of the political difficulties of contracting heavy industries but more importantly because this would imply government interference with detailed technical decisions in industry concerning the relative merits of different materials. However, a carbon tax, apart from giving greater incentives to improve the efficiency of industrial processes, would also improve the position of less carbon-intensive materials. This might have a large long-run impact on industrial structure and demand. RD&D support in materials science might also take carbon intensity into account and so have an impact.

Such measures could make structural changes around the margins of development, but they could not reverse the energy implications of continuing underlying needs for ever more materials. The existing and future trends of materials consumption are therefore of great interest.

A study of the US experience of 1973-85 concluded that 'this [energy] decline was due almost equally to a shift of production from energy-intensive manufacture or materials to lighter industry and a reduction in sectoral energy intensity'.[38] The review by Howarth et al. cautioned about wide international variations in these trends[39] but acknowledged that overall 'structural change had a modest but measurable impact'. A global analysis concluded that 'The raw material economy has ... come uncoupled from the industrial economy, with tremendous implications for the industrial economy and social policy as

---

[37] In order of total use (in 1985): petroleum refining, chemicals, paper, steel, glass and stone, cement, transportation equipment, and aluminium.
[38] R.H.Williams, E.D.Larson, and M.H.Ross, 'Materials, Affluence, and Industrial Energy Use', *Annual Review of Energy* 12, Annual Reviews Inc, 1987. Another study estimated greater contributions from direct efficiency improvements but also noted the importance of structural changes (L.Schipper, personal communication).
[39] 'Structural change drove energy use down by 15% in the US; by 11 to 12% in West Germany and Japan; and by 5% in France. Almost no change occurred in Sweden and the UK, while structural change drove energy use sharply upwards in Norway.' (Howarth et al., *Manufacturing Oil and Energy Use in Seven OECD Countries*).

well as economic theory, in developed and developing countries alike'.[40]

The picture is clouded by the fact that the period in question followed major energy price shocks, and it could therefore reflect temporary adjustments rather than deeper changes. Also, some of the trends in OECD countries, certainly in the US, reflected some migration of heavy industry to developing countries, which is of little help with respect to global carbon emissions. The review by Williams and his colleagues therefore examines in more detail the long-term trends and pressures in materials markets.[41]

They identify four influences: improvements in efficiency of materials use; development and substitution of better materials; saturation of bulk markets; and shifts in consumer preferences at high incomes. Energy prices have an important influence on the first two in particular. Saturation of some bulk materials use is readily apparent: the authors noted that 'infrastructure building [railroads, factories, highways, etc.] accounted for a large part of economic activity in the 19th and early 20th centuries in the US. Today the demand for materials for infrastructure is confined mainly to replacement markets.' Finally, 'marginal income is being spent not on more of the same, but rather on a wide range of products characterised by a low ratio of material content to price' - for example, home entertainment, home computers, and various services.

The rise of electronics throughout the economy is a very significant factor; various 'new age' materials, which currently have a small market share, may also become increasingly important particularly if prices rise. As a result of all these factors, and compared with some specific market projections, the authors conclude:

> Our analysis indicates that this [the recent trend] marks the passing of the era of materials-intensive production and the beginning of a new era in which economic growth is dominated by high-technology products having low materials content.

This is perhaps an oversimplification; another review, for example,[42] notes various limits on 'dematerialisation' and gives some examples of

[40] P.F.Drucker, 'The Changed World Economy', *Foreign Affairs*, Spring 1986.
[41] Williams et al., 'Materials, Affluence and Industrial Energy Use'.
[42] R.Herman, S.A.Ardekani, and J.H.Asubel, 'Dematerialisation', in J.H.Asubel and H.E.Sladovich (eds), *Technology and Environment*, National Academy Press, Washington DC, 1989.

materials use which show no sign of saturation, if anything increasing with the pressures of the 'use and throw away' society. This may modify but does not invalidate the central trend. Rather, it points to another factor which may limit industrial energy demand, namely the existence of other wide-ranging pressures to limit waste.

Ayres,[43] drawing an analogy with natural metabolisms which tend to be very efficient in their use of materials, notes that 'the biosphere as it now exists is a very nearly perfect system for recycling materials. This was not the case when life began ... the industrial system today resembles the earliest stage of biological evolution.' Industry consumes prodigious amounts of raw materials stock and leaves wastes, and 'although residuals do not disappear from the real world of human health and environmental quality, they do tend to disappear from the market domain. Thus many environmental resources are underpriced and overused.'

This particular chicken is coming home to roost with a vengeance in the Eastern United States, where waste disposal is a major political issue, and the price is rising fast; contracts have even been signed for shipping wastes across to the UK for disposal in disused mines.[44] Some European countries, especially in Scandinavia, have always been sensitive to waste and have sought to promote efficient material use and recycling; other industrialised countries may have this forced on them.

There are at least two implications for energy. One way of reducing the volume of problems posed by waste is to burn the combustible components, which, as noted in Chapter 5 and some of the country studies, can be a significant source of energy. Second, waste can be reduced if materials are recycled where possible. In some cases recycling can use as much energy as production from virgin materials, but in others the savings are large. In perhaps the most carbon-intensive of all industrial processes, namely aluminium manufacture, recycling of cans reduces the unit energy consumption by a factor of twenty, and recycling of steel scrap takes less than half the energy of virgin ores. In the United States it has been estimated that a national programme of recycling based on current practice could save over 13Mtoe, over 2% of total industrial demand; with time, and more extensive programmes, larger savings

---

[43] R.U.Ayres, 'Industrial Metabolism', in ibid.
[44] *The Times*, London, 29 August 1989, p.8.

would be achieved.[45] In the past, even if incentives existed the role of recycling has been limited by continuing expansion in the demand for materials, but as this demand stabilises or even declines, recycling can assume a much more important role.

Yet again, existing pressures and trends seem to be pushing in a direction which will tend to limit growth in energy demand. In this case, unlike the broader structural trends, there are clear roles and opportunities for governments to assist the changes. Governments may or may not favour 'depletion taxes' to reflect the depletion of limited resources, but there is little disputing the fact that industries rarely pay in full for the costs of the wastes they generate either directly or indirectly.

Deposit-refund systems have proved effective ways of encouraging the return and recycling of some products. Government schemes and incentives for separating wastes into various categories and incentives for recycling or burning rather than dumping wastes (as well as extraction of the methane produced when organic wastes are dumped) all have an important role to play in reducing waste from industry and consumption, and, in so doing, helping to limit the use of fossil fuels.[46]

Finally, there is a more speculative factor which may limit industrial energy demand in developed economies. This concerns the broader goals and direction of economic development. Only the more radical 'Greens' have dared to question the holy grail of general economic growth as the prime objective of society. However, because of its potential importance in the debate about longer-term options and prospects it is worth clarifying what a broader change of attitudes and objectives might mean. There have been few attempts to study seriously the real meaning and implications of 'green economics.' One notable exception occurs in the book *De-industrialisation and Foreign Trade*,[47] which in its concluding chapter examines a number of energy-economic scenarios

---

[45] All data from the US case study. In addition to explicit recycling and public use of wastes for energy, use of waste products for energy by industries, most notably in paper and pulp but also in others, could make a substantial contribution. The same applies to a greater extent in some areas of agriculture, for example sugar, where use of the wastes for energy could result in sugar becoming the by-product of an energy-producing industry.

[46] Various schemes are reviewed in OECD, *Economic Instruments for Environmental Protection*, OECD, Paris, 1989.

[47] Rowthorn and Wells, *De-industrialisation and Foreign Trade*.

for the UK. The authors adopt a broadly conventional approach to assessing energy-economic interactions, and conclude that long-term GDP growth based on manufacturing output is not possible without a substantial increase in energy consumption and, ultimately, reliance on nuclear power. They also examine a Green scenario, where the emphasis is on reduced working hours, equity, and provision of non-material services, under which:[48]

> labour-saving technology would be introduced only gradually and would be used primarily to reduce working time rather than to increase real incomes. There would be some economic growth ... but additional output would be used mainly to help those who are currently poor and/or out of work ... the benefits come mainly in the form of reduced working time and improved public services.

> From a theoretical point of view the Green Scenario is perfectly feasible and has much to recommend it. It is certainly preferable to what has been happening in recent years [i.e. the collapse of UK manufacturing and unemployment during the early 1980s] ... it challenges the conventional wisdom that the only route to human happiness is through indefinite increase of material wealth. On any rational calculation the UK already has sufficient material wealth to enable all of its citizens to live in reasonable comfort. However this wealth is either maldistributed or is of a socially irrational kind ... although not rejecting growth entirely, the Green Scenario is just as concerned to remedy these defects as to increase the amount of wealth available. Many economists would consider this to be a defect. We consider it to be a virtue. Another advantage of this scenario is in the use of energy ... total energy requirements fall quite rapidly ...

> Having said this, we must admit that, given present attitudes and aspirations, the Green Scenario is politically impractical.

Despite the wave of environmental concerns there is little sign that 'green economics' of this nature is becoming much more acceptable at present, but such a shift in attitudes and aspirations in the developed countries, implying either a comprehensive redefinition of GDP growth or its abandonment as the primary goal, certainly cannot be ruled out in the long term.

---

[48] Ibid., p.313

6.5 Energy prospects in developing countries: what blocks the tunnel?

The previous sections suggest that the long-term pressures for growth in energy demand in developed economies may be much weaker than is often supposed, or at least that wide opportunities exist for further economic development without large increases.

Moving to less developed economies is to move to a different world. Even in the industrialised countries of Eastern Europe and the USSR, the desires to improve lifestyles and increase material consumption seem set to increase energy consumption for a long time, unless this is offset by painful contraction of existing industries. In newly industrialised countries, as well, enjoying and spreading the fruits of their heavily concentrated industrial success seems likely to generate pressures for increased demand. As for the poorer developing countries, in most of which commercial energy consumption per head is barely a tenth that in industrialised countries, everything at present points in the direction of energy demand growing as fast as supplies can meet it.

The immense potential for growth in these countries has been indicated briefly in Chapter 2. The following chapter attempts to put the pieces together in discussing global energy prospects. Before embarking on this, however, the crucial question which needs to be asked is whether developing countries must follow in the footsteps of the past carbon-intensive development of others, or whether they can largely avoid this by the use of advanced technologies combined with a move directly towards some of the advanced institutional and structural conditions sketched out in this chapter.

Technically the prospects seem bright. One of the major factors dampening developments towards lower carbon emissions in the OECD countries is the extent of carbon-intensive infrastructure, institutions, and habits, and the political implications of this. The vast majority of buildings reflect an age when energy was of no concern. Utilities have grown around large thermal power stations, fundamentally limited to less than 40% efficiency, usually sited well away from areas where the waste heat might be used, and usually powered by coal; gas turbines were thought to be highly inefficient machines running on expensive secondary fuels. Coal industries developed as the primary energy source; oil, gas, hydro and nuclear power came later. Industries still use processes and sometimes plant from the early decades of the century, and are loath to move away from things which work and are familiar, even if new processes could save energy and perhaps money as well.

Developing countries do not carry any of these handicaps, and this has led many people to argue that they should be able to 'tunnel through' to a Nirvana of high energy efficiency and reliance on gas and non-fossil sources. It is indeed true that this is technically quite possible,[49] and such developments could be by far the most important factor in limiting long-term global carbon emissions.

Unfortunately, this gargantuan technical and political fix, so convenient for the Western conscience, appears to be most improbable. The Chinese and Indian case studies display with brutal clarity the naiveté of such a vision. Energy efficiency, innovative institutional reforms, and unfamiliar, capital intensive and unestablished non-fossil sources are the last things on the agenda of most countries struggling to develop the infrastructure for providing food, shelter and other basic needs with reasonable quality and reliability.

A number of specific issues can be disentangled.[50] The first is that energy in many developing countries is dominated by supply companies to an even greater extent than elsewhere. This is partly because of the political implications of poverty: people have neither the time nor the inclination to worry about the environmental and other impacts of energy production when their concerns are focused on much more basic needs, and the main worry about energy is whether they can get enough of it. Even though greater efficiency would improve the situation, economies without sufficient energy supply create an environment in which supply industries reign. They *may* develop an interest in efficiency as a cheaper alternative to extending supplies, but this requires a very major shift in

---

[49]Some specific examples are summarised in G.H.Kats, 'Slowing global warming and sustaining development - The promise of energy efficiency', *Energy Policy*, Butterworth, January/February 1990. The author emphasises the contribution not only to reduced emissions, but to development itself.

[50] The report of the Brundtland Commission gives a broad analysis of the constraints upon developing countries, and the role of the international economy in these (World Commission on Environment and Development, *Our Common Future*, Oxford University Press, 1987, especially Chapter 3). For a fuller discussion of the technical potential for improving energy efficiency in developing countries, and the nature of some of the political and institutional obstacles to it, see J.Goldemberg, T.B.Johanssen, A.K.Reddy, R.H.Williams, *Energy for Development*, World Resources Institute, Washington DC, September 1987.

attitudes, and without a concurrent change in regulation it may well be against their interests to do so. None of this seems very likely. Industries which are attacked for not meeting demand are unlikely to win many friends by saying that demand should be reduced instead of building new supplies, and even if they do promote efficiency, there is no guarantee that this will much reduce the pressures on supply for the reasons sketched in Chapter 4, section 4.2.

Because of this situation, governments are often captive to the supply industries, or at least share the same focus on supply. Even where this is not the case, the difficulties of promoting energy efficiency are formidable. As noted in Chapter 3, grinding poverty may often not be a very good economic rationale for energy subsidies but it is an excellent political one, and this makes price reform very difficult. Similarly, Least Cost Planning may be fine in theory but it is unlikely that regulatory systems exist which could effectively police it, even if the managerial and analytic capabilities for gathering and processing the considerable data required, and then implementing the relevant incentive policies, were given sufficient priority - which again seems unlikely. Efficiency standards are much simpler, but even these might face managerial problems and might discriminate against domestic products in favour of those from richer countries.

Many measures would also soon run foul of the chronic shortage of capital available to industry in general and to domestic consumers in particular. Consumers who have saved for a year to buy their first refrigerator will not wait another six months to buy a more efficient one, even if the more efficient ones are available, which is unlikely, and they have information about and interest in the difference, which is still less likely.

Of course these difficulties can be exaggerated. There are success stories in energy efficiency programmes.[51] Various policy reforms should be possible, including pricing, given the political will and skill as discussed in Chapter 3. This could also extend to transport pricing, with petrol taxes, if not road pricing; the Indian case study lays particular emphasis on the need and possibilities for developing transport infrastructure more in the directions sketched out in section 6.3 of this volume.

---

[51] Kats, 'Slowing global warming'.

Also, most developing country governments can wield considerable capital, including large amounts spent on military equipment and large energy projects, such as coal mines, dams and in some cases nuclear developments, all on quite long time horizons. As elsewhere, the plea of poverty is relative, though it is more justified in developing countries than others. The way in which the limited resources are spent, however, often simply reflects many of the other factors noted above: various political pressures for focusing on large supply options, and managerial and institutional limitations on implementing policies which require more disaggregated approaches.

There is a widespread view that the key to more efficient development lies in technology and resource transfer. This is a gross simplification. Insulation, for homes or process heat, is not a high technology business. Replacing the filament bulbs used to light streets in some towns by sodium lamps would require far less capital than building a power station with output equivalent to the energy saved. Some kinds of energy efficiency require high technology, and are capital-intensive - but many are not. The key problem for improving efficiency is not one of resource shortage itself, but the overall social and political implications of poverty, inadequate supplies, and the short time frame created by capital shortage.

In principle, much can thus be achieved by domestic policy reforms. In practice this seems most unlikely, partly for the reasons sketched above, but also because external relations currently exacerbate many of the difficulties rather than easing them. The technologies for both energy production and use transferred to developing countries are often the dregs of foreign production rather than the cream, as companies seek to get the utmost from old production capacity, rather than directing new and more efficient products to countries which have lower expectations and can only afford the cheapest. More generally, the burden of debt worsens the scramble for capital, and the focus on supply. Supply investments can be justified by pointing to the fact that supply shortages would clearly reduce output and the country's ability to service debt; turning the money to improving efficiency may make more sense, but can be politically harder to justify domestically and to lenders. Also lending countries often provide supply technologies, and so have more interest in supporting this rather than domestic, less advanced technology.[52] The trappings of

---

[52] 'Generally, the elite put great emphasis on big projects .. as it happens, these interests coincide nicely with the interests of major international credit and aid agencies

debt, perhaps more than anything, help to block the tunnel to a high efficiency future.

The obstacles to basing energy development upon non-fossil sources are much simpler. Most are just too capital-intensive. The solar village is a beautiful concept, but it makes little sense if people who want energy today have to save for five years to afford the capital cost, even if the energy is almost free thereafter. In addition, it is more likely that non-fossil technologies will have been developed and perhaps manufactured abroad. Therefore, although institutional obstacles arising partly from the focus on supply may be much less for non-fossil sources than for efficiency - depending somewhat on their nature (ie whether centralised or decentralised) - resource and technology transfers would be much more important. There could also be difficulties with patents, as countries would not want to become dependent on foreign-controlled technology. Attempts to transfer renewable sources also have to face up to other realities, as argued by Foley:[53]

> It is sometimes argued that without extensive practical experience and a reasonable market for manufacturers, renewable technologies will never become technically and commercially viable. This is true. It does not mean that the villages of the Third World should be used as test-bed for the development of technologies which will primarily benefit manufacturers in the industrial world ... it is not acceptable that people should have their lives disrupted and expectations raised by projects which temporarily increase their standards of living but leave them with equipment which they can neither maintain nor replace.

International lending institutions, including the World Bank, have often focused on energy developments. The general implications of capital shortage, and other factors, do point to a central role for international aid, which will be crucial especially for developing non-fossil sources. But overall the nut of effective technology transfer, which might offer a realistic hope of 'tunnelling through' to an era of high efficiency, non-fossil based systems, has not yet been cracked. It is far from clear that the nutcrackers yet exist, in terms of the willingness of the rich

---

... aid money is spent primarily on technologies and consulting and engineering services from the aid-giving countries ... much of the aid ends up back in the industrialised countries.' (J.Goldemberg etal., *Energy for a Sustainable World*, p.101)

[53] G.Foley, *Electricity for Rural People*, Panos Institute, London, 1989.

countries to offer the scale of assistance implied, or the mechanisms for managing such transfers and using them effectively to alter the structure of development. Much has been learnt about how not to proceed with energy assistance,[54] and some clear successes have been achieved with the World Bank ESMAP[55] work, for example, but the conclusions drawn by Schumacher in another context still seem apposite: 'it was easy for the rich to help the rich .. it was possible for the poor to help the poor .. but for the rich to help the poor was very hard indeed'.[56]

Some observers, either recognising these difficulties or simply unwilling to countenance serious resource transfers, place their hopes in the assertion that the developing countries would in any case be forced to take a much more efficient track because their local environments could not stand the consequences of following the path of industrial development taken by the richer countries. For some of the most densely populated countries, primarily the Indian subcontinent and perhaps China because of its very uneven population distribution, this may be true, particularly concerning transport, though this does not exclude further major increases in carbon emissions.

For most developing countries these 'constraints' are simply wishful Western thinking. As indicated in Figure 2.4, the projected population densities even forty years ahead in the rest of Asia, Africa and Latin America are all considerably *below* those in much of Europe and in Japan, and it is far from clear why environmental constraints should prevent them from following the Western path. Certainly, there is no sign of such constraints on energy expansion as yet. The Chinese case study notes that city pollution from coal is a major problem, which may affect the way in which coal is used, but it will certainly not significantly impede coal's overall expansion.

If developing countries can develop along a path of high energy efficiency and predominantly non-fossil sources, it will undoubtedly be an immense contribution to limiting future carbon emissions; it could

---

[54] US Agency for International Development, *New Directions for AID Renewable Energy Activities*, Report No.88-01, Office of Energy, Bureau for Science and Technology, US AID, February 1988.

[55] Energy Sector Management and Assistance Programme, 'Greenhouse Gases and the Potential for Global Warming: Energy Options for the Developing World and ESMAP's Role', ESMAP, World Bank, Washington DC, November 1989.

[56] B.Wood, *Alias Papa: a Life of Fritz Schumacher*, Oxford University Press, Oxford, 1984, p.342.

also be of great direct benefit to the countries concerned. Yet achieving this may be a greater challenge than any of the possible changes in developed economies discussed in the earlier sections of this chapter.

*Long-term energy projections span a very wide range, from reductions
in global energy use to more than fivefold increases by the middle of the
next century. These reflect wide variations in assumptions, but also
differences in the methods used. The higher estimates tend to use broad
macroeconomic relationships between economic growth and energy,
while many of the low projections make explicit estimates of the energy
required for different purposes. The difference between the two to an
extent reflects the theoretical scope for economic energy savings, as well
as differing underlying assumptions.*

*Despite the shocks of the 1970s, the underlying trends are still clearly of
slow to moderate growth in many developed economies and rapid growth
elsewhere, with a continuing reliance on a mix of fossil fuels including
steady expansion of coal use. As a result, in the absence of abatement
policies, it is likely that global fossil carbon emissions will double over
the next thirty to forty years, and will have risen by a factor of three to
four by the middle of the next century.*

*Abatement policies could have a large impact on this prospect. Policies
to improve energy efficiency could begin to affect emissions very quickly,
and if sustained, their impact could accumulate throughout the next
century as technology and infrastructure adapt to these and other
pressures.*

*Accelerated use of gas could also have an important short-term impact,
sustained over several decades. Reforestation to absorb carbon could
act on similar timescales and, perhaps together with other absorption*

measures, might extend further as a significant contribution. Options for removing and disposing of carbon, if feasible, would come in more slowly and their long-term impact would be limited by constraints on disposal.

Non-fossil energy sources might expand more slowly initially, but their impact would continue to accumulate and accelerate, so that by the middle of the next century their contribution might be as large as all other options combined.

The combined effect of feasible abatement policies remains uncertain but, barring dramatic climatic shocks, a stabilisation of net global carbon emissions at current levels is probably the most that can be expected for many decades to come. The key factors which will determine whether or not carbon emissions can be controlled to this extent are neither technical nor economic. They concern, rather, whether the energy and political culture in key countries and regions can be changed, to allow the kinds of domestic policies and effective international assistance which could steadily reduce carbon emissions from the industrialised countries, and constrain their growth in developing ones.

Introduction

The previous chapters in this book have focused upon the options and issues raised by energy policies aimed at limiting carbon emissions, and how they may relate to underlying trends and pressures. In this chapter, these strands are brought together to consider more quantitatively the global prospects for carbon emissions, and the extent of impact which abatement policies might have on them. The final section reviews the main uncertainties, and the key factors which will determine how far the world is likely to go in approaching suggested targets for reducing carbon emissions.

7.1 Energy projections: a brief review

The breadth of energy projections is astonishing. Whether considered in terms of total energy demand, the costs and impact of energy savings, or energy prices, it seems that specialists can be found to support almost any view. Projections of global energy consumption for the year 2050, as illustrated in Figure 7.1, range from 5TW to well over 50TW,[1] compared with about 11.3TW (8000 Mtoe) in 1989. Lovins[2] claims that US consumption of oil and electricity can be reduced by 75%, saving trillions of dollars in the process, while Manne and Richels[3] estimate that merely constraining carbon emissions to 20% below 1990 levels (phased in by 2020) could cost the US trillions. Many assume that energy efficiency can be compared directly with the need for new supplies, while some maintain that this is false, because 'there is no evidence that using energy more efficiently reduces the demand for it'.[4] What is any observer to make of such diversity?

It is useful to start by briefly reviewing the recent history of debates over energy projections.[5] The late 1970s saw an extensive debate between advocates of 'hard' and 'soft' energy paths. The 'hard' path saw

[1] B.Keepin, 'Review of Global Energy Forecasts', The Beijer Institute, Stockholm, Royal Swedish Academy of Sciences, 1984.
[2] A.B.Lovins, 'End-use/Least-cost Investment Strategies', *14th Congress of the World Energy Conference*, Montreal, September 1989.
[3] A.S.Manne and R.G.Richels, 'CO$_2$ Emission Limits: An Economic Cost Analysis for the USA', *The Energy Journal*, April 1990. See Chapter 8, note 5.
[4] Len Brookes, 'The greenhouse effect: the fallacies in the energy efficiency solution', *Energy Policy*, March 1990. See discussion in section 4.2.
[5] For a fuller review of these and later debates, and their relation to external events, see W.Patterson, *The Energy Alternative*, Boxtree Press, UK, 1990.

Figure 7.1 A selection of primary energy projections

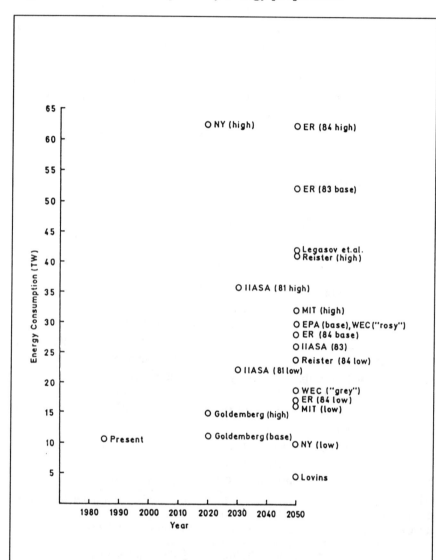

Source: B.Bolin, B.R.Döös, J.Jäger, R.A.Warrick (eds), *The Greenhouse Effect, Climatic Change and Ecosystems, SCOPE 29*, John Wiley & Sons, Chichester, UK, 1986.

increasing energy use as the cornerstone of economic and social development, and predicted a future with continuing exponential growth of demand which, in view of limited fossil resources and environmental constraints, could be met only by massive nuclear programmes founded on fast breeder reactors. The 'soft' proponents viewed this with horror, as not only dangerous but alien to real human needs, and advocated a path which stressed changing attitudes towards energy use and supply, with more humble lifestyles emphasising conservation and the use of local, natural resources.

There were substantial clashes of detail and numbers, as revealed by exchanges between the leading figures, Wolf Haefele, the project leader for the major study for the International Institute for Applied Systems Analysis, *Energy in a Finite World*,[6] (see box) and Amory Lovins, author of *Soft Energy Paths*.[7] Lovins accused Haefele of predicting absurdly low improvements in efficiency, and of 'choosing whatever costs he likes'.[8] Haefele retorted that 'one can pile optimistic assumptions about the performance of components and people on top of one another and eventually build a sky-high (but shaky) tower,' and emphasised the painstaking detail in the IIASA study.[9] But as a fascinating account of the clashes noted, 'the real differences between the two lie in the realm of social, moral and political assumptions, visions and values'.[10]

The high/low debate continues, but the 1980s have changed its character. Whatever the philosophy of the advocates, the 'me' decade showed no signs that people in developed economies would in practice move towards simpler and more humble lifestyles. Yet OECD energy demand remained almost constant, and it came to seem likely that

[6] J.Andere, W.Haefele, N.Nakicenovic, A.McDonald, *Energy in a Finite World*, Ballinger, Cambridge MA, 1981. Subsequent criticisms and some responses are summarised in B.W.Keepin and B.Wynne, 'The Roles of Modelling - What Can We Expect From Science? A Study of the IIASA World Energy Model', in T.Baumgartner and A.Midtthun (eds), *The Politics of Energy Forecasting*, Clarendon Press, Oxford, 1987.
[7] A.B.Lovins, *Soft Energy Paths: Towards A Durable Peace*, Penguin, Harmondsworth, 1977.
[8] A.B.Lovins, 'Expansio Ad Absurdum', *The Energy Journal* 2(4), 1981.
[9] W.Haefele, 'Energy in a Finite World - A Rebuttal', *The Energy Journal* 2(4), 1981.
[10] D.Meadows, 'A critique of the IIASA Energy Models', *The Energy Journal* 2(3), 1981.

Conventional energy futures: the *Energy in a Finite World* study

The IIASA study led by W.Haefele was the largest international assessment effort ever made of energy futures. End-use energy models with economic feedbacks were constructed to estimate future energy demand on the basis of future economic activity and growth, with the world divided into seven regions.

Two main scenarios were developed. In the high-energy scenario, world energy demand nearly quadrupled to 40TW by 2030; related studies extended this to above 50TW by 2050. In the low-energy scenario, which envisaged much faster improvements in energy efficiency consequent upon stronger conservation policies and lower economic growth, per capita energy demand in the developed countries increased very slowly, and global demand by 2030 was little more than doubled, to 22TW, reflecting continued very low per capita consumption in many developing countries. In both scenarios, large-scale nuclear power was judged an essential economic component of meeting energy requirements, though 'more than 50 years would be necessary to complete the transition towards a sustainable energy future'.

The 'objective, consistent modelling basis' of the IIASA study proved to be fallacious. Subsequent critiques (see note 6) demonstrated that the automatic feedbacks between different models were never achieved; in defence, the IIASA team placed increasing weight on the importance of 'craftsmanship and judgement' in determining inputs and in linking the outputs of the models. The supply model, like all optimising linear programmes, proved extremely sensitive to input cost assumptions, and with a different set of figures which appeared more credible in the later 1980s, the nuclear futures were replaced by coal. The specific numeric conclusions on supply were therefore almost worthless.

However, far less specific criticism has been levelled at the analysis of energy demand, which was unique in its scope and combination of approaches. The IIASA scenarios are often still taken as a reference, though there was little explicit discussion of conservation policies or their impacts. The summary book to emerge from the project, *Energy in a Finite World (Vol.1)*, remains in many respects one of great insight into some of the principal issues in world energy development.

advanced societies could neither accept nor manage vast centralised energy systems based on the plutonium economy - and that continuing discoveries of fossil and uranium reserves meant that there was no need for this either.

The terms of the debate have thus narrowed. The low-energy advocates talk less of lifestyle changes, and more of efficient technologies. The opposite camp has abandoned grandiose nuclear visions, and is more concerned with the 'realities of the energy market' and the 'need to recognise the contribution that nuclear can and does make.' Yet the gulf, in quantitative terms, remains very large.

A central question concerns the scale of the savings that might be achieved if current technology and practice were replaced by the most efficient options. This is the basis claimed for Lovins' estimate that cost-effective savings of 75% are possible in the United States. It must assume not only complete adoption of the most advanced technologies - including at least retrofitting insulation and other measures on all housing - but almost perfect performance and maintenance, together with cessation of wasteful behaviour (such as leaving doors and windows open). The more sober and thorough *Energy for a Sustainable World* study[11] (hereafter referred to as ESW - see box) estimated that OECD energy consumption might be halved over a 30-year period by full adoption of efficient technologies and practice. A detailed industry-based study of *electricity* options[12] (restricted to those 'readily available nationwide' rather than test or demonstration models) concluded that 'if by the year 2000 the entire stock of electrical end-use stock were to be replaced with the most efficient end-use technologies, the maximum savings could range from 24-44% of electricity consumption'.[13] The

---

[11] J.Goldemberg, T.B.Johanssen, A.K.Reddy, and R.H.Williams, *Energy for a Sustainable World*, World Resources Institute, Washington DC, September 1987; an extended version was published as a book of the same title by Wiley-Eastern, New Delhi, 1988.

[12] Electric Power Research Institute, *Efficient Electricity Use: Estimates of Maximum Savings*, EPRI CU-6746, March 1990.

[13] The study does not include cost-effectiveness constraints, but in practice this is unlikely to affect the results. Hardly any of the more efficient options already on the market are uneconomic in terms of life-cycle costs at supplier discount rates, let alone social ones.

Low-energy futures: The *Energy for a Sustainable World* study

The End-Use Global Energy Project (EUGEP) resulted in a global study of energy end-uses and the impact which efficient technologies could have on future energy demand. The report discusses the developments in energy demand technologies, their affect on costs and performance, and attempts to place them in the context of energy and economic trends in the developed and developing world. It discusses a number of broad themes for domestic policy and international action. The primary conclusions are:

> Building on detailed studies of the energy economies of the US, Sweden, India, and Brazil, the EUGEP global energy scenario for 2020 suggests a per capita energy use in the industrialised countries of about half [3.2kw/cap] what it was in 1980 ... In the developing world, an average of 1.3kw/cap (contrasted with the present average of 1.0kw/cap) supports a living standard up to that of Western Europe today ... Global energy use is only 10% higher than it is today.

> The EUGEP analysis is neither a projection nor a policy prescription. It is rather an illustration (a rather conservative one in that it employs only commercially available or near-commercial technologies) of what is technically possible.

In other words, a halving of energy use in the industrial countries, and the adoption of equally advanced technologies in the developing countries, almost offsets the impacts of world population and economic growth.

An Appendix to the study places this result in terms of macroeconomic variables. The base year is taken as 1972 (on the grounds that this is the last year in which the energy-economic system was in some equilibrium). The authors wisely refrain from making specific macroeconomic predictions, but note that for a range of broadly plausible coefficients, 'For industrialised countries ... our energy demand projection is consistent with a 50-100% increase in per capita GDP ... and 2020 energy prices 2 to 3 times the 1972 values', whilst with similar price increases in developing countries, per capita GDP growth rates could be as high or higher than those assumed in the major high-energy futures.

IEA has documented a wide range of sectoral studies showing economic potentials for saving 20-50% of current demand.[14]

What no-one disputes is that the technical potential is very large. Why, then, do most analysts conclude that energy demand must grow, and that constraining carbon emissions would be very expensive? One answer is that many such studies make no explicit attempt to model the potential for energy efficiency. They may include an allowance for improvements, usually expressed as a steady growth in energy productivity (GDP/energy ratio), but it is assumed that this cannot grow by more than 1-2%/yr (often less), while GDP is usually projected to increase at 2-3%/yr. So energy demand must grow.

It is immediately apparent that there is a deep gulf in the way different analysts think about energy. Some - often trained in the physical sciences - concentrate on the physical end-uses for energy, and potential savings. Others - often economists - consider energy as one of the factors involved in economic production, with aggregate use developing over time in response to economic circumstances. The two approaches often seem to lead to completely different conclusions.

Undoubtedly, political and social perspectives also affect both the choice of methodology and assumptions,[15] but alone cannot explain the deep differences in technical assessments. Some economists have argued that the differences arise because end-use analyses do not take economic reactions into account - in the extreme form, that direct intervention to increase energy efficiency does not in fact reduce demand, because it simply makes the energy services cheaper and hence stimulates demand for them. This claim was discussed briefly in Chapter 4, and more fully in the references contained in notes 7 and 8 of that chapter. The underlying arguments provide an explanation of why energy demand has in the past increased alongside static or improving technical efficiencies, but this does not imply that policy-driven measures cannot achieve reductions.

However, it remains clear that for economies to develop towards the goals of the efficiency enthusiasts would require radical changes in the energy-economic trends that have marked past development. The

[14] IEA, *Energy Conservation in IEA Countries*, IEA/OECD, Paris, 1987 (Tables 5 and 6).
[15] A point graphically illustrated by various case studies in Baumgartner and Midtthun, *The Politics of Energy Forecasting*, (see note 6).

coefficients which have characterised the relationship between energy and economic growth would have to take very different values from anything experienced before.

Few low-energy studies have attempted to consider the macroeconomic perspective, the main and notable exception being the ESW analysis, which argues that its end-use projections are consistent with plausible macroeconomic coefficients, while not denying that major changes would be required. Yet neither is it true that end-use analysis automatically leads to a 'low-energy future'. Indeed an end-use analysis formed part of the most famous high-energy projection of them all, the Haefele/IIASA study *Energy in a Finite World*. Like nearly all projections, it did allow for improved energy efficiency, both in terms of national energy productivity and in specific end-uses. The question is over how much efficiency improves, and the extent to which new uses of energy arise.

Surveying the expanse of the hard/soft, high/low, debate, two features seem to stand out. One is the extent of the divide between mainstream energy economists and industrial forecasters, on the one hand, and end-use oriented advocates of efficiency on the other. The former focus on the broad macroeconomic perspective and try to predict what will happen. The latter focus on the technical potential for efficiency, and what they think should happen. Only rarely do experts cross the divide. This is a pity, because both perspectives seem necessary in understanding the nature of the problem. Indeed, to an extent, by pointing to the likely implications of current trends and assuming no major changes in the way that energy develops, macroeconomic studies point in the broad direction of a 'business-as-usual' baseline. The end-use studies reveal the theoretical potential for energy savings, and a central question is how much of the potential can really be tapped.

The second feature is the extent to which the debate has focused upon projections, rather than policies. This is despite the fact that the main participants recognise the enormous uncertainties in making any energy projections, and maintain that the purpose of their analysis is to indicate appropriate policies. Various reasons can be advanced, but it remains a remarkable fact that with literally hundreds of scenario studies, some involving many years of effort, it is still hard to find serious quantified studies of the impact of the main policy instruments on either macroeconomic development or energy savings. It is because the analysis of policies for efficiency is such an infant science that it seems necessary to rely heavily on judgement rather than modelling results in drawing conclusions about possible energy futures. The first step is to clarify where overall energy developments in the absence of abatement policies are likely to lead carbon emissions.

7.2 Where leadeth the supertanker?

Those arguing for low-energy futures have taken great inspiration from the period 1973-86, when despite continuing economic growth (and in contrast to the expert predictions, which doggedly continued to predict rising demand), energy consumption throughout the OECD was more or less static despite limited conservation policies.

However, this need not indicate that OECD energy use has become saturated, and can now be pushed down. With almost no economic or political incentive towards efficiency before the price shock of 1973, large and easy savings were available. OECD demand fell immediately following the 1973 and 1979 price rises, and as prices stabilised, it began to rise again, and has done so rapidly following the price collapse in 1986. Also, despite improving efficiency in all sectors, the demand was only stabilised by the fall in industrial use, which offset growth in other sectors. As discussed in Chapter 6, section 6.4, there are grounds for thinking that industrial demand may be limited but such large and rapid savings seem unlikely in the future.

After 1986, the trend towards improving efficiency at the micro levels ceased, whilst in some OECD countries the underlying factors still driving demand up strengthened. Leading analysts concluded:[16]

The underlying factors that restrained energy use in the OECD have been shaken up. Present thinking about low [slowly increasing] demand in the year 2000 may be inaccurate.

The world in fact seems well back on course for the low to mid range of conventional long-term energy scenarios, and if the growth patterns of the late 1980s are sustained they could lead to some of the higher-energy scenarios.

The underlying reasons for this have been summarised in Chapter 2: continuing economic expansion in the industrialised countries, and

[16] L.Schipper and A.Ketoff, 'Energy Efficiency - the perils of a plateau', *Energy Policy*, December 1989.

primary industrialisation combined with population growth in the developing world.

The discussion in Chapter 6 argued that energy growth in developed economies might well be curtailed by natural evolutions in the structure of demand and supply infrastructure. For the most part, however, these arise as constraints on further expansion: as requirements for materials level off, transport adapts to the problems of excess, and services and domestic use become important enough to make utility changes in favour of greater efficiency worthwhile - and consumers become rich enough and environmentally sensitive enough to make all this probable. These factors do not preclude further slow growth even in these countries, with plateaus or declines at times of price rises followed by periods of more rapid growth when prices stabilise or fall.

The evidence at present is ambiguous. Despite the price falls of the 1980s, total energy demand has remained static in Western Europe, and indeed declined slightly in some of the 'greener' European countries towards the end of the decade. Yet demand grew quite rapidly in the US and Japan. Also, clearly, transitions such as those indicated are unlikely to impose themselves on developing countries for many decades.

Putting these factors together with the studies cited in the previous section, and many other reviews, suggests that world energy demand could easily double over the next three to four decades, and by the middle of the next century could well be three to five times the levels of the late 1980s. Furthermore, even a fivefold increase, with doubled population, would still imply a global average per capita consumption around the current levels of Japan and Western Europe today - half that of the US - so that especially if demand in developed economies did continue to grow this would still imply large global inequalities, with potential for further growth.

The outlook for supply is no more promising in terms of carbon emissions. Gas, oil and coal all seem set for global expansion. Fossil fuel price shocks would probably prevent the highest ranges of demand projections discussed above if the contributions from non-fossil sources were small. Some penetration of non-fossil sources is likely, but in the absence of policy measures to remove the barriers facing them they seem unlikely to start growing seriously until fossil fuel prices rise steeply; the inevitable delays in penetration, discussed further below, suggest that as a result their role up to 2030, perhaps even to 2050, could be marginal.

With a relative increase in natural gas, carbon emissions may lag behind the overall demand increase, but not by much, and a resurgence of coal following oil and then gas price rises could undo even this. The 'business-as-usual' outlook thus seems to be for a doubling of global fossil carbon emissions between 2020 and 2030, and a three or fourfold increase by the middle of the century. This is consistent with many other projections (eg. see Figure 7.1), and is somewhat lower than the reference case presented by the Intergovernmental Panel on Climate Change Energy and Industries Subgroup,[17] which projected a doubling before 2020.

How can such futures be justified when so many opportunities for cost-effective improvements in efficiency have been identified? As the review of recent energy trends cited above[18] continued:

What about all the least cost studies that reveal an enormous potential for saving energy? These studies show that the potential is still there, even at present [1989] prices. But the necessary investments are not likely to be made in the coming years.

So we come back to the 'efficiency gap', and other opportunities for reducing emissions - and the critical questions of how rapidly and how fully these might be exploited by feasible policy measures, if desired.

7.3 Energy efficiency: how fast, how far?

Chapter 3 discussed energy prices and carbon taxes as an instrument for reducing carbon emissions, and Chapter 4 examined the various policy instruments available for trying to narrow the 'efficiency gap' which prevents uptake of many cost-effective options for improving efficiency. Both concluded that such measures were most unlikely to have adverse general economic impacts unless applied very heavily; rather, the key questions concerned the extent to which they might be applied and the impact on energy which they would have.

No-one really knows how much impact the policy measures discussed might have, because no country has ever tried to apply the full range of available instruments - taxes, information, standards, fiscal incentives, Least Cost Planning, and various other measures, starting with the

---

17] 'Report of the Intergovernmental Panel on Climate Change Response Strategies Working Group' ('Working Group III Policymakers Summary', unpublished.).
18] Schipper and Ketoff, *'Energy Efficiency'*.

removal of existing incentives to over-use energy. The evidence of the piecemeal efforts to date is sobering. Least Cost Planning has certainly helped to constrain demand in the US utilities that have practised it, but overall electricity use has still grown rapidly. The intensive efforts in Japan from 1973 to 1986, focused primarily on the industrial sector but also going broader, held demand almost constant despite strong economic growth (the ratio of energy to GNP declined by an average 2.7%/yr), but did not reduce it, and demand has leapt since the oil price fall (Japanese case study). Denmark, with some of the most advanced energy conservation policies including broad and successful promotion of CHP, held demand constant to 1988; there was a dramatic but uncharacteristic fall in 1989, and government forecasts project a slow increase despite continued emphasis on conservation policies.

Given time and a more concerted mix of policies, it is not unreasonable to suppose that the majority - perhaps 60-80% - of the cost-effective technical measures will be taken up. To judge from earlier discussions and the most stringent country study scenarios (see Chapter 2) this might enable reductions of around 25-40% in the energy required to meet current uses, perhaps up to 50% with a high carbon tax, in developed economies - still based on current technology, and roughly equivalent to the ESW scenario.

The speed with which this might occur would depend on the policies used, but there are clear limits. The rate of efficiency improvement is usually expressed through the ratio of energy to GNP (E/GNP), but this may not be very helpful in this context. When economies are growing fast, new stock is coming in, which is often more efficient and is certainly more easily affected by policy. Applying maximum rates of E/GNP reductions to periods of lower economic growth may thus give a very misleading impression of what might be achieved. When considering actual reductions it seems more helpful to focus on constraints on absolute changes.

Modelling studies of housing stock turnover for the UK case study suggest that reductions of just over 1%/yr (down from a more or less static baseline) might be expected from a broad-ranging package of standards at least over the next decade. Modelling of strenuous vehicle efficiency standards suggested a 1-1.5%/yr improvement in efficiency, but compared with a baseline of similar growth resulted roughly in a stabilisation of road emissions, turning into a decline of up to about 1%/yr when other measures were included (see Chapter 6, note 19). Industrial demand in the UK declined more steeply in the early 1980s, due partly to real economic contraction; the possible rate of energy reductions in more prosperous times remains obscure, but some stock is long-lived.

The present author has not seen other studies which model the impact of specific policies over time, though some must exist, but the broad message seems to be that reducing energy demand by more than about 1%/yr on average through technical measures would be extremely difficult because of limitations of stock turnover. Deliberate price shocks (as opposed to more gradual increases) or other measures to affect behaviour could obtain faster responses but would not be politically sustainable.

This suggests that the ESW (2020) scenario for developed economies, even if ultimately feasible, maybe premature despite the 30-year timescale. Nevertheless, combining the technical assessments with the review of possible underlying developments in Chapter 6 does suggest that in many developed economies, long-term steady reductions in energy demand, perhaps up to 1%/yr sustained for several decades, might be feasible. This would not be easy in any of the countries, but given a sufficient level of concern, concerted actions do seem possible in most OECD countries. To judge from the country studies, by far the most difficult would appear to be the United States, despite the fact that it is starting from the highest level.

There are two jokers in this particular pack, apart from the political issues, and they point in opposite directions. The first concerns the potential for genuinely new technologies. As noted in Chapter 1, section 1.7, the theoretical potential for energy efficiency, on the basis of thermodynamics, is much larger than any of the figures discussed above suggest. Policies which create a more favourable environment for efficiency would help to stimulate new technical developments, which might present opportunities which are not foreseeable.

The second joker is the pressure of new demands, rather than the efficiency of meeting existing ones, and the impact of increasingly profligate and wasteful attitudes to energy as consumers become richer. It seems clear that the underlying causes of growth in energy demand in developed economies are shifting 'from production towards pleasure'. It is less clear whether this makes them more or less amenable to limitation. Ultimately, after the technical options have been pursued as far as possible, the long-term future of energy demand lies in the behaviour and desires of increasingly wealthy individuals, and in the very meaning and constituents of 'economic growth', as touched upon in Chapter 6.

Turning to other countries, it seems harder still to disentangle the technical issues from the political and institutional ones. The situation in the Soviet Union and Eastern Europe is obviously fluid at the turn of the decade. The Soviet case study argues that, despite this, reduced energy consumption is most implausible even under quite strong pressures. Only substantial industrial contraction could alter this conclusion, but it is far from clear whether such analysis necessarily applies to the Eastern European countries also, where the hurdles arising from size and institutions developed around indigenous resources are much less, and the political and economic changes currently appear to be faster and deeper. For many of them a convergence towards the patterns of Western Europe, implying significant reductions for some, seems more possible.

In some of the rapidly developing countries which have by now largely established an industrial base, per capita demand is fast approaching the levels of Japan and Western Europe, and for them much will depend on how the rest of the infrastructure expands. This may be strongly affected by government policy. However, on a global level this is a relatively small issue compared with the great potential for further growth in the poorer developing countries.

The broad factors influencing the outlook for abatement policies in these countries have been outlined in Chapter 6, section 6.5. As discussed there, technically a trajectory of very high efficiency should be possible but in practice it seems impossible. The discussion, together with the Chinese and Indian case studies, suggests that feasible improvements might include price reform and a modest change in the focus of energy developments to include more emphasis on efficiency, if external pressures alter. This might lead to a path somewhere between the very high energy growth implied by attempts to follow in the tracks of the industrialised countries, and the more modest increases implied by visions of 'tunnelling through' to an era of very high efficiency. In particular, if the higher rates of economic growth could be based on efficient technologies, in both demand and supply, this could bring down the very high energy growth rates in much of Asia at present. Overall the effect might be to bring down growth rates from the currently typical

4-7%/yr to levels of 3-4%/yr, perhaps declining closer to 2%/yr after a few decades. Because the starting point for many of these countries is so low, the end point of this process remains obscure.

This in fact is not so different from the developing country scenarios of either the IIASA or the ESW studies, though the underlying assumptions about how it might be achieved differ widely from the IIASA work. The larger differences concern the implications of 'low' scenarios for industrialised countries.

The aggregate effects of these savings are illustrated in Figure 7.2, which is presented after discussing the other components of trying to limit net fossil carbon emissions - supply changes and measures for absorbing carbon dioxide.

7.4 Decoupling carbon from energy

Whatever perspective is taken on these and other energy issues, global demand seems likely to continue increasing for the foreseeable future. This reinforces the message that, however optimistic a stand is taken on energy efficiency (and population growth), long-term reductions in global emissions of fossil carbon are not possible for as long as the world runs on a predominantly hydrocarbon economy, barring fundamental breakthroughs in options for disposing of CO_2.

Technically, it is already clear that the world could run on non-fossil sources, through nuclear technologies and/or a range of renewables with photovoltaics as the centrepiece, and with hydrogen as the carrier for non-electricity uses. Politically and economically, however, this is not possible at present.

It has been observed that, in the past, global transitions between different energy sources have taken about fifty years.[19] Without a clear rationale of this timescale it is difficult to know if it will apply in the future, or how much it might be changed by policy. But clearly there are major reasons, relating to the requirement for large and concurrent investments in the infrastructure of production, delivery, and use, why it is always a slow process.

Partly on these grounds, the authors of the IIASA study *Energy in a Finite World* concluded that, to their surprise, 'the possibility of a

[19] C.Marchetti and N.Nakicenovic, *The Dynamics of Energy Systems and the Logistic Substitution Model*, International Institute for Applied Systems Analysis report RR-79-13, Laxenburg, Austria, 1979.

Figure 7.2 Global carbon emissions and the impact of abatement measures: illustrative scenarios

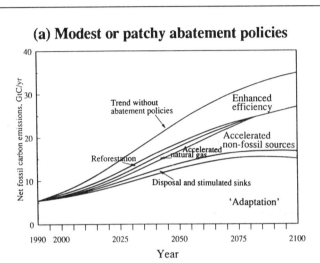

(a) Modest or patchy abatement policies

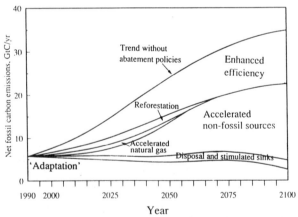

(b) Concerted and widespread abatement policies

'Net fossil carbon emissions' is here defined as carbon emissions from fossil fuels minus the carbon extracted by deliberate measures to remove carbon in addition to that absorbed by natural processes.

The shading indicates the emission levels which could stabilise atmospheric concentrations if net deforestation is halted.

sustainable global energy system is at least fifty years away'. This difficulty was compounded by the problems their leading 'sustainable' supply option - fast breeder reactors - faced in chasing a rapidly expanding demand. But, on the other hand, the transition envisaged - from relying on centralised fossil energy sources to relying on centralised nuclear sources - was in many respects a relatively simple one.

The transitions required to approach more plausible forms of sustainable systems are likely to be of a far deeper nature than simply replacing one centralised technology by another. They include major restructuring of energy industries to promote increased efficiency (including CHP) and inputs from dispersed renewable energy sources; far-reaching changes in both attitudes to and the infrastructure of transport; and various other developments as noted. These would involve changes in deep-rooted economic and political perceptions and processes.

Furthermore, as discussed in Chapter 5, nuclear power seems to have stalled and, despite some successes, most modernised renewable sources are as yet hardly into the earliest stages of deployment, with the potentially most important ones still requiring further technical developments. The deployment of many could only follow on the kind of institutional and infrastructural developments sketched out above. Progress in the industrialised countries could be further impeded by the fact that, if efficiency policies did succeed in reducing demand, there might not be a need for new supply at all in some countries. Displacing existing and well functioning fossil fuel supplies and generating capacity by non-fossil sources, would clearly raise far greater political difficulties than simply installing them as and when capacity was required.

For these reasons, again, the arena in which non-fossil sources could make the greatest impact over the coming decades would be in the developing countries. However, as outlined in Chapter 6, section 6.5, substantial resource and technology transfers, probably combined with some degree of deployment in industrialised countries to establish a manufacturing base, viability and confidence, would be quite essential in achieving this vision - far more so than for efficiency developments.

There is little doubt that the long-term potential for non-fossil energy is immense. It is equally apparent that the policies adopted by governments in the industrialised countries concerning R&D, the removal of existing obstacles and further encouragement in domestic markets, and the provision of capital to support their deployment in developing countries, will be crucial in determining their actual development. With such policies, some renewables could move fast - especially the modernised biomass technologies which could rise on the back of existing capital and interests and potentially resolve existing dilemmas concerning excess agricultural land. Overall progress of non-fossil sources may still be quite slow but over the course of several decades they could mature towards being the major energy sources for the second half of the twenty-first century. Without such policies, that prospect could be delayed by many decades.

Even with supportive policies, the simple combination of efficiency and non-fossil energy sources leaves a gap in the first half of the next century where carbon emissions would be destined to rise. There are, however, many interim options. One is to accelerate the progress of natural gas. As discussed in Chapter 5, section 5.2, this could occur quite rapidly, though market reactions would limit the extent and duration after a few decades.

It is also on this timescale that some options to absorb or otherwise remove carbon from the system could be of most importance. Tree planting programmes could be developed fairly quickly, and overall peak absorption might be maintained for a couple of decades. Thereafter, carbon absorption would decline back to zero if no new areas were found, the trees were allowed to mature and the cut trees allowed to decay. If, on the other hand, the trees were replaced when mature and the wood effectively stored, net absorption would continue at much the same pace; using the wood to displace fossil fuels, if well managed, might have a net effect almost as large. The practical scope for such an afforestation programme is a matter of conjecture, but as discussed in Chapter 1 it seems improbable that, even with a global effort, absorbing more than about 1GtC/yr would be feasible.

Other possibilities for removing carbon from the system were also noted in Chapter 1. Ocean stimulation might make a small but continuing impact; the impact of artificial plant stimulation on land, to increase biomass and transfer carbon to soils, would be of a similar form, and perhaps larger. Currently it is not known if either option is really feasible; the impact, if any, might therefore be slow as better organisms and methods were developed. For reasons discussed in Chapter 1 the total impact is unlikely to be much compared with those of broader land-use changes and the natural land uptake arising from increased CO_2 levels. An opposite pattern might emerge from attempts to remove carbon from coal. If strong measures for reducing CO_2 emissions are required, intensive R&D by the coal industry into these possibilities might follow. If this did result in successful application of the Utrecht/Williams or similar processes, this might spread rapidly to coal-fired power stations near suitable CO_2 disposal sites. This could be locally of great importance to some industries, but probably a rather small percentage overall. As these sites filled up - at very variable rates, but on a span of years to decades - this contribution would decline. A few stations might be located in conditions suitable for deep injection into ocean downcurrents. The apparent limits on this and other disposal options have been discussed in Chapter 1.

7.5 Putting the pieces together

There are many components to the jigsaw of limiting the growth of atmospheric CO_2, and they can operate on many different timescales. Waste can be reduced over very short periods. Developing and implementing policies to get more efficient available technologies into markets may take a few years, and the technologies will penetrate over a decade or two, or longer in the case of new building designs and some industrial processes. Further development of efficient technologies may follow these trends.

Accelerating the penetration of natural gas can operate on a similar timescale, as can efforts to limit deforestation and promote reforestation to absorb carbon. These measures, coming in over the next decade or two, can extend for several decades but are ultimately limited. Efforts to develop and deploy techniques for removing and disposing of carbon from fossil fuel use, and/or for stimulating the re-absorption of carbon in oceans, might well bear fruit on similar timescales, using the available carbon sinks at the maximum rate possible.

In parallel, further development and initial deployment of non-fossil sources including various renewables will occur, together with high efficiency coal technologies. A nuclear revival may begin using existing technologies, or alternatively, if the prospects do not improve, efforts may focus on developing and demonstrating alternative nuclear technologies and systems. Attitudes and institutions for handling dispersed renewables and/or a nuclear revival will also evolve over this period, but large-scale expansion of either does not seem likely until well after the turn of the century, when technology, infrastructure and fossil energy prices - including carbon taxes - combine to provide the means and incentives.

On a longer timescale still, transport infrastructure and alternative fuels may develop to the point where communal transport and non-fossil fuelled vehicles can combine to provide an effective and competitive alternative to the choked finalé of the petrol-driven automobile economy. An international hydrogen economy, the centrepiece of a sustainable global energy system, could emerge in parallel.

Figure 7.2, starting with the baseline prospect for emissions sketched out in Chapter 7, section 7.2, and drawing on the discussions of magnitudes and timing, illustrates how these various options might contribute to limiting net carbon emissions through the twenty-first century.

Perhaps the most likely outcome, at least given current attitudes and pressures, is for policy responses which are modest or which are not pursued very widely. In this situation, energy efficiency could still make a significant impact as compared with 'business-as-usual' trends; efficiency policies might nearly stabilise demand in developed economies, and future growth would be dominated by the process of developing countries catching up. Accelerated gas use, reforestation and perhaps other measures to absorb carbon could also contribute, but without substantial encouragement and other changes in policy, non-fossil sources seem unlikely to make large inroads for many decades. Carbon emissions would continue to grow, heading to double perhaps around the middle of the next century. This is broadly the pattern sketched out in Figure 7.2(a).

If stronger policies were applied, on a wider basis and including all the major players, the impact would be much greater. The energy consumption in the industrialised world might decline slowly, and this would do much to offset the reduced expansion in developing countries. Of even greater long term impact, non-fossil sources might expand much more rapidly, especially if a regime for large scale technology transfer were successfully established - though still, given the constraints, their contribution seems unlikely to dominate the response for several decades. Accelerated gas and measures to absorb carbon might also make greater contributions. Such a scenario is illustrated in Figure 7.2(b).

There would of course be variants on such scenarios, and many shorter term variations. Radical restructuring in Soviet and East European industries combined with renewed turmoil in the Middle East could lead to global carbon emissions falling for a few years. Renewed growth combined with falls in oil prices could lead to growth spurts such as seen in the late 1980s. But overall, the second scenario suggests that broad application of feasible, if still politically difficult, abatement policies could hold net global fossil carbon emissions roughly to the levels of the 1980s through much of the twenty-first century. If there is one message, it is that the responses to the greenhouse effect - and related pressures of continuing worldwide economic development - have to be very diverse, but if applied widely, could ultimately have an immense cumulative impact as compared with the baseline.

Set against the pressures described in Chapter 2, global stabilisation of net carbon emissions appears as a major achievement. Yet it falls far short of the targets proposed by environmentalists.[20] Combined with the longevity of CFCs and the equal or even greater difficulties of limiting methane, it would still imply that humanity would be altering the planet, thereby running unknown risks. If the climatologists are right, the changes would probably be more rapid than anything known to have occurred in the past; there would still clearly be a need for adaptation policies. Yet the changes would be slower, the risks less, and adaptation much easier than if emissions grew without limit.

---

[20] For example, a major international non-governmental study examined the global measures which might be required to ensure that the rate of warming did not exceed 0.1 deg.C/decade, and that the total warming compared with pre-industrial times did not exceed 2.5 deg.C. Proceeding from these criteria, the study estimated that the total allowable carbon emissions from 1985 to 2100 were 300GtC, assuming that measures were taken to address other gases as well. As a result the authors suggested a schedule which involved the global total returning to 1985 levels by 2005, reducing 20% below this by 2015, by 50% by 2030, and by 75% by 2050. The authors suggested that a reasonably equitable arrangement would be to allocate the total budget equally between the industrialised and the developing worlds, implying roughly that the above schedules would apply to industrialised countries 10 to 20 years earlier, while developing countries should have returned to their current emission levels by 2030. (International Project for Sustainable Energy Paths, *Energy Policy in the Greenhouse, Vol.1, From Warming Fate to Warming Limit: Benchmarks for a Global Climate Convention*, IPSEP, El Cerrito, CA, September 1989.)

Despite its environmental shortcomings, a scenario of stabilising global carbon emissions, with its implication of steady and long-term reductions from the currently industrialised countries, is very radical compared with any conventional energy projections. Even with the mid-term contributions of carbon absorption, many energy specialists would hold it to be incompatible with widespread economic growth, and thus at least politically implausible. Why is it so difficult, and what are the key factors which will determine whether such limitation will occur?

It seems difficult to get much below the levels indicated both because of absolute constraints on the feasible contributions of most options, and because of the many constraints on timescales, including the nature and reactions of fossil fuel markets as discussed in Chapter 5, section 5.4. But above all, even this level of stabilising global emissions is difficult because it requires many countries to adopt a broad range of policies aimed at limiting the growth of carbon emissions. It would require very diverse countries, with varying perceptions of the problem, its implications, and the importance of fossil fuels to their economies, to converge quite rapidly towards serious and effective abatement policies.

The case studies if anything suggest exactly the opposite, with the countries which are already relatively efficient becoming more so, while those with higher emissions per person and/or per GDP achieve much less in the way of abatement; steps and developments which the more efficient countries might countenance if a real need were recognised are viewed as gross, impractical, or simply not very effective by others. If the authors of the US, Soviet and Chinese studies are right in their assessments, then by 2030 emissions from these three countries *alone* are likely to exceed substantially the current global total.

What is it that makes the prospects for serious abatement in such countries appear so bleak? Many of the specific issues identified by the authors were summarised in Chapter 2. Underlying them it is possible to discern a general factor which might be characterised as 'energy culture'. For a mixture of historical and geographical reasons, the most important of which appears to be the existence of large, cheap domestic fossil resources, such countries have developed an attitude that takes energy for granted, as something cheap and plentiful; unbounded energy consumption is assumed to be an essential component of economic growth, and in some cases it is almost treated as a basic human right. Consumers are themselves wasteful of energy in ways beyond the reach of policy, and talk of policy measures to help limit consumption - especially price rises, but also other measures - raises not only opposition from those whose interests are directly threatened, but far broader public and political hostility.

Everything else - opposition to carbon taxes and other forms of more direct government intervention to affect energy consumption, and even the promotion of alternative fuels - ultimately flows from this. There are elements of this in all countries, but they are most clear in the big energy producers.

The key determinant of whether or not the lower reaches of carbon emissions sketched in Figure 7.2(b) can be achieved will therefore depend upon whether, and by how much, the energy culture in all countries, but particularly the big energy producers, can be changed. This in turn will depend upon how key challenges posed by the greenhouse effect are resolved. It is with a review of these challenges that this book concludes.

The greenhouse effect poses unique challenges. The extent to which they are addressed, and how they are resolved, will have a strong impact on the policies adopted by countries, the extent of future changes in the earth's atmosphere, and even the shape of future societies.

Scientifically there is a clear need for improved climate modelling, especially of regional impacts, but obtaining a far broader understanding of the earth's biosphere and human impacts upon it is at least as important. The possible risks arising from various biosphere responses concerning oceanic, land-based and ice feedbacks on greenhouse gas emissions and climate, need to be clarified. Communicating scientific findings effectively to the public and policy community will also be a considerable challenge.

Current analytical methods for energy projections, including macroeconomic models, are seriously inadequate for the task of estimating the costs of limiting fossil carbon emissions. Key limitations include the fact that many studies assume energy markets to behave optimally; ignore the impact of abatement policies on technology development; project the past in terms of assumed macroeconomic relationships; and fail to model the dynamic uncertainties which lead to investment and other risks. There is no convincing evidence that limiting carbon emissions, perhaps to a quite substantial degree, need damage economic growth, but the uncertainties may take many years to resolve.

Economic theory itself faces several challenges. The traditional cost-benefit framework is probably inapplicable; 'sustainable development' may imply different criteria, but these remain unclear. The appropriate rate and perhaps even form of discounting is unresolved. New economic indicators are required to reflect environmental and resource depletion. The energy efficiency gap also presents difficulties for both theory and policy assessment which have not been fully recognised. The link between efficient environmental policy and social policy requires further study.

Energy industries face many challenges. The most successful will be those that diversify into new opportunities; limiting carbon emissions would clearly imply a decline for fossil fuel industries but also a rise of new industries. The international balance of industries would be changed. The key industrial challenge will be one of timing: running ahead of policy, but not so far as to waste money on premature investments and lost production.

Political processes will be stressed by the greenhouse effect. The regulatory and tax policies required run counter to the trends of the 1980s. Devising policies which can last through changes of government to give a clear direction to abatement efforts will require great political finesse, with the difficulties compounded by the long-term and uncertain nature of the problem. There are also serious institutional difficulties arising from the structural division between finance, energy, transport and environment in most governments. Non-governmental organisations will also face considerable challenges as policy develops.

The complex and long-term nature of the problem suggests that international approaches will have to be based on clear principles: negotiations rooted in current dispositions of political and economic power are unlikely to lead to effective and lasting agreements. The most efficient solution, and perhaps the only effective one, would be one founded on the application of a polluter pays principle at the international level. However, it remains very questionable whether it will be possible to include both the United States and the major developing countries in any substantive carbon abatement protocol. Resolving the international tensions and requirements may present the greatest challenge of all.

Introduction

If Earth is already crossing certain critical thresholds - and I believe
it is - how is it going to accommodate a further 5- to 10-fold increase
in economic activity over the next 50 years?[1]

Chapter 7 suggested that, in combination, the broad collection of policy
instruments analysed in this book could make a substantial impact on
future global emissions of CO_2. It also noted that, in many countries,
effective policy seems unlikely to be developed without major and
broad-ranging changes in attitudes on the part of both the public, and the
governments and industries involved in energy provision. The extent to
which these attitudes do change will depend upon whether key
challenges posed by the greenhouse effect can be addressed, and the way
in which they are resolved. This final chapter reviews those challenges.

8.1 Scientific challenges: understanding the earth

Much remains unknown about the greenhouse effect. Politics abhors
uncertainties, and there is considerable pressure on science to come up
with more clear answers. Yet the earth is an immensely complex system
- as complex as life itself, perhaps more so since life itself is one
interacting component of the biosphere. The challenges for science are
to separate the important issues and uncertainties from the unimportant
ones, to narrow the former as far as possible, and to find ways of
communicating the results and implications to a wider audience.

There are countless specific issues which could be addressed, but the
following would seem to rank high in any priority list.

* *Observation and verification.* In dealing with any system as
complex as the earth, people - not least the scientists involved -
distrust models in the absence of measurements to verify their
assumptions about climate behaviour and responses. There is a
continuing need for detailed measurements to check various
modelling assumptions about how the climate system responds to
radiative changes. Perhaps the most important modelling
uncertainties which could be reduced through observation concern
the nature and impact of cloud formation. Others include the

---

[1] Jim MacNeill, 'Sustainable Development - Getting Through the 21st Century',
Address to J.D.Rockefeller 150th Anniversary Conference, Institute for Research on
Public Policy, Ottawa, Ontario, October 1989.

behaviour of oceans and land in affecting both the heat balance and
the uptake of carbon.

* *Regional impacts and desertification.* Countries want to know how
they may be affected by the greenhouse effect. Uncertainties surround
all estimates of regional climate change, and they are particularly
important concerning the changes in soil moisture, and consequent
risk of desertification (or even flooding). Developing better regional
estimates requires much more intensive computer power to increase
the currently very coarse resolution of models, as well as other
developments to improve the understanding of climate processes and
how they might be represented in models. There may, however, be a
risk of too much effort going into the detail of regional estimates when
larger questions remain unresolved.

* *Unexplored feedbacks.* Climate models incorporate many physical
feedbacks, but some of the longer-term ones remain very
uncertain.[2] These include the extent of changes in vegetation and
ice cover and their consequent impact on the heat reflected directly
at the earth's surface. A few million years ago, the earth did not have
a northern icecap, and some studies suggest that the current one could
shrink with alarming rapidity.[3] Furthermore the models do not
include possible gaseous feedbacks, such as the impact of a warming
world on the carbon cycle and methane emissions from the vast
methane deposits locked in tundra and frozen near the poles. The
IPCC concluded that gaseous feedbacks seem likely to be positive on
balance - with warming producing more greenhouse gases, and
reducing the natural uptake of carbon. Such processes may amplify
the rate of change. In particular, the world needs to know clearly and
urgently whether there is any chance of unstable conditions in which
the natural sources rise faster than human emissions can be cut back,
so that global warming becomes uncontrollable.

This is a particularly daunting challenge because it involves
understanding better the overall role of life in the global system, and
how it may respond not only to climate changes in isolation, but to

[2] For a broad exploration of biosphere interactions and possible feedbacks see
J.Weiner, *The Next One Hundred Years*, Bantam Books, New York/Toronto, 1990.
[3] Various studies cited in ibid. The Antarctic, because it rests on land, is much more
stable and could indeed grow as a result of increased snowfall in a warmer world.

the combination with other human impacts. The questions, however, cannot be dodged.

* *Unexplored impacts.* Further layers of uncertainty are added by the possibility of unexplored impacts. What would it imply for climate if the Arctic icecap did shrink? Could ocean currents change? What might this imply for climate, or other impacts; could it, for example, trigger subterranean mudslides and consequent tidal waves? All these are hypothetical, but the present limited understanding of the global climate system makes us vulnerable to surprises such as that which atmospheric scientists received with the discovery of the ozone hole. Humanity needs to know as far as possible the bounds on the risks which it could be running.

* *Human impacts and responses.* The uncertainties do not reside solely with the biosphere. The human response to climatic change adds further layers. How much can societies adapt; and at what stage might some start to migrate? Refugees are already a major political issue in some areas; if mass migration occurred, driven by climate changes attributed to industrial activity, how would societies respond?

* *Sources, sinks, and policy focus.* At the more practical level, the policy-making community is still looking for a better understanding of the sources and sinks of the different gases involved, and the relative importance of tackling each, including questions of timing. Will the problems be greater, and if so by how much, if responses are delayed?

Underlying all of these there is a challenge of communication. It is a common joke in Washington to ask for a 'one handed scientist' who will not burden the policy process with uncertainties by stating 'On the other hand ... '. But many important uncertainties may be irremovable. The Policymakers Summary of the IPCC Working Group I report is in many respects a masterpiece of distinguishing between what is known, what seems probable, and some of what may be possible, together with some of the implications, without drowning in a sea of caveats and generalisations. As the stakes rise, and scientists have to explore some of the more speculative but more alarming possibilities, the art of communication will become more difficult still.

The scientific challenge is not primarily one of more modelling, though that is important, but of broader exploration of the earth's system and of humanity's role in it, and of making the findings intelligible and relevant without inducing a destructive clash between those who are panicked by more speculative environmental possibilities, and those who are alarmed by the possible impacts of trying to do something about it. Assessing the latter may also pose great challenges, and nowhere is this more clear than in attempts to assess the potential for, and costs of, reducing fossil fuel emissions.

8.2 Analytical challenges: costing abatement

The greenhouse effect has brought energy forecasting back into fashion.[4] There were many forecasting efforts during the 1970s, when energy projections became both a tool in debates about the scarcity of resources, and about the need for nuclear energy. Forecasting has inevitably risen again as people try to work out where carbon emissions may be heading, and how much it might cost to do something about them. It is far from clear how far the decade of quiescence has helped the art to develop.

Energy efficiency is not a new discovery. The technologies for providing heat and light have been improving more or less ever since *homo sapiens* lit the first fire, and cost-effective opportunities for improving efficiency have probably existed for as long. Many anti-nuclear studies during the 1970s pointed to the opportunities for improving efficiency as an alternative to supply. But often, the figures advanced have assumed near-perfect take-up of more efficient technology and a cessation of wasteful behaviour. Quite how ordinary human beings and firms were supposed to start behaving in such an uncharacteristic way was rarely addressed.

Calculating the potential for energy efficiency is a useful exercise, and an important precursor to further study, but it is not enough to draw the kind of conclusions which many have tried to draw from it. The message that there are large technical opportunities for economic improvements seems finally to have sunk in, and the need is now for more sophisticated

[4] Twenty-nine recent studies are summarised in S.T.Boyle, *Limiting Climate Change: an assessment of global/regional/national energy-CO_2 scenarios*, Association for the Conservation of Energy, London, 1990.

studies, which set the technically possible against real lifestyles, and connect tomorrow's vision with today's real world.

Recent studies have paid more attention to policy, but the interaction between policy and impacts - let alone policy and politics - has never been properly established. The fact is that policies for exploiting more than a relatively modest fraction of the 'efficiency gap' are not easy. Assessing the real potential for energy efficiency cannot be separated from the question of what is and what is not feasible in policy terms, and what the actual human and macroeconomic reactions to efficiency policies would be in financial and other terms. Chapters 3 and 4 in this book have tried to grapple with some of these issues, drawing on existing work where possible, but there is clearly much that remains uncertain.

However, these failings seem minor compared with those of the opposite extreme. Broad macroeconomic modelling has never been an easy task. With respect to energy, it is particularly difficult because of the special features and failings of the energy market, as discussed in Chapter 3. Despite the best efforts to date, the gap between macroeconomic modelling and the real world seems to remain painfully large.

The broad approach used in macroeconomic modelling is to project energy demand on the basis of various trends, usually related to price and GNP growth, through elasticity coefficients. Frequently, the model then calculates the least-cost supply investment pattern to meet this demand, given various input costs. The economic impact of constraints, such as on the maximum level of CO_2 emissions, can be estimated by comparing the cost with and without the constraint imposed.

The most famous of the studies estimating the total cost of CO_2 abatement have become those conducted by Manne and Richels,[5]

[5] A.S.Manne and R.G.Richels, 'CO_2 Emission Limits: An Economic Cost Analysis for the USA', *The Energy Journal*, April 1990. From the primary analysis the paper states: 'The effects of a carbon constraint do not begin to have measurable macroeconomic consequences until 2010. At that point the rise in energy prices begins to have a significant effect upon the share of gross output available for current consumption. By 2030, roughly 5% of total annual macroeconomic consumption is lost as a consequence of the carbon constraint. This percentage remains relatively constant for the remainder of the time horizon. Adding over all the years from 1990 through 2100, the present value of these losses would be $3.6 trillion, discounting to 1990 at 5% per year.' The analysis studied other cases, and emphasised that successful R&D might substantially reduce these costs.

which are the primary source of statements that meeting the 'Toronto Target' for a 20% reduction in CO_2 emissions could cost the United States trillions of dollars. If the comments below seem unduly to relate to their studies it is only because they were the first to manage the great complexity of developing and interfacing an energy systems model ('ETA' - Energy Technology Assessment) with a general macroeconomic equilibrium model ('MACRO'), and formulating inputs and assumptions over the next century so as to make an estimate of the economic costs of constraining CO_2 emissions. A subsequent paper extends their analysis to the global level, and highlights the importance of regional differences, and the impact of developing country growth on the targets which other countries would have to meet to obtain global reductions.[6]

The most obvious difficulty with such analysis concerns the assumptions used - projecting technology costs and fuel prices over the next century. This is a difficulty which all those involved recognise. It means that any numerical conclusions are subject to large uncertainties, and places a great onus on modellers to reflect that uncertainty, and the range of opinion, in their results. This does not in itself invalidate the modelling exercise. The Manne and Richels results have stimulated a number of other papers criticising their assumptions and arguing that the costs of carbon constraints would in fact be much lower than they have suggested,[7] to which Manne and Richels have responded with further sensitivity studies, concluding that 'The direct economic losses are quite sensitive to assumptions about both demand and supply ... for the losses

---

[6] A.S.Manne and R.G.Richels, 'Global CO_2 Emission Reductions: the Impact of Rising Energy Costs', *The Energy Journal*, forthcoming 1990. They conclude that if the main policy instrument used is a carbon tax, then 'under the assumptions adopted here, it turns out that the long run equilibrium tax (for a 20% reduction in global fossil carbon emissions) is the same in all regions - $250/tC. a five-fold increase in the price of coal.'

[7] Various papers in the *The Energy Journal*, forthcoming. One critique argues 'There are strong reasons to regard the Manne/Richels quantitative findings skeptically, and to believe that the costs of constraining carbon dioxide emissions will be much lower than they have estimated ... [however] ... the model itself could prove to be a valuable tool in framing more sharply the important policy issues relating to global warming ... an important application would be to try to identify the combinations of key parameters that would lead to low (or even zero) cost scenarios for constraining carbon dioxide emissions.' R.H.Williams, 'Will constraining fossil fuel carbon dioxide emissions really cost so much?', *The Energy Journal*, forthcoming.

[from carbon constraints] to approach zero, however, the most optimistic combination of supply and demand assumptions must be adopted.'[8]

Underlying these debates, several specific difficulties facing macroeconomic modelling analysis can be identified.

The assumption of optimal markets. Implicit in many optimising models is the assumption that markets behave so as to find the overall 'least-cost' solution. For reasons discussed throughout this book, energy is a commodity subject to unusually large distortions which mean that overall it is rarely anywhere near an overall 'least-cost' solution. It would, for example, be interesting to know how the ETA-MACRO estimates of costs to the United States would have been changed if, instead of formulating energy price increases as a carbon tax distortion in optimal energy markets, they had modelled explicitly the effect of reducing existing US subsidies to fossil fuel industries outlined in Chapter 3, and of reducing various other supply-side imperfections.

Concerning the cost of reducing carbon emissions, perhaps the most important form of 'non-optimality', however, is the efficiency gap. Efforts to remove the obstacles which cause this, or otherwise to compensate for its effects, will usually result in both reduced emissions and lower total costs. Most energy models do not include specific analysis of demand-side options, or for that matter other cost-effective options which are not taken up because of various market imperfections. One which does is the MARKAL model, a 'technically rich energy model that consistently compares energy supply and efficiency options', which was recently applied by the Brookhaven Laboratories and the US Environmental Protection Agency to estimate the costs of carbon abatement in the United States.[9] The key problem of their analysis was that, as soon as the model was allowed to optimise the system, obtaining a base case anything like official or macroeconomic forecasts proved almost impossible: as compared with these, 'the base case [ie without carbon constraints] results in lower annual growth for all fossil fuels, with a higher growth rate for renewables'.[10]

---

[8] A.S.Manne and R.G.Richels, 'The Costs of Reducing US CO$_2$ Emissions - a Further Sensitivity Analysis', *The Energy Journal*, forthcoming.

[9] S.C.Morris, B.D.Solomon, D.Hill, J.Lee, G.Goldstein, 'A Least Cost Energy Analysis of US CO$_2$ Reduction Options', in J.W.Tester and N.Ferrari, (eds), *Energy and Environment in the 21st Century*, MIT Press, Cambridge MA, 1990.

[10] This did not mean that large CO$_2$ reductions were necessarily much cheaper; given the authors' assumption that efficient technologies did not continue to improve or

Manne and Richels argue that their analysis can and does capture the effect of end-use efficiency options because it includes an allowance for the rate of 'Autonomous [ie not price-induced] Energy Efficiency Improvements'. There is much merit in this but it is not the same thing as accounting directly for the effect of market distortions. One difficulty is that this parameter has been widely interpreted simply as an uncertain number - the initial M&R analysis used zero, with 1%/yr as an extreme case; others suggest that higher rates of improvement would be possible. The change from 0 to 1% halved the M&R estimate of the costs of the carbon constraint. In fact this value is likely to be a very strong function of policy, notably the kinds of policy discussed in Chapter 4 aimed at narrowing the 'efficiency gap'. In this light, the M&R studies point not just to abatement costs but also to the large savings of both money and carbon which could be made by exploiting the efficiency gap. Such a modelling framework, indeed, could be a useful one for assessing the benefits of such policies if the link between policy and impact, in terms of non price-induced efficiency improvements, can be established.

Technology development and feedbacks. A second area of difficulty concerns technology development. Projecting technology costs far into the future presents irreducible uncertainties which are universally recognised. The important point is not merely that technology development is uncertain, but that it is affected by policy in both R&D *and* in the markets available to it. As another review of modelling difficulties notes, this has been demonstrated yet again by the technological response to restrictions on CFCs:[11]

> ... in 1987 when the protocol on CFC reductions was signed, the US EPA estimated a total cost to the economy of meeting the target of $1.8bn. Recent breakthroughs in developing CFC alternatives have driven those costs down to around $500m. For some applications, the replacements will cost less than the CFCs themselves. Indeed, it is only because of these recent breakthroughs that elimination of CFCs

---

respond to changing conditions 'most end-use conservation measures are selected in the base case; leaving little to be added to meet CO_2 constraints ... [additional] CO_2 reductions are primarily the result of substitution of renewables and to a less extent nuclear power for coal' (ibid.).

[11] M.B.Zimmerman, 'Assessing the Costs of Climate Change Policies: the Uses and Limits of Models', Alliance to Save Energy, Washington DC, April 1990.

is now regarded as one of the most cost-effective means of mitigating global climate change.

An example of equally direct relevance comes from the Japanese response to the oil shocks. A representative of the Japanese Environment Ministry noted with heavy irony that 'twenty years ago we argued over exhaust emissions, and MITI said that reducing emissions would lead to local car makers being dominated by GM and Ford ... '[12] The superior fuel and emission performance of Japanese technology subsequently proved a strong selling point. Both Japan and West Germany, drawing on its experience of sulphur limitation, show signs of regarding the greenhouse effect as a technical challenge which, if confronted, might be addressed with profit.

The costs of low-carbon technologies are bound to be lower when carbon emissions are constrained than in any 'business-as-usual' projection, because more effort will be put into them and there will be larger markets for them. It is impossible to quantify this effect, and as a result it is usually ignored, thus by default giving the feedback between technology and carbon constraints a value of zero. As with the failure to include many environmental externalities, this is perhaps the only value that is certain to be wrong. This is primarily an issue of assumptions rather than modelling structure, though some attempts could be made to model economies of scale in deploying new energy sources.

The assumption of perfect foresight. The third generic area of difficulty is that optimising models assume perfect foresight. This is not to say that they do not reflect uncertainties; most models are run many times to reflect different possible future values. The problem is that, within each run of the model, all investments are made assuming that all conditions over the rest of the model period are known. For an optimising model to do anything else would be extraordinarily difficult. But the real world is not like that.

Consider, for example, the following scenario. After all other issues have been resolved as far as possible, analysts still conclude that severe constraints on carbon would be very costly, while climate models remain ambiguous. As a result, pressure for low emission targets is successfully resisted, and investment in mines etc. continues as planned. Fifteen years later, as these massive investments are just beginning to mature, dramatic

---

[12] Quoted in 'Japan seeks to end emissions dispute', *Financial Times*, London, 19 May 1990.

climatic events and/or improved models elevate greenhouse concerns to the status of crisis, and heavy curbs on the use of fossil fuels follow. Not only are the supply investments wasted, but fifteen years in which to improve efficiency and gain experience with other technologies have been lost; the resulting costs of response are very much higher than they would have been if action had been taken earlier, and CO_2 concentrations are still considerably higher.

Of course, it is also possible (though it seems less likely) that measures will be taken to limit carbon emissions, and that, after a few decades, improved climatic understanding will show conclusively that their consequences will be far less serious than was originally conceived, so that constraints on fossil fuels are relaxed. Which carries the higher cost?

The point is simply that current models can reflect uncertainty but not risk, and consequently, they cannot reflect the benefits of insurance policies.[13]

Projecting the past. The final difficulty with macroeconomic modelling is the tendency to project the past, in terms of the coefficients and behaviour it assumes. The relationships between energy demand, price, and GDP are obvious examples; elasticity coefficients are generally derived from past data applied decades into the future. Again, this is primarily an issue of assumptions rather than of structure, but concerning energy developments it may be an exceptionally deep problem. The energy history analysed by economists consists of three main periods: the long post-war boom combined with steadily falling energy prices, tracing the expansion of Middle East oil; the 'crisis management' period of energy responses to the oil price shock and the decade of widespread stagflation from the early 1970s; and the period following the likewise rather sudden reversal of the mid-1980s. How much can any of these periods really tell us about the responses of energy systems to steadily developing and coherent policies for limiting carbon emissions over decades?

Furthermore, the structure of energy demand changes over time. Chapter 6 considered some of the future pressures on energy demand in developed economies, and argued that many of these were undergoing profound changes which would tend to constrain future energy demand almost irrespective of prices. Why, for example, should energy use in car

---

[13] Manne and Richels report that their model is currently (August 1990) being extended to address this issue (R.Richels, personal communication).

travel depend upon energy prices if the cost of driving is eventually dominated by congestion and urban pollution taxes?

These are four generalised problems facing macroeconomic modelling attempts to evaluate the costs of carbon abatement. In addition, there are generic uncertainties surrounding the macroeconomic role of energy prices and taxes, the employment impact, the stability benefits of a 'price smoother' tax, and the feedbacks between abatement measures and international energy prices, as discussed in Chapter 3.

These are not trivial issues. Economic analyses of the costs of carbon abatement have been widely cited, and strongly influence political attitudes in some quarters. Studies citing high abatement costs have been used to bolster the 'energy culture' in many fossil fuel economies.

Yet the difficulties listed above, combined with the general uncertainties in projecting fuel and technology costs, mean that estimates of high abatement costs are extremely questionable. Given time to develop and to respond to different policy considerations, the way in which total energy system costs vary with the level of carbon emissions may be as sketched in Figure 8.1. The real shape of this curve is unknown, but as with many economic optima, the minimum may be broad, and the curve sketched is consistent with discussions in this book. Furthermore, current markets clearly do not settle at the minimum overall cost, but at a point some way to the right, with both higher emissions and higher costs. If the situation is as sketched in Figure 8.1 then, if efficient policies can be found to exploit these opportunities, carbon emissions could be reduced by over 50% with no increase in overall costs.

In the author's view, there is no convincing evidence to suggest that limiting carbon emissions, perhaps to a quite substantial degree given time, need damage economic growth. Indeed, some abatement policies would aid it. Studies which come to the opposite conclusion seem universally to ignore the most cost-effective options, and to overlook the likely impact of abatement policies on technology development and on fossil fuel prices and price stability. Their failure to model risk could indeed tempt governments and industries into incurring the highest costs of all, if responses are avoided now but are forced at a faster pace by later climatic events.

The analytical challenges are formidable. The limitations listed above add greatly to the complexity of what is already a very complex modelling task. Developing adequate macroeconomic modelling of

**Figure 8.1 Global energy system costs: possible form of variation
with carbon emissions**

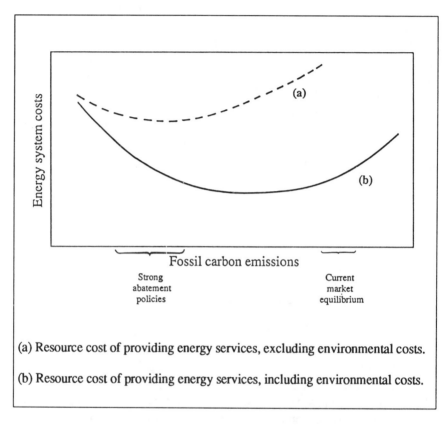

(a) Resource cost of providing energy services, excluding environmental costs.

(b) Resource cost of providing energy services, including environmental costs.

abatement policies (particularly at the global level), and gaining
sufficient understanding of energy systems and possible technical
developments to reach a broad consensus concerning input assumptions,
may take as long as developing adequate regional climate models - and
arguably longer because future economics, depending upon human
behaviour and technology developments, is to an extent inherently
unpredictable.

However, there are more manageable tasks which could be addressed
in the relatively near term. The present need is not for long-term
projections but for policy modelling. What *are* the most attractive
policies for trying to exploit the efficiency gap, and how much impact
would they really have? What policies could help to remove the obstacles

to new energy technologies, and how much encouragement would they need? It is in the area of explicit and broad-ranging appraisal of specific policy instruments that better analysis is more feasible, and is sorely needed. This in turn could lead to the development of *policy scenarios*, which, however uncertain the baseline projections, could give an indication of the extent to which changes might be made.

Ultimately, however, all modelling studies reflect the underlying economic ground-rules on which they rest. This in itself provides an equally important area of greenhouse challenges.

8.3 Economic challenges: tools for sustaining development

Countries are doing political handstands today to open their economies to market forces ... what they haven't yet discovered is that it [the market] can drive development in two ways - sustainable and unsustainable. Whether it does one or the other is not a function of an 'invisible hand' but of man-made policy.[14]

The greenhouse effect is a problem of unique dimensions, and as such it poses unique problems for economics. The Oxford English Dictionary offers a definition of economics as 'the science of political economy', and of political economy as 'the art of managing the resources of a people and its government'. Few issues so clearly encompass the whole human race - including innumerable future generations - as 'the people', and the planet itself as 'the resources', with some of the largest industries in the world central to the whole process. The mix between science and art in the definitions seems particularly appropriate.

Three main questions may be asked of economics with respect to the greenhouse effect: how much to act; how best to act; and how much will such action cost in terms of human and material resources? These questions are obviously interrelated but many strands can be separated.

An economic answer to the first question would require some estimate to be made of the likely cost of the greenhouse effect. This is extremely uncertain at present and for reasons discussed in Chapter 3, section 3.1, it is arguable that attempts to put numbers to the cost betray a fundamental misunderstanding of the nature of the scientific, human and

[14] MacNeill, 'Sustainable Development'.

philosophical uncertainties involved.[15] This may be an extreme view, but since few dispute that cost assessments will remain extremely uncertain for many years, and that action will have to be taken in the face of great uncertainty, this makes little practical difference. This poses a serious question as to whether economics can suggest any alternative criteria - for example, criteria following from some interpretation of 'sustainable development', which may be far different from a cost-benefit framework.

For the present, the degree of abatement is likely to be determined far more at the level of gut reaction and politics than as a result of any attempt at an economic cost-benefit analysis. There is still plenty of scope left for economic challenges.[16]

The economic instruments of costs and prices remain the primary signals for decisions on how to use resources; GDP growth is taken as the prime indicator of national success; and the extent to which measures to limit carbon emissions would affect this indicator is usually taken as the key determinant of the pain involved. Consequently it is disconcerting to recognise the uncertain basis on which many costs are founded, their limitations as a guide to optimal decisions, and the weaknesses of the GDP indicator.

Perhaps the most obvious example of these problems, also implicated in the difficulties of costing the greenhouse effect, is that of how much weight to give to the future - the discounting conundrum, as outlined in Chapter 3, section 3.3. The absolute and relative costs of different energy supply and demand options may vary greatly according to whether they are assessed at the market, the societal or some intermediate or mixed rate. In global energy models, the choice of discount rate may have as much impact on results as all other technology cost assumptions combined.

---

[15] For a fuller discussion of the problems facing the application of cost/benefit analysis to environmental issues see J.G.U.Adams,'Unsustainable Economics', International Environmental Affairs, University Press, New England, Vol.2, No.1, 1990.

[16] At least two recent special issues of journals have considered problems of economics and the environment (*Oxford Review of Economic Policy*, OUP, Spring 1990; *Energy Policy*, 17(2), April 1989). At the risk of dangerous generalisations, it appears that papers considering specific policy instruments and issues have often pointed to quite clear conclusions, while those considering more general issues, such as evaluating environmental damage and discounting, pointed to at least as many problems as they resolved.

The discounting conundrum is hardly a new problem in economics and there is little reason to suppose that further work directed at the greenhouse effect will resolve the inherent difficulties, though further exploration of modified approaches such as those outlined in Chapter 3, section 3.2 would be of interest. Certainly, some clarification from economics as to the bounds on rates and perhaps methods which other analysts might reasonably explore in their costing studies would be of help to the whole business of cost and policy analysis.

The GDP is an indicator of great symbolic importance. Economic theory is far more aware of its limitations than are the political and public processes which treat GDP growth as the holy grail of national aspirations. Many economists have emphasised its weaknesses: namely the fact that it only reflects material consumption without reference to other aspects of the quality of life, and in particular does not reflect environmental costs. Many economists are now advocating at least a set of satellite accounts which reflect the degradation of the natural capital of limited resources off which economies feed, and internalisation of environmental costs, for example through a carbon tax.

Given the great uncertainties in attempts to quantify most environmental resources in monetary terms, especially the greenhouse effect, attempts to translate environmental degradation into comparable economic indicators which could actually affect GDP itself would be fraught with difficulty and uncertainty. However, whether or not such environmental accounts were so translated, or just kept in terms of a high-profile physical report on environmental status, the symbolic value of having established environmental indicators could be considerable. Anything which tended to counteract the emphasis on material consumption in modern market economies would presumably help to lessen the pressure on environmental resources, including energy.

If and when such changes are adopted, they may moderate the picture, but they seem unlikely to change it fundamentally. Given all the intervening uncertainties, it is much too early to say whether never-ending economic growth, as conventionally defined, is ultimately incompatible with stabilising the atmosphere. But it is clearly a possibility. As noted in Chapter 6, section 6.4, changes in attitudes could raise more fundamental questions about what constitutes 'economic growth', with a consequent abandonment or drastic revision of the GDP indicator. At present it seems unwise to rely on such developments to help cope with the greenhouse effect; but it is also clearly grossly premature to talk of the greenhouse effect heralding the end of economic growth.

An economic challenge of more direct and immediate relevance concerns the efficiency gap. There may be no free lunches, but some are unusually large and cheap, and improving energy efficiency is the most obvious example. Yet in comparison with discounting and even the limits of the GDP indicator, where problems are recognised if not entirely resolved, economics seems still to be at the pre-natal stage when it comes to handling the implications of the particular market issues discussed in Chapter 4 which create such large but untapped opportunities for improvements in efficiency. With respect to this, and with but few honourable exceptions, many macroeconomic analyses and discussions of energy economics seem reminiscent of Galileo's critics refusing to look down his telescope at Jupiter's moons: the efficiency gap does not fit into the theory, therefore it does not exist, or if it does then it is an insignificant artifact which is best ignored in the hope that it will go away.[17] This may be something of a caricature, but a variant on the theme - that governments can or should do nothing about the 'efficiency gap' - carries little more validity.

Again this poses issues at both the theoretical and the practical level. There is no reason why economic theory should not be developed to encompass the reality and implications of the widely differing consumer and producer discount rates, or the 'don't know don't care' threshold, below which consumers seem to pay little or no attention to operating costs, and which breaks the assumed symmetry in consumer responses to price changes.[18]

---

[17] A recent study by two US economists surveys the evidence concerning the efficiency gap and notes that: 'The existence of numerous opportunities for paybacks of one or two years is clear evidence of a non-equilibrium situation that has not yet been clearly recognised [by economists]', R.Ayres and J.Walter, *Global Warming: Abatement Policies and Costs*, IIASA research report, International Institute for Applied Systems Analysis, Laxenburg, Austria, forthcoming (draft, January 1990).

[18] Elasticities reflect the assumption that, if prices rise, demand will decrease, and if they fall, demand will increase, other things being equal. If there is a threshold below which consumers 'don't know and don't care', price rises may take them above this threshold, stimulating the uptake of better technology for example, but there is no reason why the savings should reverse when the price falls again.

Perhaps of more practical interest are the nuts and bolts of how the large potential for cost-effective improvements in energy efficiency might best be exploited. Various options have been explored in Chapter 4. These have varying attractions and drawbacks. It is hard to judge the real impact which most of them would have on energy demand, or the disbenefits in terms of greater government intervention in private decisions and/or greater bureaucracy. There is clearly much that can be done, but the risks of getting it wrong could also be high. There is a clear need for further work in assessing the overall implications of such policy instruments, and exploring the possibilities for better ones, both in relation to the efficiency gap and to the much broader policy options for trying to limit carbon emissions.

Beyond the efficiency gap, it seems likely that economically efficient policies would rely to an extent on financial incentives to create moves away from carbon and other environmentally damaging activities. Carbon taxes and road pricing are two clear examples. The economic perestroika arising from really applying the principle that polluters should pay for their external impacts could have a considerable impact on prices. The first consequence of many efficient responses would be to make many things relatively more expensive.

This could raise perhaps the longest-running tension in economic theory, namely that between efficiency and equity. Market-based responses may be efficient, but if they result in the poorest people shouldering a relatively greater share of the environmental burden, they can hardly be described as desirable. There are ways of reconciling the two, as discussed in Chapter 3 in relation to carbon taxes. Environmental taxes could be offset against lower tax rates, and/or higher thresholds for lower income groups. Alternatively, special energy allowances could be created: this is a special case of the general concept of 'merit goods' to which people should have a general minimum entitlement. The extent to which efficient environmental policy and broader social policy will need to be tied is clearly an area requiring further study.

Finally, like many other spheres, theory is clearly limited in dealing with the dynamics of economic development over time, rather than the much simpler long-term optimal condition - which in practice never arrives because conditions change. In the case of the greenhouse effect, the dynamics are clearly important in several respects. One concerns the timing of abatement measures, as illustrated in the previous section. But also, whether or not abatement did have any impact on GDP growth, there would clearly be major impacts at the microeconomic level of specific activities - such as coal mines and the communities which surround them. The failure to reflect the 'pain of change' can be considered as another limitation of the GDP indicator. The pain could be substantial; it will drive the most important political obstacles to abatement; and it is, naturally, the reason for the greatest concern on the part of the industries involved.

8.4 Industrial challenges: timing transitions

The fossil fuel industries sell packaged carbon. No matter how they are dressed up, and whatever the policy priorities, the discussion in Chapter 1 suggests that these industries cannot escape the implications of the greenhouse effect. Taking it seriously is incompatible with the assumed long-term growth of coal and oil, and ultimately even gas; the limit of how much is in the ground, at what cost, is replaced by environmental limits.

A large-scale move away from fossil fuels would be the largest industrial transition in history. Managing decline has never been an easy business, and trying to prevent it is perhaps going to be an inevitable part of industrial responses. This may achieve success in some countries, but is hardly a means of ensuring a secure future. In-situ gasification and processes for coal use without CO_2 emissions could ease the transition for coal, and are obvious areas requiring further work. But one of the key elements in responding successfully would undoubtedly be diversification, with an eye to some of the new business opportunities presented.

The pressure for increased end-use efficiency would first lead to increased inter-fuel competition, and the rise of new industries focused on energy-use services. The supply industries could become more involved in the energy management companies, in order to exploit new business opportunities, and to help keep the market share for their fuel. Different divisions of the same company might then be operating in ways which would directly compete, and this might present managerial difficulties; the importance of the energy service operations would gradually rise.

Similar remarks would apply to renewables. Several major energy producers became involved with renewable energy during the 1970s, with varying degrees of enthusiasm. Many have given up, having concluded that renewables will remain poor business for many decades yet. If the discussion in Chapter 5, section 5.6 is correct, and if governments do adopt measures to remove the obstacles and to promote renewables, that assessment will have to be reversed. Again, if the fossil fuel industries became involved, they would have to resolve the problems of having two competing arms of business. But with the increasing liberalisation of many energy markets, simply trying to squeeze out the competition is unlikely to be very successful.

Another theme to emerge would concern the international balance of fossil fuel industries. For reasons already discussed, continued growth in the developing countries seems inevitable for some time. Attempts to reduce global reliance on fossil fuels, with decline in industrialised countries, would greatly accelerate the increasing importance of developing country markets. The implications of this for the structure and focus of international fossil fuel industries could be profound, and the extent to which company resources devoted to industrial country markets could be switched to developing countries could be a key determinant of success in managing the transitions.

Quite apart from this specific shift, the greenhouse effect may well promote trends towards the internationalisation of energy-related industries, including those which have hitherto had a national focus. Electricity systems are becoming more interlinked, and exploiting non-fossil sources more fully would increase this trend, both to promote access to distant non-fossil resources (such as areas rich in hydro, geothermal, or nuclear) more fully, and to manage better the inputs from variable sources such as wind and solar energy. Accelerated use of gas would imply greater international flows. The development of hydrogen might well be an international industry almost from its inception, with 'niche' production sites in one country - depleted gas wells or other opportunities for CO_2 storage, or deserts for PV hydrogen - being developed to supply 'niche' hydrogen markets - such as the most intolerably polluted cities - in another.

Bound up in much of this will be the issue of technology transfer to developing countries. This will involve a wide range of industries, and their exact role will depend heavily upon how transfers are managed, but it clearly has to be an important theme which will further the links between development in some countries and deployment in others.

All of these transitions pose challenges to industries, but underlying them is the challenge of timing. Currently the signs are that many fossil fuel companies intend to ignore greenhouse concerns in the belief that they will never reach a level sufficient to change their business, or at least that they can wait until the political response is clear, and that they can then dampen down the response to give them time enough to adapt without undue difficulty.

This could be a disastrous strategy. It is already apparent that some of the European OECD countries are taking serious steps which will affect fossil fuel industries. It may be right to believe that greenhouse concerns will abate, perhaps following a few cool years and a relatively toothless international framework convention. The problem for the industries is that the politics is likely to depend upon the weather. Some time in the next decade or two there is almost bound to be a collection of relatively severe climatic events (to a degree they tend to occur together, because causes are interrelated) which galvanise public opinion and politics. The US climatologist Schneider[19] graphically sketched a scenario in which the United States successfully resisted pressures to take action, and some years later was hit by an intense and prolonged heat wave and drought, finally breaking in unprecedented hurricane and storm surges. The legislative reaction could be devastating for any companies which had sunk their future in the continued expansion of fossil fuels.

Given the timescales involved in developing the technologies and expertise for energy management and renewable sources, the companies which stand to benefit are clearly those which develop such capabilities well in advance of any panic legislation. There is, however, a limit to how far ahead of the field companies can afford to go, and how much they can cut back on fossil fuel investments in advance of political signals that retreats from such investment will not simply be filled by competitors perhaps at higher profits.

In all, industries could do a lot either to help or to hinder the transitions, and could benefit or suffer accordingly: but they are ultimately dependent upon the political processes which determine the nature of the game.

8.5 Political challenges: managing the trade-offs

The 1980s saw widespread though not universal trends towards reducing government economic intervention, both in general and, specifically, in

[19] S.Schneider, *Global Warming*, Sierra Club Books, San Francisco, 1989.

energy. These included attempts to reduce the 'regulatory burden' on industry, to reduce the scale of government finance, and to reduce the impact of the tax system on business. Surveying the kinds of policy instruments discussed in Chapters 3-5, there are clear tensions between these trends and the measures which would be needed to reduce emissions of greenhouse gases.

The most efficient responses in resource terms are those which encourage the take-up of cost-effective opportunities for improving energy efficiency. However the economic challenges in this area are resolved, it seems inevitable that measures to exploit the efficiency gap will involve greater regulation, to push investments in directions where the free and highly imperfect energy markets would not normally lead. Making the trade-off of regulatory burden against the waste from *laissez-faire* will be a highly political issue, for, as noted, the gap between making markets work and letting them work in this area seems an unusually large one.

Removing the market obstacles which impede new energy sources, and providing RD&D and other subsidies to encourage their development, may not be a much simpler political process. Vested interests may have a stronger sway here. The rationale for subsidies is very clear but so is the risk of slipping on the 'banana' problem (see Chapter 5, section 5.8) of not being able to control subsidies effectively. To put it another way, politics needs to recognise the danger of herds of white elephants charging along under the greenhouse banner.

Carbon taxes are a very different matter. Administratively, they are relatively easy. Politically, they may be among the most difficult steps. Yet if they are phased in over an extended period, it is hard to see what can go wrong with them, other than the problems of success in environmental terms adding to the problems of domestic coal industries in some countries already declining under competition from gas. Minimising the transitional pain involved could imply hitting the international coal trade harder than domestic production, which might raise complex political issues in terms of trade provisions.

Apart from this and the obvious issue of political opposition, as already discussed, the main political problem would lie in creating a realistic commitment to phasing in such taxes at a timing and rate sufficient to have a real impact on industrial planning, without creating the disruptions and reactions which might destroy the tax itself or make progressive implementation impossible.

Logically, regulatory and price-based measures would be complementary. Politically there may well be trade-offs. Many countries may face a prospect of uneven swings in the degree and mix of policy responses, as governments change to reflect differing ideologies and to differing degrees the public pressures for highly visible and probably non-price-based measures, and the business pressures for minimum regulatory interference. Such fluctuations would add needless costs. A key political challenge will be to devise and implement policies which have sufficiently broad acceptance, or which are sufficiently deep-rooted, to persist through changes of governments to give a clear long-term direction for abatement measures.

The political challenges concern institutions as well as policy. Most governments are deeply divided by discipline. Energy departments traditionally see their role as ensuring energy security and the health of domestic energy industries. Most transport departments still see their task as the provision of a transport network which can meet all demands for personal and commercial mobility. Environment departments generally have no business in either. MacNeill notes:[20]

> During the '60s and '70s, governments in over 100 countries, developed and developing alike, established special environmental protection and resource agencies. But governments failed to make their powerful central economic, trade and sectoral agencies in any way responsible for the environmental implications of the policies they pursued, the revenues they raised and the expenditures they made. The resulting balance of forces was and is grossly unequal.

Changing this situation, and integrating environmental factors including greenhouse gas emissions into the entrenched structure of sectoral government decision-making, will not be an easy task.

The political challenges in developing countries are still greater. Domestic political tensions can be exacerbated by the considerable external pressures. These forces push in many contradictory directions. In many respects the politics of poverty reinforce the economic trap. Much as capital shortage and high discount rates tend to reinforce each other, for example, poverty creates immense pressures for subsidies, but subsidies can help perpetuate poverty - higher resource prices discourage

---

[20] MacNeill, 'Sustainable Development'.

waste, and the increased expenditure is recycled through the economy anyway. The greenhouse effect adds but one additional complication for both internal and external politics, with both traps and opportunities.

The political challenges posed by the greenhouse effect do not only concern the policies and structure of governments. Non-governmental organisations (NGOs) have been critical in bringing many environmental issues to the current levels of concern. The challenge they face, as with other groups, is to adapt to a changing world, in particular to a world in which global environmental issues are established as a legitimate political issue. The US case study notes how the public support behind many 'causes' has disappeared as the issue moves into policy formation, and the real implications of doing something become apparent; the study argues that the same is almost certain to happen concerning the greenhouse effect. Trying to galvanise support with forecasts of doom sometime in the next century may cut progressively less ice as the realities of higher energy prices, declining coal industries, and perhaps large-scale international resource transfers become apparent.

NGOs have prospered largely on criticisms, and often by avoiding the harder choices. On the occasions when governments have taken steps in line with NGO concerns, recognition or support has rarely been very noticeable. If there are major changes in government attitudes, then lobbying on behalf of government to facilitate unpopular decisions - such as carbon taxes or measures to tackle transport - could become as important as earlier criticisms. This in turn might require greater NGO involvement in the dirty business of policy formation and its inevitable compromises, whether they remain outside government or obtain a degree of political power. As events with the Greens in Germany have shown, this could be just as divisive as issues in conventional political parties.

But even at the level of continued opposition there are clear political challenges for NGOs. In particular, an ambivalent or flatly contradictory attitude to renewable energy sources in practice - as opposed to theoretical support - could greatly inhibit their development, since many rely on deployment at a large number of small-scale sites. NGOs, with their strength in local organisations, are also in a unique position to influence the attitudes and behaviour of consumers in ways beyond the reach of governments.

The political problems of taking decisions now to avoid uncertain environmental impacts sometime in the next century are obvious: politicians are concerned about the next few years, not the next few decades. As a scientist coming into policy, the author also finds it hard not to be struck by the immense gulf between scientific and political attitudes to uncertainty. Uncertainty is the lifeblood of science, and scientific knowledge advances largely - some say exclusively - by proving previous theories wrong or inadequate. Politics abhors uncertainty concerning either the risks for or impacts of policies, and politics sometimes appears as the art of admitting neither errors concerning the past nor uncertainty concerning the future. This is a caricature, but a sufficiently valid one to indicate the fundamental nature of some of the political obstacles to effective action concerning the greenhouse effect.

Nevertheless, it seems likely that many political systems will deliver some policies to limit greenhouse gas emissions, partly because of the pressure of public concerns, but more because of the growing conviction that measures such as improving energy efficiency, removing subsidies and other market distortions, and perhaps even instituting carbon taxes, could be economically beneficial.

This reflects a growing belief that responses to the greenhouse effect will be divided into two distinct phases. The first phase will be dominated by unilateral action concerning measures which are judged desirable anyway, or at least not damaging. To judge from the analysis in this book, measures which are not necessarily economically damaging could extend a very long way indeed. However, as the public and industrial impact of such measures becomes more visible, pursuing abatement policies is likely to become more and more difficult even for those countries which are broadly favourable towards it. Furthermore, various international economic reactions, as discussed in this book, could offset some of the gains in terms of carbon emissions, and a failure on the part of other countries to act would provide a running and growing sore which would be exploited to oppose further policy measures. Irrespective of the actual economic issues involved, sustaining and extending effective abatement policies on a unilateral basis would increasingly require effort akin to that of wading through treacle, and they would be of steadily declining benefit in terms of global carbon emissions.

Effective international action would in the longer term quite clearly be central to any major limitations of carbon emissions. This is likely to present the greatest challenges of all.

8.6 International challenges: efficiency, equity, and international politics

The greenhouse effect is a issue of exceptional complexity in terms of international negotiations. It is a global problem, without even the regional links of an issue like acid rain. Decisions will be required while the likely impacts are still highly uncertain. Different gases need to be considered, differing in their relative importance, atmospheric residence times, measurability, controllability, and the likely costs of limitation. Policies will need to address both sources and sinks, as well as attempt to reflect the trade-off of emissions abatement against adaptation. Control of some, notably CO_2, would have far-reaching implications for some of the world's largest industries, and for land-use policies in the developing world.

Furthermore, trying to address the greenhouse effect is likely to bring in a wider range of still more complex issues. Chapter 6 has illustrated the way in which energy developments in both developed and developing economies are inextricably linked with a range of other issues. MacNeill[21] comments:

Experts ... presume that an agreement can be negotiated within parameters that are essentially technical and scientific. Yet ... both climate change and the measures needed to address it raise a range of more fundamental issues, including economic and ecological security, debt, trade, aid, access to science and technology, and North-South equity issues generally ... A meaningful international agreement, one which is capable of being implemented, will not be possible unless and until these issues are addressed.

Because of these complexities it is now widely accepted that the first stage of the process will have to be a 'framework convention'. This would be a formal international recognition of the problem and expression of concern about it. It could summarise recognised aspects of the science, the need to take action in principle, and include general

[21] J.MacNeill, 'The Greening of International Relations', *International Journal* XLV, Canadian Institute of International Affairs, Toronto, Winter 1989-90.

commitments to minimise emissions of greenhouse gases as reasonably practical. It could also give recognition to some of the underlying political issues, for example the need for assistance for developing countries. Issues such as international relief for victims of climatic disasters, and assistance with protection against them, could also fall within the purview of a convention.

However, as the name implies, the most important role would be to provide a framework for protocols which attempt to tackle the many areas of concern. Among these would be protocols involving explicit measures or targets for reducing emissions of greenhouse gases.

It is an open question where the boundaries between a framework convention and protocols might be drawn. There is growing concern that an entirely toothless convention would delay the whole process. MacNeill comments that 'a framework convention is a little like an author selling a book on the basis of a table of contents and a statement of intent to write the text at some later date'. Nitze[22] argues that a framework convention should involve some specific targets, and in particular should bind parties into a regular process of assessing their domestic policies and justifying them to the international community.

However, no-one expects a framework convention to provide the kind of impetus which could make countries greatly alter domestic policies on the major issues - like energy. This would be left to the subsequent protocols. What forms could a protocol on CO_2 take which would induce the kind of policy developments and impacts discussed in this book?

Like-minded groups, like-minded limits. An effective global protocol which could have a major impact on CO_2 looks to be so difficult that many have begun to argue that in fact it would be unwise to attempt such an agreement on a global basis for the foreseeable future. Instead, it is suggested that groups of 'like-minded' countries should develop agreements among themselves concerning the control of greenhouse gases.

This is fine with respect to groups which seem prepared to countenance serious action to limit CO_2 emissions, such as the European Community. Extending such efforts to the full OECD membership could clearly have a substantive impact. But an equally obvious like-minded group on this issue, despite their differences in other spheres, might comprise the

[22] W.A.Nitze, *The Greenhouse Effect: Formulating a Convention*, Royal Institute of International Affairs, London, October 1990.

United States, the USSR and China - the really big energy producers which together emit more than half of the world's CO_2, and which, to judge from the country studies, will extend that pre-eminence into the foreseeable future. The kinds of measures, policies and targets which this 'like-minded group' would come up with might not be so conducive to global carbon abatement.

A process in which countries were divided according to their stage of economic development might be better on this score, but it would still face severe drawbacks. For example, any process in which countries split into different groups could leave the crucial issue of developing countries and their relationship to the industrialised world high and dry. This book has emphasised both the importance of the developing country potential for growth in emissions, and the extent to which avoiding this increase might depend both upon assistance from richer countries and upon developing a broad consensus that carbon abatement is something that all countries should be and are taking serious action on, with the industrialised countries taking the lead.

Some regional agreements are quite likely, and they could be very important in shaping the process towards a broader protocol. Furthermore, it is, of course, impossible to force any countries into an agreement if they are determined not to join. But that is a very different matter from admitting defeat at the outset by encouraging countries to split into separate groups, rather than striving for a more broad-ranging agreement. This would be a politically important process which would put considerable pressure on recalcitrant countries - even if at the end of the day there were some, perhaps even major ones, which were not prepared to join.

Guiding principles: flexibility and equity. The key international challenge is therefore to find an approach to negotiations which is difficult for any of the major countries or groups to dismiss as unfair, but which would nevertheless develop real pressures for control, while dealing as far as possible with the various technical complexities of the issue. These complexities, the scale of the problem, and its global and very long-term nature, suggest that in order to create a long-lasting and effective control regime new forms of agreements may be required, founded on clearly defined principles rather than the more usual *ad hoc* national targets in some other environmental agreements, which have often been based on relatively short-term political trade-offs.

At least two major guiding principles can be advanced: *flexibility*, to enable maximum efficiency in responses and room for domestic political manoeuvring; and *equity*, to encourage a global dialogue which could give some hope of leading to a stable and long-term basis for emissions control.

The political and economic importance of energy points to the great importance of efficiency and of giving countries flexibility in choosing policy instruments and in making various political trade-offs.[23] One implication of this principle is that, if possible, targets should be set at the global rather than the national level, and expressed through a system designed not to bind countries to individual targets, but rather allowing them to decide where and how to focus abatement efforts. Both the Japanese and the US case studies emphasise the perceived importance of being able to invest in other countries as a cheaper and perhaps politically more promising route to reducing emissions; some of the other country studies emphasise the importance of receiving help in the form of joint ventures or more direct assistance.

These observations seem to emphasise further the probable drawbacks of negotiations which focus on country-specific emission targets. The present author has reviewed these drawbacks elsewhere,[24] and argued that the most hopeful option for an effective long-term agreement, which allowed inter-country flexibility, would be through the use of International Leasable Emission Permits (ILEPs). No discussions since have altered this broad conclusion, though there are obviously many detailed issues which need to be considered. The greatest political issue concerns that of allocating the permits in the first place. This leads immediately to the questions raised by the second guiding principle, namely that of equity.

International equity: a tale of (at least) two cities. Equity has rarely featured prominently in international affairs. If there is to be an effective agreement on greenhouse gas emissions, it may have to, for several reasons. One is the very long-term nature of the problem: as indicated in

[23] A fuller discussion of the implications of flexibility is given in M.Grubb, 'Issues and Options in Implementing Greenhouse Gas Control Agreements', Paper for IPCC Energy and Industries Subgroup workshop on emissions of greenhouse gases, London, June 1990.
[24] M.Grubb, *The Greenhouse Effect: Negotiating Targets*, Royal Institute of International Affairs, London, December 1989.

Chapter 7, societies will probably still be trying to limit greenhouse gas emissions a century from now. The balance between countries is likely to change greatly over that period, and any agreement which simply reflects current emissions and dispositions of political and economic power is unlikely to form a stable basis for control. In addition, because control of CO_2 is such a politically contentious issue, any approach which is perceived not to share the burden of abatement equally, and to give assistance to those requiring it, is unlikely to gain widespread participation.

There are, however, several possible interpretations of equity, particularly in international politics. In particular, there is a serious divide between *equality of burden* and *equality of responsibility*. The former implies that all countries should be affected by abatement measures to the same degree. The latter implies that countries should be held responsible according to the level of their emissions - a Polluter Pays Principle.

On the surface, the former interpretation has a great deal of attraction from the point of view of *Realpolitik;* if all countries share an equal burden, the prospects for their joining the agreement, once these levels have been determined, are presumably quite promising. There are, however, massive drawbacks to such a process. Firstly, it is highly debatable whether a criterion of 'equality of burden' is in fact fair at all, given that the one-fifth of the world's population represented by the industrialised countries have been responsible for almost the entirety of the problem, and that the developing countries are already heavily burdened by debt and poverty. Furthermore, if interpreted as meaning that countries should face equal difficulty in reaching given targets from their current position, it would clearly lead to the most inefficient and polluting countries simultaneously being the most lightly treated. This could hardly form a long-term basis for allocation, but would need regularly to be revised according to changing circumstances. It would also remove much of the rationale for a flexible inter-country system, since if the initial allocation really reflected 'equality of burden' there would be little need to trade, and the system would not lead to any significant resource transfers.

Worst of all, the innocuous phrase 'once these levels have been determined' in fact points to a process which creates a direct incentive for negotiators to amplify the burden which their country would face in reaching any suggested target. Countries would be induced to plead exceptional circumstances, and to project large increases in emissions to make even stabilisation appear a severe burden. This interpretation of 'equity' is highly dubious in principle and in practice raises again most of the problems of trying to negotiate country-specific targets, concerning which the present author noted that 'the difficulties in limiting carbon emissions are great enough without the diplomatic prizes going to those who can amplify them the most'.[25]

When faced with these observations, it will be (and has been) suggested that the concept of 'equality of burden' really means seeking a basis for emissions which is grounded in real physical conditions that affect the energy a country 'needs', so that an index of 'reasonable' carbon emissions can be drawn up as the basis for targets or initial permit allocations.

What factors might affect this 'reasonable' level? Clearly, population and the level of economic development are very important, but per capita consumption does vary widely even between countries of similar economic development. Also, the discussion in Chapter 6 suggests that any clear relationship between economic development and energy consumption could be even weaker in the future.

Many other factors could claim a role. Unfortunately, most seem highly ambiguous. Cold countries require energy for heating; many hot ones use it for air conditioning; and ones in between may want both, according to season. Less densely populated countries may involve more energy for travel, but they are also likely to have relatively more non-fossil sources (and more densely populated countries might also claim an allowance for congestion!). Corrections might be applied for the availability of non-fossil sources, but, as illustrated briefly in Chapter 5, it is impossible to quantify these to any useful degree of accuracy, and countries already vary greatly in the extent to which they do or can exploit the resources available to them. The list of possibilities and difficulties could be extended almost indefinitely. Reaching a consensus on the formula used to estimate a 'reasonable' level of energy consumption or emissions could be almost as difficult as negotiating country-specific emission targets.

In fact, this whole exercise is founded on the incorrect assumption that energy consumption reflects primarily questions of geography and

[25] Grubb, *The Greenhouse Effect: Negotiating Targets*, p.22.

economic development. The country studies reflected in this book and presented in Volume II make it abundantly clear that this is simply not the case. There are wide variations in per capita consumption between countries at similar levels of economic development. Apart from population and the level of overall economic development, the dominant factors which determine energy demand are not ones which can be readily quantified, because they concern the energy policy, institutions, and overall 'energy culture' of countries. Not only does a rational basis for 'reasonable' carbon emissions seem to be impossible, but any approximate formula derived would be far from satisfying most countries' political interpretation of 'equality of burden'. The process might in fact be driven to some criterion based on current emission levels as a guide to 'unquantifiable' factors, with many of the drawbacks discussed above.

This does not necessarily mean that any agreement along these lines would be impossible. It does, however, suggest that any such approach would result in relatively weak targets, and that the process of trying to negotiate them could itself be damaging, by encouraging countries to focus on the difficulties. Far from easing the treacle-like process of unilateral policy, attempts to reach formal, binding international agreements along these lines could turn the treacle into tar. They would also be a poor basis from which to deal with issues of technology transfer and other intrinsic issues arising from current inequalities and international energy trends, and explicit international energy issues of industrial migration and international transport fuels.

Polluter pays: an international principle? The alternative interpretation of equity resides with the principle that polluters should pay in proportion to the emissions that they generate. This is a much clearer, simpler, and economically more logical approach to limiting emissions. Few would dispute that economically it is the most efficient one. Applied at the international level, it creates an incentive for all countries to reduce emissions, irrespective of the current situation. Those that wish to continue emitting more than the global average can do so, but they do not have the option of arguing a 'special case' which would allow them to do so for free: the real costs of their behaviour remain explicit and are not hidden.

An International Polluter Pays Principle (IPPP) could readily handle most of the international energy issues discussed in this book.

Energy-intensive activities remain free to move internationally, but wherever they go, the emissions they generate are reflected in some way. If governments pass through the costs to industries in the form of taxes, the price of goods directly reflects the cost of the emissions involved; if they do not, the costs to the government are all the higher, and the incentives to adopt other measures to reduce emissions all the stronger.

An IPPP could also help to resolve the issue of resource transfers. Applied to fossil carbon emissions, the principle would clearly imply a net transfer of resources from industrialised countries to developing ones. Unlike other approaches, such transfers would not be based on an ad-hoc and largely arbitrary process of North-South negotiation, which would add further immense difficulties to the negotiating process, but would be determined directly by the relative differences in emission levels involved. The transfers would be less clear if other emission sources, notably deforestation, were brought in; such broadening might in principle be desirable but in practice be unwise, for reasons discussed in the box.

A final important argument for a polluter pays principle lies in its political strength and implications. It is really very hard to argue against, especially in the rich market economies which consume the most fossil fuels, because it is so clearly grounded in market economics itself. The OECD formally adopted a form of polluter pays principle in 1974 as a guide to environmental policy.[26] In the context of the greenhouse effect, it would immediately force countries to recognise how their emission levels compare on a global basis. The US case study notes that 'global equity concerns are barely noticeable on the national political scene'; an IPPP would force a broader recognition of how US emissions compare internationally. Quite apart from the financial pressure to do something about emissions if the highest emitters did join such an agreement (an issue examined below), domestic debate surrounding the question would ram home how emissions compared at the global level,

---

[26] The OECD Polluter Pays Principle states that *if* measures are adopted to reduce pollution, the costs should be borne by the polluters. The costs 'should be reflected in the cost of goods and services which cause pollution in production and/or consumption. Uniform application of this principle ... would encourage the rational use and the better allocation of scarce environmental resources and prevent the appearance of distortions in international trade and investment'. (OECD, 'The Implementation of the Polluter Pays Principle', Council recommendations adopted on 14 November 1974, C(74)223, Paris, 1974).

Polluter pays, deforestation, and the past

The rationale for an IPPP applies to all gases and sources, but application to many sources other than fossil fuels may face practical difficulties (and may be less important, or less appropriate than agreements based on targets or technical measures). One problem is that measurement of many is so uncertain that it hardly seems possible to link emission levels to payments. With sufficient evidence and incentives measurements might be improved sufficiently, and/or conventions adopted for approximating them, to overcome this difficulty. A second problem might then emerge for some, notably deforestation. Per capita greenhouse gas emissions from some developing countries rank high if deforestation is included.

This duly reflects the fact that deforestation makes an important contribution to global carbon emissions, and to other environmental problems. It is possible that the developing countries with high deforestation rates could change their path sufficiently to avoid net payments under an IPPP, so the implications in terms of resource flows are not certain. However, it is clear that including deforestation would at best greatly complicate development of an IPPP for carbon emissions, and could result in some poor countries paying out rather than receiving, which might simply be impractical, apart from deeper concerns.

Including deforestation would lessen the difference between the industrialised and developing worlds, and industrialised countries might be tempted to insist on including it in an IPPP for this and other reasons. It could be argued as a matter of equity that developing countries should not be exempted from responsibility just because their emissions come from different sources.

But attempting to extend equity arguments in this way would be a dangerous business. It would also be valid to bring in historical responsibilities, and the current disparity is as nothing compared with the dominance of industrialised countries in terms of past emissions. An IPPP applied to contemporary fossil fuel emissions already involves writing off a large portion of 'natural debt' incurred by the industrialised countries. This is probably politically essential, and not without some justification (Grubb, *The Greenhouse Effect: Negotiating Targets*). But the global greenhouse would not be a good place for the industrialised countries to start throwing stones with equity arguments written on them.

and perhaps as a result improve understanding of the outlook in different countries. Since no-one likes to think of their country as a major polluter, or likes to argue that polluters should not pay, it would do so in a way which could well help to create the political conditions required either for more serious measures to limit CO_2 emissions, or for large-scale resource transfers to the poorer countries - or both.

The main complaint against such a principle would be that it is inherently unfair precisely because it does not reflect an 'equality of burden'. Although the above discussion indicates the probable impossibility of defining and applying such a concept, clearly the ease with which different countries could respond to meet the global average conditions would vary considerably. In addition to the very real political factors highlighted throughout this book, there are also wide variations, for example, in the endowment of non-fossil sources; those with large hydro resources would clearly benefit.

This criticism entirely misses the point of the IPPP, which is to reflect the cost of activities which lead to atmospheric changes. There are already wide variations in the endowment of all energy resources; this is not considered grossly unfair, but a fact of geography. An IPPP would alter the relative value of different resources to reflect their atmospheric implications. The relative value of non-fossil resources would be increased; that of high carbon resources decreased.

In fact, as pointed out in Chapter 5, many renewable resources are more evenly distributed than fossil resources, so the net effect of an IPPP would be to reduce slightly the current overwhelming disparities in energy resource endowments. Since the major renewable resources also depend largely on land area, increasing their value would also add marginally to the pressures discouraging high population densities.

In practical application, one way of reflecting the principle could be by an international tax. However, this would result in all the revenues generated going through a central agency, managing and disbursing a budget which could be ten to a hundred times the total budget of the UN.[27] An ILEP system would keep the exchanges decentralised, and they could be tied directly to development and abatement assistance. In such a system, the polluter pays principle would be reflected by initially allocating permits on a basis which was not determined relative to current emission levels, nor by attempts to share the allocation 'fairly' in terms

---

[27] Grubb, *The Greenhouse Effect: Negotiating Targets*, p.32

of national resources, climate, etc., but by using a fundamental basis reflecting an equality of responsibility in limiting greenhouse changes. There are strong arguments for suggesting that this implies a per capita entitlement, modified to avoid rewarding population growth,[28] but arguments can also be advanced for including an element reflecting economic activity. This does raise practical difficulties concerning the definition and measurement of economic activity, but some flexibility of this or some other kind may be needed politically.

The important thing would be to establish the principle that global pollution should be paid for, not excused on the basis of special circumstances. Given all the complexities and the almost endless potential for claiming special cases concerning greenhouse gas emissions, it is hard to see how any other approach can lead to an effective long-term solution.

The international political challenges. If it is correct that an international polluter pays principle offers by far the best and perhaps the only route to an effective international protocol on carbon emissions, this poses an international challenge of the first order. It is an open question how large the transfers implied would be; they would depend on the global target set, and the way in which countries responded. But clearly they would be much larger than those considered in any previous agreements, at least for some decades while countries adjusted their energy systems accordingly.

Yet such transfers may be necessary anyway to resolve the environmental and other dilemmas posed by the situation in developing countries. Resource transfer is a crucial element of any global abatement strategy for many reasons, as highlighted at several points in this book: to persuade developing countries to join; to pay for more efficient infrastructure and deployment of non-fossil sources; and to speed up the development process in order to give the best prospects for population control. Large transfers would be needed to reverse the current situation in which the poorer countries are in aggregate paying the richer ones tens of billions of dollars annually in debt servicing, on debts which are still

---

[28] Grubb, ibid., suggests that an adult per capita allocation would break the incentive for population growth; an allocation based on current (eg. 1990) population could also achieve this.

growing. MacNeill[29] supported other estimates[30] that transfers to developing countries need to be of the order of US$100bn annually, a hundred to a thousand times greater than the figures usually discussed in relation to environmental and development assistance. This is an extremely large figure by most measures, but still around one-thousandth of the global expenditure on military forces.

The interwoven nature of debt, development and international energy flows has been clear for decades. The greenhouse effect adds a new twist. If the nettle is grasped, an IPPP could do much to resolve the economic disparities and heal political sores. But the political obstacles remain immense.

To judge from the country studies and the existing political landscape,[31] it may not be inconceivable that the West European countries and Japan would agree to a system which met many of the key concerns of the major developing countries, perhaps including sizeable international transfers based on an IPPP.

The obstacles to the USSR and East European countries joining such a process would seem to be much larger, because of their relatively high emissions combined with their current severe economic difficulties. However, the Soviet Union has shown a strong desire to be seen as taking a leading position in international environmental affairs, and recognises that its high emission levels reflect great inefficiencies. Also the Soviet case study indicates that the political leaders recognise increasing energy efficiency and a reduction in coal use as desirable goals, and might thus not be entirely averse to some forms of external pressure towards this end. If the economic position does improve, if emissions do decline with industrial restructuring, and especially if in addition European aid is used as a bargaining lever, it is not impossible that the Soviet Union and some East European countries would also consider joining the process.

Canada might be very wary because of its current high emissions, and the perceived difficulties of controlling them, but it has taken a forward position on the greenhouse effect. Australia, as a large coal and heavy minerals exporter, would probably be hostile, though New Zealand might

[29] MacNeill, 'The Greening of International Relations'.
[30] L.R.Brown et al., *State of the World 1988*, Norton, New York, 1988.
[31] A broad review of the political situation concerning carbon dioxide emissions existing in mid-1990 is given in Nitze, *The Greenhouse Effect: Formulating a Convention*.

not. But economically and in terms of carbon emissions, Canada and Australia are not large enough for their failure to participate seriously to undermine an agreement, and all would be under considerable pressure to join if other major countries did.

Amongst all the industrialised countries, by far the biggest question mark surrounds the US position. As of mid-1990 the US Administration is sceptical about the need for action on the greenhouse effect, but that could change. More important are the underlying constraints discussed in the US country study combined with the high per capita emissions of the United States. Most other countries believe the US should reduce emissions by more, and should contribute more, than other countries. Yet the US may be the most reluctant of the OECD countries to accept even stabilisation or equal reduction targets, and there are clear signs that it is very wary of commitments to large-scale resource transfers. It remains an open question how much impact the generous streak in US popular culture might have as the issues develop, but clearly the stage could be set for an extremely bruising international clash, exacerbated by wide differences in perceptions of historical and current responsibilities.

The United States has led many of the world's former environmental efforts, often dragging other reluctant countries behind it,[32] and consequently regards with some hostility attempts to lecture it concerning global environmental affairs. It has also nearly always been the largest single contributor to international funds, and so regards charges of international meanness with equal distaste. Strong domestic environmental policies have been charged with substantial economic losses, and powerful lobbies now exist to oppose any further major environmental measures or agreements. Furthermore, most US citizens are entirely unaware of the extent to which their whole lifestyle is so exceptional in its use of energy as compared with other countries: heavy reliance on large cars, large houses with large refrigerators, buildings heated often without any timing controls, and with air conditioning regarded as one of the necessities of life in much of the country.

Most US citizens see nothing exceptional about their position, and in so far as they are aware of how US emissions compare internationally,

[32] For an excellent account of the US view of CFC negotiations and the extent to which the US set the pace, and the implications of this for US attitudes on climate change, see R.Benedick, 'US Environmental Policy', *International Environmental Affairs*, 1(1), Spring 1989.

many believe theirs to be a justifiable special case. Yet what is considered normal in the United States, most other countries see as immense profligacy with energy. To most observers in other OECD countries, and above all in the developing countries, the US is rich, wasteful and irresponsible both in its domestic energy consumption and policies, and in its international attitude to the greenhouse issue and resources transfers more generally.

The divide across the Atlantic is a very deep one. Across the Pacific it seems less so as of mid-1990, but the Japanese situation and attitudes towards the challenges posed by the greenhouse effect are so disparate that Japanese support for the US position, already wearing thin, seems unlikely to persist.

An agreement on carbon emissions among the OECD countries and not including others is clearly possible. But the gulf between the US position and attitudes and those of most developing countries is so large that it is almost impossible to see how they could be accommodated within one agreement, unless that agreement were so emasculated as to achieve very little of substance. To judge from the situation in 1990, the language which would be required to accommodate both India and the United States, for example, would be entirely inadequate to create either the kind of incentives which could break the US 'addiction' to fossil fuels, or the kind of assistance and motivation which could prevent India from getting hooked further on them as it developed.

If this analysis is correct, and if it is also true that relying on a process of 'like-minded groups' cannot deliver either, then the world may be faced with the prospect of having the centrepiece protocol of global efforts to tackle the greenhouse effect lacking in one of three key aspects. Unless there are major changes in attitudes, it must lack one of: the United States; the major developing countries; or all teeth and impact.

None of these is attractive. The last may be the most likely but it also seems the least desirable. The developing countries hold the key to long-term emissions growth, and their participation, at as early a stage as possible, seems immensely important. A protocol without the world's largest emitter of greenhouse gases is hardly appealing. But if forced, moving along this road could perhaps be the best of a bad bunch.

In 1980, the idea of a major international agreement on the biggest of all environmental issues proceeding against the wishes of the United States would have been unthinkable, but the relative decline of the US economy during the 1980s means that this is no longer the case, though it would still be an extremely serious departure. But an alliance between the European Community, Japan and the major developing countries, especially if the USSR also joined, would now place immense pressure on the US.

If under these conditions the US attitude did change to such an extent as to allow an agreement including all the key countries, probably based on a form of the IPPP, the prospects for the kind of global scenario sketched out in Figure 7.2(b), with net CO_2 emissions roughly stabilised, would be good, because the energy culture in the key countries would be forced to change. Perhaps even more could be achieved. But there would presumably also be some chance of such a process driving the United States into isolationism on this issue, probably taking some other countries with it. This would give far poorer prospects for global emissions. If the protocol contained provisions which involved economic sanctions against non-participants - and many would argue it must, to survive - this could have serious repercussions on the overall structure of international affairs.

Pointing to these unpleasant prospects and choices is as far as this book can go. The sooner the parties are aware of the potential clashes, and the depth of the political forces involved, the better may be the chances of resolving them. If there is a recognised need seriously to limit global carbon emissions, resolving the resulting international tensions may be the greatest challenge of them all.

8.7 Conclusions

The events of the late 1980s, culminating in the IPCC report and the Second World Climate Conference, mark the end of the period when the greenhouse effect was the concern of a small group of scientists. However countries respond, the realisation that human actions themselves are changing the planet will haunt humanity throughout the next century. In few activities will the spectre's presence be felt as keenly as in the provision of energy.

This book has examined the trends and pressures in global energy developments, and the possible implications of the greenhouse effect for energy policy, supply and demand. The conclusions are mixed. Technical options exist, though clearly further development is important. The costs of limitation may not be nearly as great as is widely supposed, and some measures could clearly be of economic benefit. Yet for decades ahead, reducing global emissions of CO_2 from fossil fuels much below today's levels seems barely credible, and even stabilising global emissions seems immensely difficult.

The major technical responses in the energy sector can be divided into a triad in terms of both form and timescale. The cornerstone is improved energy efficiency in both conversion and end uses in all sectors. This offers the greatest scope for cost-effective saving, and much can be done relatively quickly. Reduced energy demand will make all supply-side responses more effective and more manageable. The second element is accelerated use of natural gas, including for power generation; the technologies and infrastructure are largely established, though both can be improved, and other pressures are already pushing for more gas, so this can move quite quickly compared with the glacial pace of most supply-side changes. But gas is not a panacea: the resources are neither infinite nor evenly distributed, and gas still emits substantial amounts of CO_2. Gas would thus be a long bridge to the third component of the triad, namely the dominant use of non-fossil energy sources. This could consist of various renewables, nuclear energy, or both, and the mix would vary among countries. But with few exceptions, neither nuclear nor renewable sources are in a position to expand rapidly at present: non-fossil sources may eventually emerge as the most important technical response, but this would take decades, and will depend strongly upon policies adopted earlier.

Energy policy responses can also be separated into a triad. The first component consists largely of unilateral measures to exploit the cost-effective opportunities for improving energy efficiency, and lower cost responses such as R&D. Removal of market obstacles, and various interventions to circumvent the 'efficiency gap' are likely to feature prominently. The second component would be marked by increasingly sophisticated use of these instruments and a growing emphasis on carbon taxes. Special support for the deployment of major non-fossil sources, and revived debates over the expansion of nuclear power, may also become important. There are likely to be wide differences between countries, but also attempts to extend measures internationally, in terms of international product efficiency standards and other agreements attempting to minimise the international repercussions of widely differing measures and tax levels. The third component would hinge upon the development of an effective international regime for controlling CO_2 emissions; with measures for streamlining energy markets for greater efficiency well established, domestic policies might then focus more on substantial carbon taxes to stimulate further savings and to bring in non-fossil sources on a large scale, and structural changes in the nature of, and attitudes towards, energy services.

In concluding his *History of the World*, Roberts[33] wrote that 'only two general principles emerge from the study of history. One is that things tend to change much more, and more quickly, than one might think. The other is that they tend to change much less, and much less quickly, than one might think.' The greenhouse effect, long identified by research studies as potentially a more important constraint on fossil fuels than resource limits, has risen from political obscurity to the stage of world politics with astonishing rapidity. The dominant attitude in many energy industries, government departments and agencies - that it is a problem so big, so uncertain and so amorphous that it is best ignored - may change just as fast. Yet developing effective national and international policies to turn the supertanker of energy developments may take many years of debate, trial and conflict; and even if effective policy responses are pursued, the process of changing energy supply and demand infrastructure may span many decades, far longer than those who perceive both technical options and the urgency of the issue would dream possible.

Yet for all the likely difficulties, many of the measures for limiting carbon emissions from fossil fuels may in fact be beneficial, and could indeed emerge from and merge with other concerns. It seems increasingly clear that Western energy industries cannot carry on business as they once did. The public wants energy services but does not want new mines, power stations, port and other energy transport infrastructure, oil spills, sulphur and nitrous emissions, or gypsum dumps - if it can possibly avoid them. Nor do people want to sit choking in traffic jams, or cope with ever-mounting volumes of garbage arising from energy-intensive, once-through industrial processes. Combined with an increasing appreciation of the economic benefits of some abatement measures, pressures which limit the use of fossil carbon, directly or incidentally, are likely to grow irrespective of the greenhouse effect.

[33] J.M.Roberts, *The Pelican History of the World*, Penguin, Harmondsworth, 1980, p.1019.

What the greenhouse effect does mean is that policies which help to address such concerns may be applied sooner, and in the long-term to a much greater extent, than would otherwise be the case. Fossil fuel consumption must eventually hit environmental or resource limits; it may be no bad thing if greenhouse-related measures help to avoid later and still sharper shocks which could render large national and international infrastructure unusable, or which even provide a touchstone for war. Greenhouse concerns could even force the richer countries to address international inequities before the power and resentment of the poor, but large and fast-growing, developing countries rise to levels which could threaten serious international strife.

It is impossible to tell at present how far policies can go, how much they may cost, and whether anything approaching atmospheric stabilisation is in fact plausible. Arguably these are not important questions. It is clear that there are a range of policy options which will help to limit carbon emissions, which carry few economic costs, and which often indeed yield economic and other benefits. Some of these measures have already been adopted in some countries for these reasons. They seem likely to spread in coverage and depth, hastened by domestic and international pressures to limit CO_2 emissions. Is it possible that in a hundred years time societies will look back and say that if the greenhouse effect did not exist, it would have been necessary to invent it?